P9-CAN-276

SOUTHERN CALIFORNIA
TRAVEL ✦ SMART®

HUNTINGTON BEACH

Unicorn Stock Photos / © Jim Hays

SOUTHERN CALIFORNIA
TRAVEL ✦ SMART®

SECOND EDITION

Gary Gordon

John Muir Publications
Santa Fe, New Mexico

Dedication

This book is dedicated to my family; especially to my nephews David and Jesse Rabinowitz, in the hope that they will travel, travel, travel! With thanks to John Gabree, Bonnie Wolfe, Doug Brodoff, Elizabeth Hornbeck, Brent Weber, Lisa Dawn Sterling, and Ira Luft.

John Muir Publications, P.O. Box 613, Santa Fe, New Mexico 87504

Copyright © 1999, 1997 by John Muir Publications
Cover and maps copyright © 1999, 1997 by John Muir Publications
All rights reserved.

Printed in the United States of America
Second edition. First printing June 1999.

ISSN: 1523-0686
ISBN: 1-56261-446-0

Editors: Jill Metzler, Nancy Gillan
Graphics Editor: Laura Perfetti
Production: Rebecca Cook
Design: Marie J.T. Vigil
Cover Design: Janine Lehmann
Typesetting: Kathy Sparkes, White Hart Design
Map Style Development: American Custom Maps—Jemez Springs, NM USA
Map Illustration: Kathy Sparkes, White Hart Design
Printing: Publishers Press
Front cover photo: small—© Arthur Grant/Leo de Wys Inc.
                        (Santa Barbara, California, rooftops)
                        large—© Christian Heeb/Gnass Photo Images
                        (Laguna Beach, Southern California)
Back cover photo: © Mike Howell/Leo de Wys Inc.
                        (Sailboats on Mission Bay, San Diego, California)

Distributed to the book trade by
Publishers Group West
Berkeley, California

While every effort has been made to provide accurate, up-to-date information, the author and publisher accept no responsibility for loss, injury, or inconvenience sustained by any person using this book.

SOUTHERN CALIFORNIA TRAVEL•SMART: A GUIDE THAT GUIDES

Most guidebooks are primarily directories, providing information but very little help in making choices—you have to guess how to make the most of your time and money. *Southern California Travel•Smart* is different: By highlighting the very best of the region and offering various planning features, it acts like a personal tour guide rather than a directory.

TAKE THE STRESS OUT OF TRAVEL

Sometimes traveling causes more stress than it relieves. Sorting through information, figuring out the best routes, determining what to see and where to eat and stay, scheduling each day in order to get the most out of your time—all of this can make a vacation feel daunting rather than fun. Relax. We've done a lot of the legwork for you. This book will help you plan a trip that suits *you*—whatever your time frame, budget, and interests.

SEE THE BEST OF THE STATE

Author Gary Gordon has lived in Southern California for eight years. He has handpicked every listing in this book, and he gives you an insider's perspective on what makes each one worthwhile. So while you will find many of the big tourist attractions listed here, you'll also find lots of smaller, lesser-known treasures, such as the Autry Museum of Western Heritage in Hollywood or the Madonna Inn in San Louis Obispo. And each sight is described so you'll know what's most—and sometimes least—interesting about it.

In selecting the restaurants and accommodations for this book, the author sought out unusual spots with local flavor. While in some areas of the region chains are unavoidable, wherever possible the author directs you to one-of-a-kind places. We also know that you want a range of options: One day you may crave Peekytoe Crab Tortellini with sage and shallots, while the next day you would be just as happy (as would your wallet) with a California wood-fired pizza. Most of the restaurants and accommodations listed here are moderately priced, but the author also includes budget and splurge options, depending on the destination.

CREATE THE TRIP YOU WANT

We all have different travel styles. Some people like spontaneous weekend jaunts, while others plan longer, more leisurely trips. You may want to cover as much ground as possible, no matter how much time you have. Or maybe you prefer to focus your trip on one part of the state or on some special interest, such as history, nature, or art. We've taken these differences into account.

Though the individual chapters stand on their own, they are organized in a geographically logical sequence, so that you could conceivably fly into San Diego, drive chapter by chapter to each destination in the book, and end up close to where you started. Of course, you don't have to follow that sequence, but it's there if you want a complete picture of the region.

Each destination chapter offers ways of prioritizing when time is limited: In the Perfect Day section, the author suggests what to do if you have only one day to spend in the area. Also, every Sightseeing Highlight is rated, from one to four stars: ★★★★—must see, ★★★—highly recommended, ★★—worthwhile, ★—see if you have time.

At the end of each sight listing is a time recommendation in parentheses. User-friendly maps help you locate the sights, restaurants, and lodging of your choice.

And if you're in it for the ride, so to speak, you'll want to check out the Scenic Routes described at the end of several chapters. They take you through some of the most scenic parts of the region.

In addition to these special features, the appendix has other useful travel tools:

- The Mileage Chart and Planning Map help you determine your own route and calculate travel time.
- The Special Interest Tours show you how to design your trip around any of five favorite interests.
- The Resource Guide tells you where to go for more information about national and state parks, individual cities and counties, local bed-and-breakfasts, and more.

HAPPY TRAVELS

With this book in hand, you have many reliable recommendations and travel tools at your fingertips. Use it to make the most of your trip. And have a great time!

WHY VISIT SOUTHERN CALIFORNIA?

Southern California is the land of imagination. The name "California" was itself taken from an imaginary island in a Spanish romance novel published in 1510. So let's use our imaginations. Can you imagine a place that gets less than two inches of rainfall a year, has the lowest point below sea level in the Americas, and has recorded some of the world's highest temperatures—like 134°F? That's Death Valley, and despite its name and dramatic climate, it's beautiful. Can you imagine a place where the main industry is storytelling and dreams? That's Los Angeles. Can you imagine a quiet, peaceful, almost desolate place just two hours from a major metropolitan area, where sculpted natural rock formations and spiky trees dominate the high desert landscape? That's Joshua Tree.

Can you imagine islands just off the coast with their own unique species; a park with so many wonderful museums you'd swear you were at the Smithsonian; a place where you can balloon or taste wine all day; a whole coastline where you can bike, rollerblade, and whale-watch in winter? Can you imagine camping on a bluff overlooking the Pacific Ocean; riding the tallest and fastest roller coasters; and listening to some of the best music, poetry, and comedy—all while enjoying gorgeous weather? And can you imagine a culturally diverse place that's on the cutting edge of the arts, entertainment, fashion, science, government, and many other areas of our lives?

All of this and more is in Southern California, where Native Americans imagined a peaceful life, where Spanish explorers imagined gold, where pioneers imagined abundant crops, where the folks who invented Los Angeles imagined a city in the desert, where storytellers imagined an industry, and where visitors don't have to imagine—they can realize their dream vacation.

This guide will acquaint you with what's available in Southern California. If your pleasure is the outdoors, you'll find numerous places to hike, bike, play in the water or the snow, and enjoy scenic views. If you prefer art, culture, or history, you can explore these passions in numerous ways. If you and your kids like zoos, rides, and other fun stuff, that's here, too. And if you want to explore and experience all that California has to offer, it may take more than one vacation—but you'll find the start you need with the information in this book.

HISTORY

Most of Southern California history dates to the arrival of the Spanish in 1542, but many of the area's museums display artifacts from the Chumash, Salinan, and Cahuilla Indians, residents of the area long before the Spanish arrived. When the Spanish found these peoples, they set about the task of "civilizing" (i.e., changing, oppressing, and/or exterminating) them.

Juan Cabrillo was the first Spanish explorer to discover Southern California. He found what is now San Diego, although another Spanish explorer, Sebastian Vizcaino, took the credit and named the site 60 years later. In 1769, at a time when the American colonists were preparing to revolt against the British Crown, Franciscan missionary Father Junipero Serra founded the first of more than 70 missions. The missionary's goal was to baptize and "civilize" the Native Americans, as a way of extending the Spanish influence on the Pacific side of the "New World." Spain held Southern California, exploiting its resources, for the next 50 years.

In 1822 Spain conceded to Mexico's independence, and the state of California became part of Mexico. The mission land was taken from the church and returned to the people, but few of the indigenous Indians had survived. In 1836 Texas rebelled against Mexican rule, and 10 years later, the United States and Mexico went to war. During that decade U.S. settlers began moving into California. When the war ended in 1848, California was ceded to the United States. That same year gold was discovered in northern California, at Sutter's Mill. Two years later California became the 31st state. During the U.S. Civil War (1861–1865), California's Mexican residents considered fighting against the Union to win the land back for Mexico, but the plan was never carried out.

After the war, the building of the railroads connected California to the rest of the country and the state continued to grow. In the late 1800s people began discovering the resort possibilities of places such as Coronado Isle and Santa Catalina Island, and Los Angeles began to prosper when oil was discovered in the 1890s. Hollywood blossomed as a motion picture production location starting in 1911, and the next two decades saw the Hollywood area become the movie capital of the world. Tourists flocked to Venice, Santa Monica, and other coastal towns, as Palm Springs and Santa Barbara became fashionable hideaways for the wealthy elite.

During World War II Southern California's defense industry boomed. After the war national defense joined the movie, entertainment, tourism, and high-tech industries as cornerstones of the Southern California economy. These industries greatly influenced the area's culture and lifestyle. But Southern California history is still being written today, in current discussions of citizenship, immigration, multiculturalism, affirmative action, civil rights, environmental safety, and resource protection.

THE ARTS

Sometimes it seems as if art is everywhere here. Take the sculpture poised at the intersection of Rose and Main in Venice: a bearded clown with a top hat, holding a wand and wearing a ballerina's tutu and ballet slippers. Though you may sometimes question how art is defined, you'll find lots of it in Southern California. The region offers the full range of expression of the human creative spirit, be it the work of ancient Native Americans in San Diego's History of Man Museum or the breathtaking pottery, china, and fashion collections in Pasadena's Pacific Asia Museum. Pasadena also hosts the Huntington and Norton Simon Museums, displaying seventeenth- to nineteenth-century British, French, and American art, books, and manuscripts; and Renaissance to mid-twentieth-century European, Indian, and Southeast Asian art, respectively.

Museums in neighboring Los Angeles cover the spectrum, from art (Los Angeles County Museum of Art, the J. Paul Getty Center, and the Museum of Contemporary Art), to the real and reel history of the West (the Autry Museum of Western Heritage), to Hollywood (the Museum of Television and Radio), to the history of racism and prejudice in America (the Museum of Tolerance).

But let's not be overly highbrow. There's also street art. On the Venice Boardwalk and at Santa Monica's Third Street Promenade, artists work in a variety of media (including the spray can), creating art before your eyes. (Could van Gogh have painted with one-man bands, jugglers tossing chain saws, and women in revealing fashions gathered around? On the other hand, are any of these street artists the next van Gogh? You be the judge.)

If you're looking for performance art, you'll find theater in San Diego, Newport, Long Beach, Santa Monica, Los Angeles, Hollywood, Pasadena, Santa Barbara, Joshua Tree, and Palm Springs. Cutting-edge comedy (known as "alternative comedy") thrives in such coffeehouses and bookstores as the Novel Cafe in Santa Monica, and at Borders Books in West L.A. and Westwood. You can sample critically acclaimed acoustic music in San Diego, wonderful small and large concert halls in the Los Angeles area (like McCabe's, the Wiltern, Pantages, and the Greek Amphitheater), TV shows taped before live audiences in Burbank, a weekly Thursday night open-air market and street dance in Santa Barbara, and the natural (not manmade) Artists Palette in Death Valley.

And let's not forget fashion, like the high-concept avant-garde styles displayed at the boutiques on Rodeo Drive in Beverly Hills, or their funky cousins on hip Melrose Avenue. Art is everywhere in Southern California.

CUISINE

Some people want to eat the same thing again and again (burgers and fries, steak and potatoes); others are eager to try new dishes. Southern California cuisine accommodates each of these desires and everything in between. In this territory, settled by almost every ethnic group from around the globe, variety is the standard, and mixing and experimenting are the norm. The possibilities for thrilling your taste buds are infinite.

Popular restaurants feature Southwestern, Mexican, Italian, American, Chinese, international, and California cuisine. What is California cuisine? Anything from pizza topped with Thai chicken to a dish served with blue corn chips to bits of food carefully arranged on a large plate—you admire the colors, textures, and arrangement, but wonder when you'll get a real meal.

And what is international cuisine? To Southern Californians it's a little of this and a little of that: a historical or newfangled Italian pasta, a rich French sauce (according to Woody Allen in Love and Death, the reason the Russians fought Napoleon was to save future generations from French sauces and desserts), spicy Szechwan noodle-meat-and-veggie mixtures, and specialties from every continent except maybe Antarctica.

The delicatessens in this region are real (cold cuts on white bread do not constitute a sandwich), serving lox, cod, whitefish, bagels, chicken soup, and triple-decker sandwiches on rye.

Southern California's Mexican food does not fit the Taco Bell stereotype. Rather, it's soups like caldo de camaron (shrimp soup), milaneza (breaded steak), *huachinanago* Colorado (red snapper in red sauce), *camarones al mojo de ajo* (shrimp in garlic sauce), and more.

All the things that can be done with salmon, sea bass, lamb, veal, steak, lobster, shrimp, and chicken are being done in Southern California. The same goes for noodles, pastas, rice, and fresh vegetables.

From tacos and enchiladas to pizzas and pastas to sushi and seared tuna, you'll taste food both as the originating ethnic group intended and as modified by clever chefs who add just a touch of "whatever" to make it different and delicious.

Every destination in this book offers a variety of culinary possibilities; the bigger the city, the more variety you'll find (Los Angeles and San Diego offer the most choices). But the smaller destinations also offer more extensive choices than you might expect in a small town or city, and you don't have to be seated oceanside to enjoy imaginative, luscious cuisine.

A Southern California meal is incomplete without wine and sweets. Fanciful and calorie-laden desserts and a variety of homegrown wines make your dining adventure complete.

FLORA AND FAUNA

Southern California's enormous diversity also extends to its plant and animal life, which are so varied that they're almost impossible to summarize.

The coasts provide habitat for coastal sage, beach weed, marshland (around Malibu and Oceanside), and protected wetlands (such as Newport Beach's Upper Newport Bay Ecological Preserve). In Malibu Creek you find sycamore, cottonwood, bay laurel, coffeeberry, wild rose, and bigleaf maple. At certain times of year the blossoming jacarandas turn L.A.'s streets purple. And Venice has plenty of palm trees, imported by the developer Abbot Kinney around the turn of the century.

In some areas the forests closely adjoin the beach—fires almost reached the ocean in Malibu and Laguna Beach a few years ago. Other areas support chaparral and grassland, with conifers and other trees at higher elevations.

Farther east, in the high desert, such plant life as creosote bush, Joshua tree, and desert holly mix with juniper and piñon. Joshua Tree National Park is habitat for many kinds of cactus, including cholla and ocotillo, with California fan palms in the oases.

Death Valley is a world unto itself that you could spend a lifetime exploring. At its bottom are barren salt flats, around which salt grass and pickerelweed grow. Beyond the flats are desert plants such as burrobrush, arrowweed, shadscale, mesquite, rabbitbrush, desert tea, sagebrush, and cottontop, cholla, and beavertail cacti. Juniper and piñon cover the mountain slopes, while in scattered locations you'll see tamarisk and Joshua trees. Each year more than 100 species of wildflowers carpet the desert floor, but when they'll bloom is not always predictable. It's usually in January but can be as early as November or as late as March. In the higher elevations, over 11,000 feet, look for the 20-plus plant species that grow nowhere else.

The birds and animals are as diverse as the plant life. Peregrine falcons nest at Morro Bay, the swallows return to San Juan Capistrano once a year, and some areas host brown pelicans in addition to herons and seagulls. Malibu Creek birdlife includes red-tailed hawks, scrub jays, and roadrunners.

Golden eagles and prairie falcons inhabit the western boundary of Death Valley in the Panamint Mountains, and more than 250 bird species have been spotted in Death Valley, including herons, sandpipers, hawks, owls, vultures, roadrunners, and quail.

In the very different world off the coast of Santa Barbara and Ventura, the Channel Islands serve as rookeries for many seabirds. These islands also feature birds not found on the mainland, such as the Santa Rosa blue jay.

Some areas of Los Padres National Forest support condor sanctuaries and so many deer that hunting is permitted. Coyotes, gray foxes, and mule deer inhabit almost all of Southern California, and forest fauna include opossums and, in some areas, mountain lions and even elk.

Desert wildlife often includes rabbits, kit foxes, and coyotes. Other Death Valley residents are kangaroo rats, black-tailed jackrabbits, mule deer, bobcats, mountain lions, and coyotes. Bighorn sheep dwell in the remote canyons. Among the reptiles you may spot in the desert are banded gecko, desert rosy boa, California king snake, Panamint rattlesnake, and desert tortoise.

Sea lions populate the Morro Bay region, and it's not unusual to see dolphins swimming off the coast—an exciting sight any time, especially when you're rolling along the Santa Monica bike path. On Santa Catalina Island, you can spot buffalo, brought there not by Darwin but by a movie producer in the early 1900s and protected ever since, and the Channel Islands are home to seals and sea lions.

In Southern California you're likely to find whatever life form interests you— whether it blossoms, flies, trots, slithers, or swims.

THE LAY OF THE LAND

From Keys' View in Joshua Tree National Park, much of Southern California's diverse geography comes together. To the west is San Gorgonio Mountain, the region's tallest point, at over 11,500 feet. South of the mountain, San Gorgonio

Pass lets in the smoggy air from Los Angeles, more than 100 miles away. Farther to the south, at the foot of 10,800-foot San Jacinto Peak, is the city of Palm Springs, a desert oasis known for its golf courses, spas, and movie stars. Between Keys' View and Palm Springs runs the San Andreas Fault, the visible origin of immortal earthquakes. The Colorado River aqueduct, 340 miles of concrete canals, pipes, and mountain tunnels that supply water to the region, is south of Palm Springs. Also to the south is the town of Indio (famous for home-grown dates and date shakes) and the Salton Sea. This ancient lake bed, 40 miles long and 228 feet below sea level, was dry from the time before the Spanish exploration until 1905, when the Colorado River flooded and broke through its banks at Yuma, Arizona (on the California–Arizona border). Ninety-five miles away, seen from Keys' View only on the clearest of days, is Mexico's Signal Mountain.

In this one view from the high desert you'll see nearly every kind of geographic feature but the beach—and who can think of Southern California without picturing sun, sand, and surf? Southern California's miles of coastline, beaches, and offshore islands have become an internationally recognized image of the state.

Southern California would be beautiful even if its geography contained only ocean, beach, desert, hill, mountain, and valley. But these wonderful natural features combine to create sights so magical it's almost as if the land were alive, beckoning you to come and have an adventure.

OUTDOOR ACTIVITIES

Because the weather is clear and fairly warm most of the year and abundant recreation opportunities exist, California is an outdoor-activity lover's paradise. You can hike, camp, four-wheel-drive, ride horseback, skate, ski, play tennis, or just float in a heated pool on a November night gazing at the clear, starry sky above.

Southern California's coastline, islands, lush coastal mountains, wine country, high deserts, and high desert mountains afford ample opportunity for a staggering variety of land and water sports. You can continue outdoors into the evening with open-air amphitheaters, street dances, and patio dining galore.

Outside of San Diego the major hiking and/or camping areas include Mission Trails Regional Park, Cleveland National Forest, and Anza-Borrego Desert State Park. State and county parks and campgrounds dot the coast between San Diego and Long Beach. In and around Laguna Beach there are places to surf and snorkel, while La Jolla's Windansea and Mavericks near San Luis Obispo are surf spots for experts. On Santa Catalina Island's 36,000-plus acres, wildlife is protected by the Island Conservancy, hiking/biking trails and camping (permits required) are available, and Lover's Cove and Two Harbors promise excellent diving and snorkeling. Venice and Santa Monica are heaven for bicyclists, joggers, volleyball players, and rollerbladers. Los Angeles' Griffith Park, Pasadena's San Gabriel Mountains (Arroyo Seco), and Malibu's Will Rogers State Park are all great for hiking.

The Channel Islands (off Ventura and Santa Barbara) draw hikers, kayakers, snorkelers, and picnickers. Montana de Oro Park, on the coast near San Luis Obispo, offers spectacular scenery for hiking, picnicking, and camping (but reserve your campsite early).

Joshua Tree lies in a breathtaking desert, very different from Death Valley to the north. Be sure to take in Keys' View, then explore the park, hike, rock climb, or camp.

In Palm Springs, Coachella Valley, and over the mountain in Temecula, ballooning and horseback riding are popular. In San Diego, south of Coronado Isle, you can even horseback ride on the beach.

Southern California also abounds with manmade outdoor adventures: Disneyland and Knott's Berry Farm in Anaheim, Universal Studios Theme Park in Universal City, and Six Flags Magic Mountain, north of Los Angeles near Valencia. San Diego has the Wild Animal Park, Sea World, and the famous San Diego Zoo. Santa Barbara hosts another zoo, while Palm Springs showcases the Living Desert, and Newport Beach has Balboa Fun Zone. Several professional sports teams call this area home, including baseball's San Diego Padres, Anaheim Angels, Los Angeles Dodgers, basketball's L.A. Lakers, and the NFL's San Diego Chargers.

You can see why Southern California is such a popular place—there are almost too many choices for you to decide where to go first. Make your plans as early as possible, and if you plan on camping, be sure to reserve your campsite in advance.

PLANNING YOUR TRIP

Before you set out on your trip, you'll need to do some planning. Use this chapter in conjunction with the tools in the appendix to answer some basic questions. First of all, when are you going? You may already have specific dates in mind; if not, various factors will probably influence your timing.

How much should you expect to spend on your trip? This chapter addresses various regional factors you'll want to consider in estimating your travel expenses. How will you get around? Check out the section on local transportation. If you decide to travel by car, the Planning Map and Mileage Chart in the appendix can help you figure out exact routes and driving times, while the Special Interest Tours provide several focused itineraries. The chapter concludes with some reading recommendations, both fiction and nonfiction, to give you various perspectives on the state/region. If you want specific information about individual cities or counties, use the Resource Guide in the appendix.

WHEN TO VISIT
Southern California's climate is usually beautiful year-round, so when you go depends a lot on what you plan to do. For example, Santa Catalina Island water is clearest and offers the best snorkeling in winter. And the whale-watching season lasts only from roughly mid-December to late February.

In other words, to a great extent, hype is not hype at all—it's true. But it's not always warm and it's not always tropically clear. The climate is governed by the whimsy of offshore winds that behave so inconsistently, the phrase "weather pattern" is academic at best. It's better to be guided by Bob Dylan: "You don't need a weatherman to know which way the winds blows."

As unpredictable as the region's weather can be, some general statements can be made. Since Southern California encompasses such a vast territory north to south, including coastline, mountains, and deserts, it's necessary to think in specific geographical terms when considering the climate. Year-round along the coast it can be windy and chilly in the morning, clear and warm in the afternoon, and windy and chilly again in the evening. Mountain areas are almost always at least 20 degrees cooler than coastal or desert areas, with winter ice and snow. And deserts can be very, very hot—dangerously so in Death Valley, where July temperatures can soar above 100°F.

In spring (March–May), high temperatures along the coast range in the mid- to upper 60s. The same months in the desert will see highs in the 80s, but low temperatures can average 20 to 25 degrees colder than those on the coast. In summer (June–August), coastal high temperatures are in the mid- to high 70s, but nighttime temperatures can drop significantly. In the desert, daytime highs reach the high 90s and low 100s. During fall (September–November), the coast continues to enjoy mid-70 highs, dropping around 20 degrees at night. In winter (December–February), high temperatures along the coast and in the desert average in the mid-60s. Again, the difference between high and low temperatures can be as much as 25 to 30 degrees.

Avoid Death Valley and Joshua Tree during summer, especially mid-summer. The desert blooms in late winter or early spring, but it's also very pretty in November, and the temperature is easier to handle. You may also want to forego the summer heat of Palm Springs and the Coachella Valley, although in the last couple of years summer has been *the* popular time to be there.

Coronado, San Diego, the Southern Coastal Region, Los Angeles beaches, Santa Barbara, and San Luis Obispo are great during the summer, though August can be pretty hot. Winter months may be overcast even without rain, and the wind can make things uncomfortable. There are days when Venice is downright bleak.

In general, spring and fall are great times to visit. And as some visitors have remarked, even if you do hit an inclement day, it's usually a heckuvalot better than the weather back home.

As in the rest of the nation, season length can vary. August in Los Angeles can be brutally hot (anyplace more than five miles from the coast is at least 10 degrees hotter, and the San Fernando Valley can be 20 degrees hotter than the beach). Winter along the beaches from Redondo to Malibu can be depressing under constant cloud cover.

Southern California receives most of its rainfall between December and February. The worst thing about the rain is what it does to the region's roads—and drivers. With roughly eight months of oil buildup on the roads, they become a slick mess when it rains, making it much more dangerous to drive and creating conditions for bad drivers to become even worse. During the rainy season Malibu may be inaccessible due to mudslides.

A final note about Southern California weather: Don't pay attention to the TV weatherfolk. If they present a five-day forecast, the third, fourth, and fifth days are usually wrong. (If I had kept track of all their errors in the last five years, I'd have a book thicker than all the volumes of the Warren Commission report.)

HOW MUCH WILL IT COST?

Southern California is not cheap, but you don't have to be a millionaire to travel comfortably and enjoy most of the attractions covered in this book. Ultimately, cost is up to you. This book includes a broad range of activities, restaurants, and lodging so that you can enjoy the trip without destroying your budget.

Some destinations, naturally, cost more. Santa Catalina Island, for example, can be costly, partly because of transportation fees and partly because everything but hiking has a ticket price. Death Valley can be expensive if you don't bring your own food and don't camp, because you're a captive of its lodging and restaurant alternatives.

If you're trying to economize, Joshua Tree, San Luis Obispo, and Venice are good picks. And Palm Springs has many budget motels, its reputation for high-end resorts notwithstanding. The same is true for the resort-like Coronado.

You can save money by traveling during "low season" (usually December–March). This is technically the "rainy season" (the song "It Never Rains in California" is wrong), but nowhere near as extreme as winter in the rest of the country. There may be a few wet days here and there, and yes, Malibu mudslides do make the national news, but unless you're unlucky, your vacation won't be ruined if you visit during that time.

In general, your costs involve food, lodging, transportation, activities, and entertainment. Depending on your tastes, breakfasts can run $5 to $12, but an average of $6 can easily be accomplished. Lunches can cost anywhere from $7 to $15 per person, and dinners can range $7 to $50 and up, depending on your taste for fine dining.

For lodging, you can expect to pay at least $45 a night for the basic amenities (bed, shower, cable TV, pool), with prices escalating ($80 to $165 and up) for larger rooms, views, microwaves, refrigerators, and spas and/or gyms at the facility. (If you decide to stay in Beverly Hills, the sky's the limit.) Camping is a great way to save money on lodging in less-urban areas, with some campsites starting as low as $6 per night. This low rate may or may not include flush toilets, running water, and partial or full RV hookups.

Gasoline prices are often higher here than elsewhere in the country. Prices averaged around $1.30 a gallon in 1997–'98. As of April 1999, those prices were closer to $1.60.

For activities and entertainment, prices vary widely. Admission to state parks, when there is a fee, is generally $5. National park admissions are increasing and average closer to $10. Admission to amusement parks can run around $30 or more per person; small museums (such as county museums) are often free, less than $5, or request a donation; larger museums can run between $5 and $10. Renting boats or bicycles, or participating in numerous beach activities, generally costs less than going to a popular amusement park (such as Sea World or Disneyland). If you want to see a movie in Los Angeles, chances are you'll pay $8 ($5 for a matinee).

Two travelers spending a week in Southern California and logging 1,000 miles could probably spend as little as $700 if they camp and spend $30 per person per day for food. Staying at budget-oriented motels would raise the trip cost to $1,200. A weeklong trip for a family of four (spending more on admissions and other activities and staying in moderately priced motels) could run $2,200.

ORIENTATION AND TRANSPORTATION

If you're flying into Southern California, the two major airports are in Los Angeles (LAX) and San Diego. Each airport is large and accommodating, with plenty of rental car companies. Most of the smaller airports in Long Beach, Orange County, Ontario, Santa Monica, Van Nuys, and Burbank also handle general aviation, and there are commercial flights into Long Beach and shuttles from the major airports. Both LAX and San Diego offer taxi and shuttle services, and both are conveniently located: LAX is 15 minutes from Santa Monica, and the San Diego airport is virtually downtown.

If you're going to be traveling by plane to visit Disneyland or the central part of Southern California (from the coast to the high desert, or, say, Laguna Beach to Palm Springs to Joshua Tree) and want to avoid L.A., there's the John Wayne Airport (SNA) near Newport Beach and Santa Ana. Located about 35 miles south of Los Angeles, this airport is served by 11 commercial and 4 commuter airlines offering more than 100 daily, direct, nonstop departures to almost 30 U.S. destinations. Airlines flying into John Wayne include America West,

American, Continental, Delta, Northwest, Southwest, TWA, United Airlines, and USAir. Commuter airlines serving John Wayne include Americal Eagle, Delta Connection, United Express, and USAir Express. And there are often direct, nonstop flights to and from Chicago, Dallas/Ft. Worth, Denver, Detroit, Houston, Las Vegas, Minneapolis/St. Paul, New York City, Phoenix, Pittsburg, Seattle, St. Louis, and Washington, D.C.

If you're planning on visiting areas east of L.A. (Palm Springs, Joshua Tree, Idylwild, Death Valley), and want to avoid L.A., try Ontario International Airport (ONT), located 35 miles east of downtown Los Angeles in the west end of San Bernardino County. This airport, which has experienced a 500 percent increase in airline passenger volume in the last 10 years, and is served by American, America West, Delta, Northwest, Southwest, TWA, United, as well as commuter lines including United Express and USAir Express.

Southern California is car country, probably because driving is still the best way to get around. Seeing Southern California by RV can also work well, although Los Angeles–area traffic and parking can be challenging. Gas stations are plentiful except in the Death Valley area, where the few stations are miles apart. Specifics on where to gas up near Death Valley can be found in that chapter.

A note about Mojave Desert driving: Many of the area's smaller, mom-and-pop gas stations have closed in the past year (because of Environmental Protection Agency requirements about replacing underground storage tanks), so stations are not nearly as abundant as they once were; it's best to start every drive with a full tank, and to fill up when your tank is half full.

Most of the destinations in this book are accessed by interstate and state roads, all well-marked and usually in good condition. Some roads, like the Pacific Coast Highway, can suffer or even close during inclement weather. For up-to-date information about road conditions, call 800/427-7623.

In Los Angeles area parlance, an interstate's number is usually preceded by "the." You may hear someone say, "To get from Santa Monica to Universal Studios, take the 10 to the 405 north, then take the 101 east and get off at Lankershim." Also, an interstate may have one name heading one direction and another name heading the opposite direction. (The 101 westbound is the Ventura Freeway; eastbound, it's the Hollywood Freeway.) You'll also hear non-freeway roads called "surface streets": "The 10's jammed at that time of day—better take surface streets."

San Diego and Los Angeles have bus systems, and many places described in this book have shuttles or trolleys. Los Angeles buses work, but they can take a while. For information, call Los Angeles MTA, 213/626-4455; or San Diego MTA, 619/233-3004. The new Metrolink "subway" now connects many areas of the Los Angeles basin; for routes, schedules, and fares, call 800/371-LINK or check the Web site: www.metrolinktrains.com.

Amtrak provides rail service to much of Southern California. The *San Diegan* heading north from Los Angeles links the city with Ventura and Santa Barbara. Heading south, it stops at Anaheim, San Juan Capistrano, Oceanside, and San Diego. Eastbound, Amtrak's *Southwest Chief* goes from downtown L.A. through Pasadena and San Bernardino to points east. Bus feeders connect Santa Barbara with San Luis Obispo. From Los Angeles, you can take Amtrak to see the Angels, Knott's Berry Farm, or Disneyland.

RECOMMENDED READING

Southern California is a wonderful and complex mix of history and culture, of absurdity and hardship, of realized dreams and dashed ones. Many of the books focus on these themes.

The Seven States of California, by Philip L. Fradkin (University of California Press, 1997), is an interesting overview of the state's personality, culture, values, and direction. Fradkin believes that California is really seven states and that Southern California contributes to four of these states: Desert, Profligate, Fractured, and Sierra.

Southern California: An Island on the Land, by famous journalist Carey McWilliams (Gibbs Smith Publisher), was originally published in 1946; a new edition was released in 1994. It offers a view of what folks thought about the area 50 years ago. *Natives of the Golden State: The California Indians*, by Rupert Costo and Jeannette Henry Costo, offers a glimpse into the indigenous past, as does *Conquests And Historical Identities in California*, by Lisbeth Haas (University of California Press, 1995). *I, Candidate for Governor*, by Upton Sinclair (University of California Press, 1994), is an excellent story and history by the Socialist writer/activist who ran for governor in 1934. *The Great Los Angeles Swindle*, by Jules Tygiel (Oxford University Press, 1994), is a look at the oil, stocks, and scandals boom in Los Angeles during the 1920s. *Dark Sweat, White Gold* by Devra Weber (University of California Press, 1994), offers vivid insights into the history and lives of the farm workers. *Los Angeles & the Automobile*, by Scott L. Bottles (University of California Press, 1991), also provides insight into the present via the past.

Modern Los Angeles is best discussed in *City of Quartz* (Vemo Books, 1990), by MacArthur Fellowship winner Mike Davis. Davis has a knack for seeing the complexity of the city and humanizing the issues it faces. His new book, *Ecology of Fear* (Metropolitan Books, 1998), picks up where *City of Quartz* leaves off. *Ethnic Los Angeles*, edited by Roger Waldinger and Mehdi

Bozorgmehr (Russell Sage Foundation, 1997), and *The Coming White Minority*, by Dale Maharidge (Times Books, 1996), are also fine discussions of modern times and the future to come.

Sex, Death & God in L.A., essays by Alexander Cockburn, Mike Davis, Jeremy Larner, and Ruben Martinez, edited by David Reid (University of California Press, 1994), presents intriguing portraits of modern Los Angeles. *Cadillac Desert: The American West and its Disappearing Water*, by Marc Reisner (Penguin USA, 1993), presents a foreboding portrait of drought reclaiming the California desert. This book served as the basis for a recent PBS series. *The Great Thirst*, by Norris Hudley, Jr. (University of California Press, 1992), also deals with the fundamental issue of water.

Past Imperfect, edited by Marc C. Carnes (Owlet, 1996), is a book of essays connecting Hollywood films to the fiber of American life. Entertainingly written, it compares various "historical" films with the "real" history. *History by Hollywood*, by Robert Brent Toplin (University of Illinois Press, 1996), is a more scholarly look at the same subject. *Adventures in the Screen Trade*, by William Goldman (Warner Books, 1989), and *Final Cut*, by Stephen Bach (Newmarket Press, 1999), are two books that look at the pop culture aspects of the film industry. Goldman, who wrote the scripts for the movies *Butch Cassidy and the Sundance Kid* and *Marathon Man*, as well as many other screenplays and novels, discusses writing for Hollywood. Bach, a former top executive at United Artists, tells in delicious detail how the making of Michael Cimino's *Heaven's Gate* bankrupted U.A. And *Easy Riders, Raging Bulls*, by Peter Biskind (Simon & Schuster, 1998), tells the complex story of the visionary and often selfish and self-destructive auteur directors of the late '60s and '70s (Coppola, Scorcese, Lucas, Spielberg, Altman, DePalma, Schrader and more)—how they changed the movie industry and how the movie industry changed them.

On the fictional side are *Devil with the Blue Dress* (and other Easy Rawlins novels), by Walter Mosley; *The Big Sleep, The Long Goodbye, Farewell My Lovely* (and other works), by Raymond Chandler; and *The Grapes of Wrath* and *Tortilla Flat*, by John Steinbeck. These books all offer excellent reading about life on the surface—and underneath it—in Southern California.

Those who access history and culture through their taste buds will enjoy *California the Beautiful Cookbook*, by John Phillip Carroll and Virginia Rainey (Collins Publishers San Francisco, 1991), and a vegetarian cookbook called *The Flavor of California*, by Marlena Spieler (Harpercollins, 1994).

For a humorous look at L.A., check out what *L.A. Times* columnist Steve Harvey has to say in *The Best of Only in L.A. (A Chronical of the Amazing, Amusing and Absurd)*. This compendium of quotes, funny street signs, ads, and other tidbits is accessible to all—you don't have to be from L.A. to get it.

If you're really keen on seeing Disneyland, there's *The Unofficial Guide to Disneyland* by Bob Sehlinger (Macmillan General Reference, 1998). He offers numerous tips on how to save money and time while the rest of the crowd is wasting theirs.

For those seeking more comprehensive information about local geology, especially that of Death Valley, *Rocks & Minerals of California*, by Vinson Brown, David Allan, and James Stark (Naturegraph Publications, 1972), and *The Explorer's Guide to Death Valley National Park*, by T. Scott Bryan and Betty Tucker-Bryan (University Press of Colorado, 1995), should be helpful. And for some hiking information, there's *San Bernardino Mountain Trails* by John W. Robinson (Wilderness Press, 1986), and *California Hiking* by Ann Marie Brown (Foghorn Press, 1997).

And, by the way, did you know that Southern California is haunted? Read all about it in *The Haunted Southland*, by Richard Senate (Charon Press, 1998).

1
SAN DIEGO

In 1542 Juan Rodriguez Cabrillo, searching for the famed Seven Cities of Gold, led his three ships into a bay off of what is now Southern California and named it San Miguel. In 1602 another Spanish explorer, Sebastian Vizcaino, arrived at the same place, claimed it was not the place Cabrillo had found, and named it San Diego.

Though today many perceive it as a quiet retirement center, "America's finest city" is the sixth largest in the United States and the second largest in California. But even though it's large, it's not overwhelming; the city's efficient layout makes it easy to visit many sights in a short time. San Diego has an active Navy base, a beautiful coastal area, a new waterfront center, and a renovated downtown area featuring shops, dining, and nightlife.

San Diego is a convention center, a museum center, and for many, a tourist center. From its beaches to the Mission San Diego de Alcala, from Balboa Park with the famous San Diego Zoo to such attractions as Sea World and the Wild Animal Park, San Diego is an exciting place to visit. You can probably find whatever you want in the city or the vicinity, and enjoy it in a climate that boasts sunny, mild weather (70°F average temperature), low humidity, and an average rainfall of only nine inches a year.

DOWNTOWN & BALBOA PARK AREA

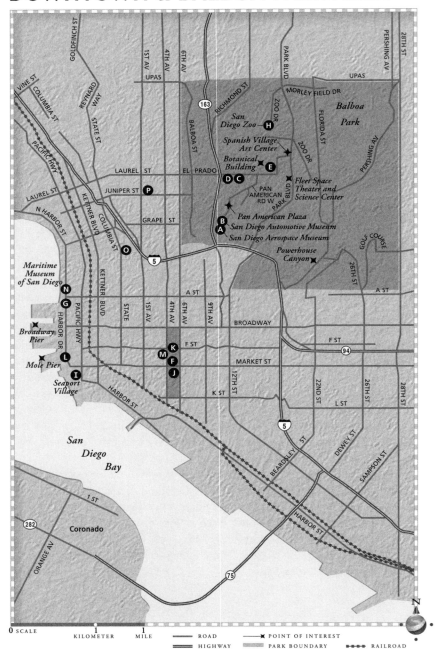

A PERFECT DAY IN SAN DIEGO

Begin your day with a stroll along Mission Beach or a drive to the Cabrillo National Monument, enjoying the brisk Pacific morning air and the ocean view. Breakfast at the Original Pancake House or any of the numerous restaurants with beach or harbor views. But don't linger—there's too much to do! Sea World, the Wild Animal Park, and the San Diego Zoo take almost a full day each. If museums beckon, head for Balboa Park. If you prefer the outdoors, go deep-sea fishing or take a harbor excursion. If history is your passion, visit the Mission San Diego de Alcala and Old Town. In the evening, dine at the Fish Market or one of many other restaurants overlooking the harbor. And if you still have the energy for nightlife, check out the rhythm and blues at Patrick's II or one of the other Gaslamp Quarter clubs.

ORIENTATION

San Diego runs long, north-south, more than wide, east-west. Starting at the northern end is La Jolla and an area known as the Golden Triangle. Moving south there are Mission Valley and Old Town, and just to the west is Mission Bay (where Sea World is). Southwest of Old Town are Point Loma and Shelter and Harbor Islands. Cabrillo Point is at the tip of this area; the airport is at its eastern side. To the east of Point Loma, the islands, and the airport is Downtown, and to the south is Coronado Isle (see Chapter 2). South of Downtown and Coronado is South Bay, then there's Mexico.

Most, but not all, of the sights, lodgings, dining places, and other activities listed in this chapter are located in Mission Bay, Mission Valley, Old Town, Point Loma, and Downtown. And although it's by no means walking distance from

SIGHTS

Balboa Park Museums:
- **A** Aerospace Historical Center
- **B** Automotive Museum
- **C** Hall of Champions
- **C** Model Railroad Museum
- **D** Museum of Man
- **E** Natural History Museum

SIGHTS (continued)

- **F** Gaslamp Quarter
- **G** San Diego Maritime Museum
- **H** San Diego Zoo
- **I** Seaport Village

FOOD

- **J** Buffalo Joe's
- **K** Croce's/Croce's West

FOOD (continued)

- **L** The Fish Market
- **M** Sammy's California Woodfired Pizza
- **K** The Star of India

LODGING

- **N** Holiday Inn on the Bay
- **O** Super 8 Bayview
- **P** Keating House B&B

Note: Items with the same letter are located in the same area.

Sea World to the Gaslamp area, it's not a great distance either, and it's relatively easy to get around.

Interstate 5 runs north-south coming from L.A., Anaheim, Oceanside, and Encinitas. I-15 enters the area from the northeast after passing through Temecula Valley and intersects with I-5 at Downtown's southern end. I-8 runs west-east, starting on the border of Mission Bay and Point Loma, running east through Mission Valley on the edge of Old Town and out into the desert.

Getting around is fairly easy by car, but mass transit is also available. The San Diego trolley (which costs between $1 and $2.25) runs through the downtown area, with routes leaving Downtown in different directions. And the bus system serves the entire area. Call 760/233-3004 for details, or for additional general information visit the Web site, www.sandiego.org.

BALBOA PARK MUSEUMS AND SIGHTSEEING HIGHLIGHTS

*Just north of downtown at 1549 El Prado (619/239-0512), Balboa Park has 1,200 acres of museums, gardens, theaters, and sports facilities, plus the San Diego Zoo. It's a lovely area to walk through, either as a destination or between museum visits. The **Reuben H. Fleet Space Theater and Science Center** offers a planetarium, hands-on science exhibits for kids, and changing IMAX films. One new attraction, **SciTours**, features "voyages" though space and the human body using motion-based simulation. The new **Nierman Challenger Learning Center** features a fun simulation of a space mission that demonstrates the cooperative learning experience necessary for scientific adventure. For show times and prices, call 619/238-1233. Evenings at Balboa Park often feature dramatic productions or opera at one of the park's theater venues.*

In many respects, Balboa Park's concentration of museums and exhibits is as exciting as the Smithsonian Institution in Washington, D.C. Each museum charges between $3 and $7 for adults, but all sell a Passport for $21, giving you entrance coupons for each museum, good for a week. In addition, most of these museums offer free admission one Tuesday each month, though not necessarily the same Tuesday. Call ahead for details.

The visitors center at Balboa Park is open daily 9–4. Meals are available at the park's few restaurants and snack counters. Following is a listing of some of Balboa Park's most noteworthy attractions.

★★★★ AEROSPACE HISTORICAL CENTER
2001 Pan American Plaza, Balboa Park, 619/234-8291
www.aerospacemuseum.org

With planes, exhibits, and memorabilia spanning the entire age of flight, featuring the Wright brothers, air-mail planes and pilots, Lindbergh, World War I aces, World War II fighters, astronauts, and space exploration, this is probably the most complete aerospace museum west of the Smithsonian. More than 65 air- and spacecraft are displayed, with numerous associated artifacts. And the center recently added a History of Model Aircraft Museum. If you are a buff, or just want to understand the evolution and impact of flight, this museum is the ticket.

Details: Open daily 10–4 (until 5 p.m. in summer). Admission is $6 adults, $5 seniors, $2 juniors (6–17), free for active-duty military. (1 hour)

★★★★ **AUTOMOTIVE MUSEUM**
2030 Pan American Plaza, Balboa Park, 619/231-AUTO
They don't make 'em like they used to, and for proof, check it out: old Fords, Packards, Oldsmobiles, even a Tucker; some with gangster whitewalls, some so loud you can almost hear the rock 'n' roll and taste the cheeseburger; all shining, gleaming, full of style and grace. The museum also features motorcycles (Indians, Harleys, and more).

Details: Open daily 10–5. Admission is $5 adults, $4 seniors, $2 children 6–15, free for children under 6. (1 hour)

★★★★ **MUSEUM OF MAN**
1350 El Prado, Balboa Park, 619/239-2001
Exhibits from Egyptian, Latin American, and various Native American cultures complement fascinating exhibits and information about early humans. The Egyptian exhibit offers interactive children's games and some stunning pottery and mummies. Latin American artifacts include towering replicas of columns and pillars from early central American civilizations.

Details: Open daily 10–4:30. Admission is $5 adults, $3 children 6–17, free for children under 6. (1 hour)

★★★★ **NATURAL HISTORY MUSEUM**
1788 El Prado, Balboa Park, 619/232-3821
Dedicated to Southern California's flora and fauna, this museum's exhibits include the Southwestern desert, a mine tunnel, and marine life habitat. It is geared for children and the curious of all ages.

Details: Open daily 9:30–4:30 (until 5:30 during summer).

Admission is $6 adults, $5 seniors and military, $3 ages 6–17, free for children under 6. (1 hour)

★★★ MODEL RAILROAD MUSEUM
1649 El Prado, Balboa Park, 619/696-0199
This fun museum houses 24,000 square feet of model train exhibits, the largest operating model railroad exhibit in America. Play in its interactive toy train gallery, or brush up on the history of railroads in the Southwest.

> **Details:** *Open Tue–Fri 11–4, Sat and Sun 11–5. Admission is $3 adults; $2.50 students, military, and seniors; free for children under 15. (1 hour)*

★★ HALL OF CHAMPIONS
1649 El Prado, Balboa Park, 619/234-2544
San Diego has contributed to more than 40 different sports. This sports museum profiles nationally and internationally known athletes and their trophies, equipment, and memorabilia.

> **Details:** *Open daily 10–4:30. Admission is $3 adults; $2 ages 55+, military, and students; $1 ages 6–17 (although occasionally admission is free—call for details). (1 hour)*

OTHER SAN DIEGO SIGHTSEEING HIGHLIGHTS

★★★ CABRILLO POINT AND CABRILLO NATIONAL MONUMENT
Catalina Blvd., 619/557-5450
For those inclined to feel the history of an area by going to a seminal place, Cabrillo Point should be at the top of the list. This was the very first place the Spanish explorers saw and the very first place they landed in the West in what we now call California, in what we now call the United States, in what we now call North America. Cabrillo, with his three tiny (by our standards) ships, sighted this piece of land jutting out from the main coastline, pulled into the harbor, and announced that it was "a closed and very good port." Okay, it's not as poetic as Neil Armstrong but maybe it loses a little in the translation.

Standing at the edge of Cabrillo Point, you can imagine yourself as a Kumeyaay Indian, eyeing the ships in the Pacific, coming from the south, or imagine yourself as a Spanish explorer and ask yourself, Would you have had the prescience to investigate this piece of territory, beginning the Spanish colonization of North America?

Cabrillo Point offers visitors the opportunity to use their imagination. And at the visitors center and museum you can view brief film presentations to learn more about Cabrillo and the Spanish settlement of the area, and about tide pools and marine life; examine a variety of historic items (including Indian artifacts that date before Cabrillo's arrival); and learn about the subsequent history of the area (this was an important link in our national defense system early in World War II, when fears of a Japanese attack ran high). From the visitors center you can view the harbor, the airport, and the military base and naval station. Also available is information and hands-on discovery of tide-pool activity. If you use your eyes and your imagination, the whole history of our civilization, from before 1542 to the present, is here.

Details: *At the tip of Point Loma at the end of Catalina Blvd. Open daily 9–5:15. Admission is $5 per vehicle; $2 per person for walk-ins, bicyclists, or joggers. (2 hours)*

★★★ SAN DIEGO MARITIME MUSEUM
1306 N. Harbor Dr., 619/234-9153

The *Star of India*, a full-rigged ship built and launched in 1863, is the centerpiece of this three-ship museum. Surviving storms, a collision, a mutiny, and other vagaries of the seas, this 278-foot ship sailed around the globe 21 times, hauling emigrants to Australia and cargo to dozens of ports of call—and it's still seaworthy! Visitors can climb aboard, gaze up the masts at the sails and rigging, explore below decks, see exhibits on the kind of life the sailors and the emigrant cargo led, and hear the docents tell you more about knots, capstans, and mizzenmasts than you might want to know—except that it's fascinating. This ship represents the high-tech of its day, with the capstan—there are no motors—representing the finest machine device of its time for increasing the power of manual labor in order to raise a two-ton sail to the top of the mast. If you're lucky, it'll be a bit overcast and drizzly when you visit; then you can feel the ship move under your feet and you can feel the wind and rain in your face. But it's a great place for kids and adults, even if it's not raining.

Two other ships, the steam ferry *Berkeley* (1898) and the luxury steamer yacht *Medea* (1904), make up the rest of the museum. These ships are not as fascinating (rich people had yachts and still do), but the

GREATER SAN DIEGO

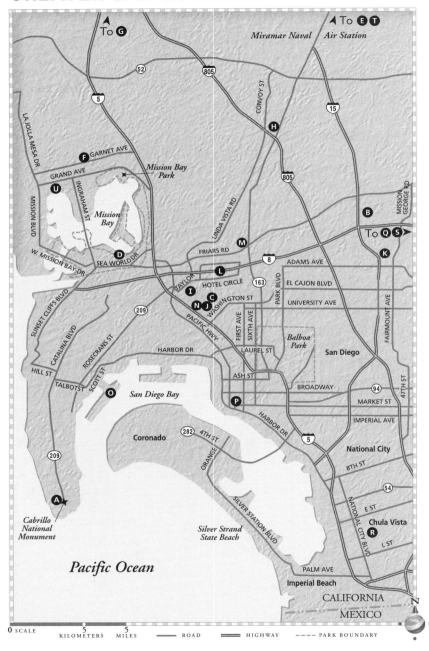

To ⓖ

◀ To ⓔ ⓣ

Miramar Naval   Air Station

52

805

CONVOY ST

5

15

ⓗ

LA JOLLA MESA DR

ⓕ GARNET AVE

GRAND AVE

Mission Bay Park

805

INGRAHAM ST

ⓤ

MISSION GEORGE RD

MISSION BLVD

Mission Bay

LINDA VISTA RD

ⓑ

To ⓠ ⓢ ▶

W. MISSION BAY DR

ⓓ

SEA WORLD DR

FRIARS RD

ⓜ

ⓚ

8

ADAMS AVE

ⓛ

HOTEL CIRCLE

163

EL CAJON BLVD

SUNSET CLIFFS BLVD

TAYLOR

ⓘ

ⓒ

ⓝ ⓙ

WASHINGTON ST

PARK BLVD

UNIVERSITY AVE

FAIRMOUNT AVE

CATALINA BLVD

ROSECRANS ST

SCOTT ST

PACIFIC HWY

FIRST AVE

SIXTH AVE

Balboa Park

San Diego

HARBOR DR

LAUREL ST

209

HILL ST

TALBOT ST

ASH ST

BROADWAY

94

47TH ST

ⓞ

San Diego Bay

ⓟ

MARKET ST

IMPERIAL AVE

HARBOR DR

282   4TH ST

Coronado

5

National City

ORANGE

8TH ST

209

54

SILVER STRAND BLVD

E ST

NATIONAL CITY BLVD

ⓐ

Chula Vista

ⓡ

L ST

Cabrillo National Monument

Silver Strand State Beach

Pacific Ocean

PALM AVE

Imperial Beach

CALIFORNIA

MEXICO

N

0 SCALE

5   5

KILOMETERS   MILES   ▬▬ ROAD   ▤▤ HIGHWAY   ---- PARK BOUNDARY

Berkeley is set up inside as an extensive museum featuring displays, artifacts, models, and a museum store. The History of Cartography (mapmaking) exhibit is excellent and educational. Altogether, this is another of San Diego's hands-on history museums: climb aboard, steer the wheel, feel the wind in your face.

Details: *Open daily 9–8. Admission is $5 adults; $4 seniors, active military, and children 13–17; $2 children 6–12; free for children under 6. (1 hour)*

★★★ SEA WORLD
1720 S. Shores Road, 619/226-3901

This Anheuser-Busch marine life entertainment park features Shamu the killer whale and 20 other exhibits and attractions, six shows, and the Shamu Backstage interactive killer whale attraction, where you can wade and play with, train, and feed killer whales! The newest attraction, Manatee Rescue, includes a viewing gallery that brings you into the river-like world of this endangered species.

Details: *Open daily, but park hours vary by season. Admission is $35.95 adults, $26.95 children 3–11, free for children under 3. Various multi-day admission packages are available. Parking is $6 for cars, $8 for RVs. (1 day)*

SIGHTS
- 🅐 Cabrillo Point
- 🅑 Mission San Diego de Alcala
- 🅒 Old Town
- 🅓 Sea World
- 🅔 Wild Animal Park

FOOD
- 🅕 Broken Yolk Cafe
- 🅖 La Especial Norte
- 🅗 Original Pancake House

LODGING
- 🅘 Best Western Hacienda Hotel Old Town
- 🅙 Blom House B&B #1
- 🅚 Blom House B&B #2
- 🅛 Days Inn Hotel Circle
- 🅣 Holiday Inn Hotel & Suites San Diego–Old Town
- 🅜 Keating House B&B
- 🅝 Ramada Limited
- 🅞 Sheraton San Diego Hotel & Marina

LODGING (continued)
- 🅞 Travelodge Hotel–Harbor Island
- 🅟 Westin Hotel at Horton Plaza

CAMPING
- 🅠 Anza-Borrego Desert State Park
- 🅡 Chula Vista RV Resort and Marina
- 🅢 Circle RV Ranch
- 🅣 Cleveland National Forest
- 🅤 De Anza Harbor Resort
- 🅖 San Elijo State Beach

Note: Items with the same letter are located in the same area.

SEA WORLD'S SHAMU

© Sea World, Inc.

★★★ WILD ANIMAL PARK
15500 San Pasqual Valley Road, Escondido, 760/747-8702
It's one thing to display animals in a simulated natural setting in the midst of a city; it's another to have them living out in nature itself. That's why I prefer the Wild Animal Park to the zoo, although the zoo is certainly superb and perhaps more affordable and accessible. This 2,200-acre park features over 2,500 animals that roam freely in settings similar to their natural habitats. Rhinos, elephants, cheetahs, and more can be spotted on the Safari Walk. Or you can pet and feed deer, goats, and antelope, and enjoy the sea creatures in the Mombasa Lagoon.

Details: About 35 miles north of downtown San Diego. Open daily in winter, 9–4; in summer 7:30 a.m.–10 p.m. Admission is $21.95 adults, $14.95 children 3–11. Parking is $3. There are no shuttles or convenient public transportation to the park. (1 day)

★★ GASLAMP QUARTER
Downtown San Diego
This downtown historic district was founded in 1850 but received its major boost from developer Alonzo Horton in 1867. It features restaurants, theaters, galleries, and shops and is a great place to stroll.

Details: Bounded by Fourth and Sixth Avenues and Broadway and L Streets. (2 hours)

★★ MISSION SAN DIEGO DE ALCALA
10818 San Diego Mission Road, 619/281-8449
Founded in 1769, this building was the first in a chain of 21 missions along the California coast that were critical to the Spanish settlement and conversion of the native population. This site includes archaeological ruins, gardens, a museum, a gift shop, and an active church.

Details: On I-15 north of I-8. Open daily 9–5. Admission is $2 adults, $1 seniors and students, 50 cents for children under 12. (1 hour)

★★ OLD TOWN SAN DIEGO AND STATE HISTORIC PARK
4002 Wallace Street, 619/220-5422
This is where the city of San Diego began in the 1820s, when the territory still belonged to Mexico. You'll find plenty of shops, restaurants, and motels, and walking tours of the many historic buildings are available.

TIJUANA/ROSARITO BEACH, MEXICO

Just minutes south of San Diego is **Mexico**. As you drive the San Diego–area freeways, you'll see yellow warning signs illustrated with figures of people running. These are to alert you that people, usually Mexican immigrants, may run across the highway; the signs are a reminder of border tensions and the disparities between life in the U.S. and in Mexico. If you go to Tijuana or farther south, prepare yourself to see a lot of poverty and many people trying to cross the border.

That said, **Tijuana** is 20 minutes from San Diego, and there's really no red tape to cross the border, 24 hours a day. U.S. citizens can enter Mexico for 72 hours or less without a passport or visa. Most shop owners and restaurant workers speak English, and most credit cards are accepted. You can bring back $400 of merchandise duty-free on great buys in perfume, watches, shoes, rugs, high fashions, and more.

To get to Tijuana, drive south on I-5 or I-805 .Cross the border in your car, or park and walk or shuttle across, as many people do. If you're going to park, take the "Last U.S. Exit Parking" off-ramp. Park safely at the Border Station Parking and walk or take the $1 **Mexicoach Shuttle**, which runs every 30 minutes between 9 a.m. and 9 p.m.

Among the Tijuana shops you may want to check out for bargains are **Discount Pharmacy**, 615 Ave. Revolución Ave., 01152/66-883838; **Sara's London Shop**, at Third and Avenida Revolución, 01152/66-850622; **Hand Art**, 967 Ave. Revolución, 01152/66-852642; and **La Fuente**, 1129 Ave. Revolución, No. 10, 01152/66-859213. For dining, try **Señor Frog's Bar and Grill**, in the Pueblo Amigo Shopping Center, 01152/66-824962, www.senorfrogs.com; and for steaks and fresh seafood in a continental atmosphere, there's **Coronet Restaurant and Piano Bar**, Seventh and Revolución, 01152/66-855551.

About 20 miles farther south is beautiful **Rosarito Beach**, with low-priced, resort-like accommodations on the beach and some fine restaurants—and it's where Titanic was filmed! If you decide to travel into Mexico beyond Tijuana and Rosarito, consider **Puerto Nuevo Lobster Village**, a few miles farther south. It has beautiful beaches, cheap to moderately priced motels, and several restaurants featuring— what else?—lobster. For more information, call 01152/66-120396.

Details: *The Old Town State Park Visitor Center is located in the triangle between I-5, I-8, and State Route 163. Open daily 10–5. The park is closed Thanksgiving Day, Christmas Day, and New Year's Day. (1 hour)*

★★ SAN DIEGO ZOO
2920 Zoo Dr., Balboa Park, 619/234-3153

This world-famous zoo, located in Balboa Park, features more than 4,000 birds, mammals, and reptiles—many endangered, many rare—plus more than 6,500 exotic plants. Don't miss the Gorilla Tropics natural habitat exhibit or Hippo Beach, viewed from underwater. There's also a Skyfari (overhead lift ride), a children's zoo, and animal shows. Restaurants, snack bars, and stroller and wheelchair rentals are available. No pets.

Details: *Open daily 9–4 (7:30 a.m.–9 p.m. in summer). Admission is $16 adults, $7 children 3–11, free for children under 3. (All day)*

★★ SEAPORT VILLAGE
West Harbor Drive at Kettner Blvd.
619/235-4014

This area features the Loof Carousel, built circa 1890, as well as 75 shops, restaurants, and eateries on the bay.

Details: *Carousel is open daily 10 a.m.–9 p.m. (1 hour)*

FITNESS AND RECREATION

It's California and it's on the coast, so you know there's boating and fishing and whale-watching. **H & M Landing**, 619/222-1144, features a variety of whale-watching tours ranging from three hours (they should call it the Gilligan tour) to 11 days, and they're guaranteed. **Seaforth Sportfishing**, 619/224-3383, offers half-day, full-day, and twilight deep-sea fishing trips. **Harbor Excursion**, 619/234-4111, provides harbor tours, a 15-minute ferry to Coronado, dinner-and-dance cruises, an on-call water taxi service, and whale-watching trips. **Hornblower Dining Yachts**, 619/234-8687, also offers dining cruises.

Or check out local air sports (**Biplane Adventures/Barnstorming Adventures** offers open-cockpit biplane rides, 760/438-7680), ballooning (**A Balloon Adventure by California Dreamin'**, 760/438-3344; and **Sunset Balloon Flights**, 619/481-9122), and biking (**Aquarius Surf 'n' Skate**, 619/488-9733).

For the less daring, there's billiards at the **Gaslamp Billiard Palace**,

379 Fourth Ave., 619/230-1968, and numerous golf courses. Contact the **American Golf Corporation**, 619/793-5416, for area information. Equestrians can get mounts and guided tours—including beach rides—from **Sandi's Rental Stable**, 2060 Hollister St., 619/424-3124. Rates vary.

Hikers will enjoy 6,000 acres of mountains, lakes, and valleys at the **Mission Trails Regional Park**, northeast of San Diego, 619/668-3275. It also has mountain-biking and equestrian trails.

Football and baseball fans can contact the **San Diego Chargers**, 619/280-2121, and the National League Western Division 1998 champion **San Diego Padres**, 619/283-4494, for game schedules.

FOOD

There are hundreds, perhaps thousands, of restaurants in the San Diego area. From traditional ethnic food to the cutting edge of American cuisine, the San Diego restaurant scene has it all. Here are a few eateries you might enjoy.

In the Gaslamp Quarter **Buffalo Joe's**, 600 Fifth Ave., 619/236-1616, cooks ribs, steaks, pastas, wood-fired chicken and ostrich, buffalo, and alligator! Burgers start around $6.95, steaks around $12.95. The restaurant serves 19 beers on tap and a late-night menu, complemented by live R&B, jazz, and Top 40 progressive dance music. Also in the Gaslamp Quarter and also featuring live jazz and R&B are **Croce's** and **Croce's West**, both located at the corner of Fifth and F Street, 619/233-4355. The restaurants are owned and operated by the wife of late singer/songwriter Jim Croce. Southwestern cuisine dominates the menu at Croce's West while pasta, seafood, chicken, and steak are the featured fare at Croce's, with entrees ranging from $12 to $22. The **Star of India**, in the Gaslamp Quarter at 423 F St., 619/544-9891, is regarded as the city's best Indian restaurant, with entrees ranging between $8 and $12. And **Sammy's California Woodfired Pizza**, 777 Fourth Ave., 619/230-8888, also in the Gaslamp, features very tasty California pizza (try the Thai chicken pizza), pasta (try the Thai shrimp linguine), and salads. Pizzas start at $7.75, pastas at $9, and salads at $6.25.

For dining with a view, the **Fish Market**, downtown at 750 N. Harbor Dr., 619/232-3474, provides a view of the bay along with a fine seafood menu, an oyster bar, and a sushi bar. Entrees range between $10 and $20.

Some of the best Mexican food in Southern California is served at **La Especial Norte**, 664 N. Highway 101, Leucadia, 760/942-1040. It's worth the drive up the coast to this family-style restaurant. Try the *camarones al mojo de ajo* (shrimp in garlic sauce). Most entrees are less than $10.

For breakfast, my favorite place is the **Original Pancake House**, 3906

Convoy St., 619/565-1740, open only for breakfast and lunch. Their claim to fame is a huge oven-baked apple pancake with a cinnamon glaze, for $7.50. Most meals are less than $10. There's also the **Broken Yolk Cafe**, 1851 Garnet Ave., Pacific Beach, 619/270-0045, open at 6 a.m. and serving meals for less than $7.

LODGING

Nationally known chain motels and hotels are scattered throughout the city and by the bay and beaches. Locally owned lodgings include **Keating House B&B**, 2331 Second Ave., 619/239-8585 or 800/995-8644, a centrally located B&B just a 10-minute walk from both downtown and Balboa Park, and a 15-minute drive to just about everywhere else in the area. Keating House has eight unique rooms: six in an 1888 Queen Anne Victorian house and two in a separate cottage. The six rooms share three baths, but the cottage rooms each have their own. A substantial breakfast is served, and rates range from $70 to $95.

The **Blom House B&B**, 1372 Minden Dr., 619/467-0890 or 800/797-2566, sits on a hilltop overlooking part of the city. It offers private baths and a deck with a Jacuzzi. This cottage-style B&B serves a gourmet breakfast, and rates run $79 to $120. A second Blom House B&B with similar amenities (and the same phone number) is near the intersection of I-8 and I-15, at 4600 Kensington.

Best Western Hacienda Hotel Old Town, 4041 Harney St., 619/298-4707 or 800/888-1991, offers quiet lodgings, microwaves, mini-fridges, and a restaurant; rates run $110 to $165.

At **Ramada Limited**, 3900 Old Town Ave., 619/299-7400 or 800/272-6232, rates start at $109. **Holiday Inn Hotel & Suites San Diego–Old Town**, 2435 Jefferson St., 619/260-8500 or 800/465-4329, features Spanish Colonial–style courtyards and fountains and complimentary breakfast and cocktails, with rates starting at $110.

Days Inn Hotel Circle, 543 Hotel Circle S., 619/297-8800 or 800/325-2525, has mini-fridges in all the rooms and rates ranging from $85 to $149.

Offering scenic views from its high-rise downtown, **Holiday Inn on the Bay**, 1355 N. Harbor Dr., 619/232-3861 or 800/877-8920, has rates starting at $115. Also downtown, **Super 8 Bayview**, 1835 Columbia St., 619/544-0164 or 800/537-9902, offers relatively inexpensive lodging, is conveniently located, and serves a complimentary continental breakfast, with rates under $80. Downtown, at the center of the Gaslamp Quarter, **Westin Hotel at Horton Plaza**, 910 Broadway Circle, 619/239-2200 or 800/6-WESTIN, offers a health club and spa and is obviously super-convenient to shopping at Horton Plaza, with rates starting at $129.

ANZA-BORREGO DESERT STATE PARK

This state park, about 85 miles northeast of San Diego, encompasses more than 600,000 acres of beautiful mountainous desert terrain, reaching an elevation of over 6,100 feet, and is the largest desert state park in the contiguous United States. There are 500 miles of dirt roads, two huge wilderness areas (comprising two-thirds of the park), and 110 miles of riding and hiking trails. The park features washes, wildflowers, palm groves, cacti, and sweeping vistas. You may see roadrunners, golden eagles, kit foxes, mule deer, and bighorn sheep, as well as desert iguanas, chuckwallas, and four species of rattlesnake. Even if you don't have time to camp or do much (or any) hiking, this is an area worth driving through. It is breathtaking, and even when the wildflowers aren't in bloom, there are stunning views. (Wildflowers usually begin blooming in January and reach their peak in March. Each year's wildflower bloom is dependent on rainfall, temperature, and winds. For an up-to-date wildflower recording, call 760/767-4684.)

The park name comes from a combination of Juan Bautista de Anza, the Spanish explorer, and the Spanish word borrego, referring to bighorn sheep.

There's a visitors center in **Borrego Springs** (easily visible and marked at the west end of Palm Canyon Drive) that includes books, maps, and short videos and slide shows. The Wildflowers of Anza-Borrego, shown during wildflower season, is a short, illustrative guide to what you will already have observed on your drive. The center is open

The **Sheraton San Diego Hotel & Marina**, 1380 Harbor Island Dr., 619/291-2900 or 800/325-3535, offers fine views and a heath club with spa, with rates ranging from $149 to $300. In the same area, **Travelodge Hotel–Harbor Island**, 1960 Harbor Island Dr., 619/291-6700 or 800/578-7878, offers bay views, a health club and spa, and the Waterfront Cafe & Club overlooking the marina; rates range from $110 to $165.

CAMPING

No tent camping exists within San Diego city limits. However, the following campgrounds are closest to the city. **San Elijo State Beach** is about 20 miles

9 a.m. to 5 p.m. October–May; weekends and holidays only June–September (when it's too hot).

If you want to stop before you get to the visitors center, **Tamarisk Grove** (on S3 off Highway 78) has picnic tables, restrooms, and drinking water.

If you do want to cool off, eat, or spend the night in a non-desert style, there are restaurants and hotels in Borrego Springs.

There is camping in the park; of its 149 developed sites, 52 have electric, water, and sewer hookups. There's also backcountry camping along 500 miles of primitive roads, and hiking and horseback-riding trails. Permits are required (a backcountry permit is $5, a weekly permit $20, and an annual permit $50) and can be purchased at the visitors center or at numerous marked self-pay stations.

If you journey to Anza-Borrego, remember: This is a huge desert area. Even if you're just driving through, carry plenty of water and drink it. Make sure your vehicle is ready. Take extra food. Wear protective clothing. Sunscreen. Bring a map. Have a plan. And if you have tendencies to walk away from your vehicle or campsite without thinking, try to remember that getting lost is one of the easiest things to do in the desert. Make sure someone else knows where you are going.

To reach Anza-Borrego from San Diego, take I-8 east to Highway 79 north, and take that to Highway 78 east; 760/767-5311 or 760/767-4205 or www.anzaborrego.statepark.org.

north along the coast, on Old Highway 101 in Cardiff, 800/444-7275. It has family campsites, fishing, swimming, and supplies. The **Cleveland National Forest**, 10845 Rancho Bernardo Road, Suite 200, Rancho Bernardo, 619/673-6180 or 800/280-2267, begins about 25 miles east of San Diego, with family camping, wilderness backpacking, and hiking available. The forest's 24-mile Sunrise Scenic Byway passes through almost 16,000 acres of wilderness, where elevations range from 1,700 to 5,000 feet and summer temperatures exceed 100°F. Visitor permits are required in the wilderness area and cost $5. The forest is accessible from many San Diego highways. It's best to call and get specific information about what areas are open and closed, and the best way to get there. Campground reservations can be made by calling the above number from 7 a.m. to 7 p.m. weekdays and 11 a.m. to 7 p.m. on weekends. Finally, **Anza-Borrego Desert State Park** (see Sidebar, pages 32–33) hosts several campgrounds.

The San Diego area offers three RV campsites. At **De Anza Harbor Resort** (RVs only, no tent camping), 2727 De Anza Road, 619/581-4282 or 800/924-PLAY, winter rates start at $27 on weekdays and $40.50 on weekends, and summer rates start at $36 on weekdays and $54 on weekends. Weekly and monthly rates are also available. South of San Diego, **Chula Vista RV Resort and Marina** (again, RVs only, no tent camping), 460 Sandpiper Way, Chula Vista, 619/422-0111 or 800/770-2878, has winter rates starting at $28.50 and summer rates starting at $34.50. Twenty miles west of San Diego, between the city and Cleveland National Forest, is **Circle RV Ranch**, 1835 E. Main St., El Cajon, 619/440-0040 or 800/422-1835. The flat rate is $23.

NIGHTLIFE
In San Diego hundreds of bars, restaurants, and clubs offer a wide variety of live music. Some of the live music scene is centered in the Gaslamp Quarter area, at places like **Cafe Sevilla**, 555 Fourth Ave., 619/233-5979, featuring salsa and Spanish rock; **Dakota Grill and Spirits**, 901 Fifth Ave., 619/234-5554, featuring piano jazz; and **Patrick's II**, 428 F St., 619/233-3077, with the best blues in town.

Professional theater choices include the **San Diego Repertory Theatre**, 79 Horton Plaza, 619/235-8025; and the **North Coast Repertory Theatre**, Lomas Santa Fe Dr., Solana Beach, 619/481-1055.

But the best way to check out what's going on is to pick up a copy of the *San Diego Weekly Reader*, a free newsmagazine available throughout the city.

SHOPPING
Horton Plaza spans seven city blocks in the Gaslamp Quarter area, with more than 140 shops in an architectural award–winning mall. But be sure to note where you've parked your car in this massive place. North of Horton Plaza, the shopping continues in **Old Town**. Some of its numerous shops sell historical wares or souvenirs, and others sell specialty items. Harborside, you'll find a collection of boutiques known as **Seaport Village**. All of these areas are perfect for window-shopping, and all have plenty of places to sit and sip a drink or have a meal.

The Pacific Coast Highway

Stretching from San Diego to San Simeon north of San Luis Obispo, the Pacific Coast Highway is one of Southern California's most beautiful drives. Known as PCH and Highway 1, it doesn't always track the coast and sometimes doubles with I-5 and I-101, but more often than not presents the driver with panoramic ocean views and a sense of what Southern California has to offer.

You could conceivably complete the 315-mile drive from **San Diego** to **San Simeon** in one or two days, but you'd be missing a lot. Many of the beautiful cities tucked along the route are destinations in this book. Take some time to stop and explore the history, views, beaches, hills, and Southern Californian charm of these areas. You might want to see the mission or the Surf Museum in **Oceanside**, or the mission and historic district in **San Juan Capistrano**; play in the waters of beautiful **Laguna Beach**; or get off the highway and visit **Santa Catalina Island**.

PCH also passes through **Newport Beach, Long Beach, Redondo Beach, Hermosa Beach**, and **Manhattan Beach**, and leads into **Marina del Rey**. There are a few places where PCH feels like just an ordinary highway and not a coastal route—Long Beach is one of them, parts of Redondo are another, and,

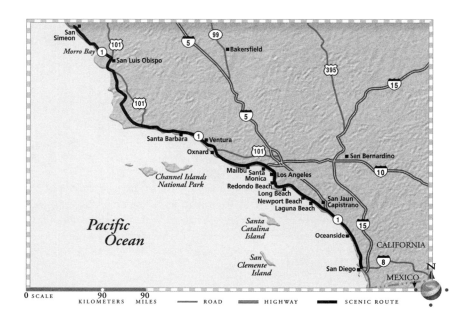

farther north, **Oxnard** is another. At times you can avoid these mundane and often traffic-heavy stretches of the highway. For instance, at Washington Boulevard, on the border of Marina del Rey and **Venice**, you can take a left, head for the ocean, and turn right on Pacific. You'll avoid all the traffic and lack of scenic views on Lincoln Avenue, and Pacific (which changes names but stays the same road) reconnects with PCH in **Santa Monica**. Within minutes you're back on track, tooling north past beautiful beaches and ocean.

It's a very pretty drive from Santa Monica into **Malibu**, though the highway occasionally closes when intense rains create mudslides. On this stretch of PCH, you'll enjoy more views of the ocean and a variety of beaches and parks. After you pass through non-scenic Oxnard, the path becomes visually pleasing again as you cruise **Ventura** and on up to **Santa Barbara**. From here through San Luis Obispo, you can enjoy the ocean and rolling hills for much of your drive.

2
CORONADO

Coronado is truly an island getaway. It is sun and beaches, biking and rollerblading, sidewalk cafés and waterfront dining, boating and fishing, all set around a huge, historic, fairy-tale hotel. Coronado is a quaint and quiet village across the bay from San Diego, convenient to but separate from that city. This popular vacation spot was enjoyed by such historical figures as *The Wizard of Oz* author L. Frank Baum, Thomas Edison, and Charles Lindbergh.

The fairy-tale hotel is the Hotel del Coronado, known by locals as the "Hotel Del" or "The Del." Built in 1888, The Del and its pristine beach form the centerpiece of the isle. Visitors, including Prince Edward of Wales, Duchess Wallis Simpson of Windsor, other royalty, 14 presidents, and numerous stage and screen stars, have come here for more than 100 years to enjoy the sands and surf.

But Coronado is not a resort island just for the wealthy and famous. While it has its luxury resorts, it is also an affordable destination for travelers seeking a village atmosphere adjacent to a fine beach, along with fine dining, 15 miles of bike paths, and plenty of other outdoor recreation.

Coronado is home port for the Pacific Fleet Aircraft Carrier Constellation, as well as other tourable surface ships and submarines.

CORONADO

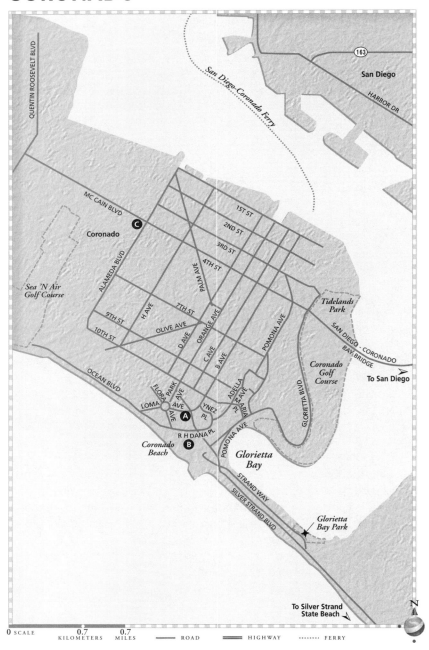

QUENTIN ROOSEVELT BLVD

San Diego-Coronado Ferry

163

San Diego

HARBOR DR

MC CAIN BLVD

Coronado **C**

1ST ST

2ND ST

3RD ST

4TH ST

PALM AVE

ALAMEDA BLVD

Sea 'N Air Golf Course

7TH ST

9TH ST

H AVE

OLIVE AVE

10TH ST

D AVE

ORANGE AVE

C AVE

B AVE

POMONA AVE

Tidelands Park

SAN DIEGO - CORONADO BAY BRIDGE

Coronado Golf Course

To San Diego

GLORIETTA BLVD

OCEAN BLVD

FLORA AVE

PARK AVE

LOMA AVE

YNEZ PL

ADELLA AVE

MARIA PL

A

R H DANA PL

Coronado Beach **B**

POMONA AVE

Glorietta Bay

STRAND WAY

SILVER STRAND BLVD

Glorietta Bay Park

To Silver Strand State Beach

N

0 SCALE   0.7   0.7
KILOMETERS   MILES   ━━━ ROAD   ═══ HIGHWAY   ········ FERRY

A PERFECT DAY IN CORONADO

As with many Southern California destinations, a perfect day in Coronado can begin with a morning stroll or bike ride along the beach. Eat breakfast at Clayton's Coffee Shop or overlooking the ocean at the Ocean Terrace at the Hotel del Coronado. Spend late morning at the beach, or play some tennis or golf. After lunch at Island Pasta or Chez Loma, where you can enjoy the village quality of life, you may want to shop along historic Orange Avenue or at the Ferry Landing. And, of course, be sure to see The Del (the Hotel del Coronado). In the late afternoon, as the sun begins its descent into the Pacific, you may want to enjoy a cold drink as you gaze at the ocean. For dinner, try Beefeaters or Peohe's near the Ferry Landing, or the Chart House, Azzura Point, or the Ocean Terrace on The Del side of the isle. After dinner, take in some live music or wander out onto the beach and enjoy the starry night.

SIGHTSEEING HIGHLIGHTS

★★★★ HOTEL DEL CORONADO
1500 Orange Ave., 619/435-6611
This National Historic Landmark features storybook red-and-white Victorian architecture with turrets, spires, and gazebos. On the grounds you'll find courtyard gardens, an Olympic-size swimming pool, an excellent tennis-court complex, a health spa, and 30 Galleria stores. Recognize the location? *Some Like It Hot* and *The Stunt Man* were filmed here.

Details: *Free as a sightseeing destination; for hotel information, see Lodging, below. (1 hour)*

★★★ HOTEL DEL CORONADO HALL OF HISTORY
619/435-6611
The Hall of History shares the hotel's bottom floor with the Galleria.

SIGHTS
🅐 Coronado Beach Historical Museum
🅑 Hotel del Coronado
🅑 Hotel del Coronado Hall of History
🅒 Ship tours

Note: Items with the same letter are located in the same area.

Its photographs depict the hotel's construction history and various famous guests. On-location celebs have included Marilyn Monroe, Jack Lemmon, and Tony Curtis (during the filming of *Some Like It Hot*); Peter O'Toole, Steve Railsback, and Barbara Hershey (during the filming of *The Stunt Man*); plus other movie and TV stars.

Details: *The Hall of History is part of a self-guided walking tour of the hotel; a cassette tape with headset can be rented for $5 at the hotel gift shop. (30 minutes, not including shopping, snacking, or relaxing on the terrace)*

★★ **CORONADO BEACH HISTORICAL MUSEUM**
1126 Loma Ave., 619/435-7242
This museum is located in a Queen Anne Revival–style structure built in 1889 and features exhibits on the history of the Hotel del Coronado, the ferry, the Navy, and the Tent City that was developed for 1920s tourists, as well as memorabilia from L. Frank Baum and other residents and visitors.

Details: *Open Wed–Sat 10–4, Sun noon–4. Admission is free. (30 minutes)*

★★ **VARIOUS TOURS OF U.S. NAVAL AND VISITING SHIPS**
The aircraft carrier USS *Constellation* is based in Coronado, along with a number of other surface ships, submarines, and, sometimes, foreign naval vessels. These ships are occasionally open for weekend tours or "open houses." Tours involve a lot of walking up and down narrow stairways. Naval ships are not equipped for the handicapped, and each child under 8 must be accompanied by a parent.

Details: *For general information about ships in port open for tours, call 619/532-3130; for general information about the* Constellation *and other U.S. Navy ships, call 619/545-1141. (1–1¹/₂ hours)*

FITNESS AND RECREATION

For enjoyment of the outdoors, Coronado offers the immaculate **Central Beach**, complete with restrooms, shower facilities, and lifeguards. You can explore tide pools or fishing areas in front of the hotel and playground equipment just south of it. Check for free parking on Ocean Boulevard. **Silver Strand State Beach**, 4.5 miles south of the village, also has showers, restrooms, lifeguards, and an underpass to the bayside beach and picnic area. Parking is $4. On the other side of the isle, at the **Ferry Landing Marketplace**, you'll find a beach adjacent to a fishing/ferry pier. It's near a grassy lawn with sweeping views of San Diego Bay, and offers restrooms and free parking. Just below the Coronado Bridge, at **Tidelands Park**, are a sandy beach, fitness course, children's playground equipment, picnic tables, and ballfields. A bike/walking path passes under the bridge. Free parking; restrooms available.

For golf and tennis players, the public **Coronado Golf Course**, 619/435-9485, features 18 holes with a backdrop of Glorietta Bay, San Diego–Coronado Bridge, and the Hotel del Coronado. Nineteen public tennis courts are found at three locations: Glorietta Boulevard at Pomona Avenue, Sixth Street and D Avenue, and on Coronado Cays Boulevard near the fire station.

Glorietta Bay Park, south of Municipal Pool on Strand Way, offers a boat-launching ramp, a grassy park, playground equipment, and a small beach. Restrooms and free parking available.

Coronado's **Loews' Crown Isle Marina**, 619/424-4000, features boat rentals ranging from paddleboats to sailboats to deep-sea fishing boats, and they also rent Jet-Skis. **Charter Connection Dining Yachts**, 619/437-8877, is anchored at Glorietta Bay Marina.

Fisherfolk can cast a line from the pier at Ferry Landing Marketplace or the breakwater at Hotel del Coronado, with abundant surf-fishing along the ocean.

For biking and rollerblading, Coronado features 15 miles of dedicated bike and inline skating paths. You can bike/blade along the bay, under the San Diego–Coronado Bridge, along the golf course, and down the Silver Strand. Bike and inline skate rentals are available at **Bikes and Beyond** (Ferry Landing Marketplace), **Mike's Bikes II** (1343 Orange Ave.), and **Holland's Bicycles** (977 Orange Ave.). Bikes are allowed on the San Diego Bay Ferry and the Strand bus route. **Coronado Walking Touring** offers one-hour easy walking tours on Tuesday, Thursday, and Saturday, departing from the Glorietta Bay Inn (across the street from the hotel) for $6. Call 619/435-5892.

FOOD

Coronado offers a variety of dining experiences, ranging from sidewalk cafés to family restaurants to fine dining with ocean or city views. A great sidewalk-café eatery is **Island Pasta**, 1202 Orange Ave., 619/435-4545, serving homemade pasta made daily on the premises. It's open for lunch and dinner, with meals around $10 to $15.

At the Ferry Marketplace, with a view of the bay and the San Diego skyline, is **Peohe's**, 619/437-4474. Serving Hawaiian seafood dishes, prime rib, and

CORONADO

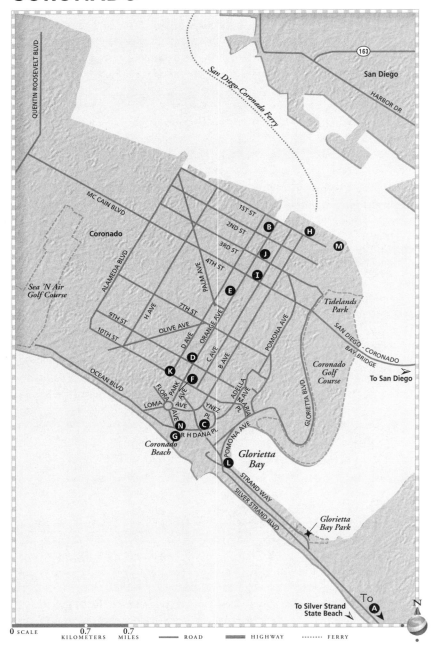

macadamia crème brûlèe, this restaurant also features lush tropical waterfalls and sculptured ponds. It's considered to be one of the isle's best restaurants; entrees range from $15 up.

On the north end of Orange Avenue is **Beefeaters**, 155 Orange Ave., 619/437-1717. Its casual family dining features carved roast beef and steaks; entrees range from $9.95 to $21.95. Also at the north end of Orange Avenue, the **Coronado Brewing Company**, 170 Orange Ave., 619/437-4452, features wood-fired pizza and special delights from their microbrewery. On the south end of Orange, try **Miguel's Cocina Restaurante Mexicano**, 1351 Orange Ave., 619/437-4237, serving a variety of Mexican dishes, with meals starting at $6.45. The **Chart House**, 1701 Strand Way, 619/435-0155, offers a restaurant and patio dining with a fine view of Glorietta Bay. Steak and fresh seafood entrees range from $14.95 to the market price of lobster tail.

Near the center of the village, **Chez Loma**, 1132 Loma Ave., 619/435-0661, located in a historical house built in 1889, offers intimate fine dining and entrees including Salmon Raifort (roast Atlantic salmon fillet with a gratinéed horseradish crust), Medallions de Veal, steaks, sea bass, duck, and lamb. The menu changes seasonally, so you may want to call for entrees and pricing. Dinner entrees generally start at $22.50 They're open evenings only; call for specific times. Sunday brunch features a fruit bowl, croissant, eggs Benedict, and other delights.

Offering views of the Pacific Ocean is the **Ocean Terrace**, 619/522-8866, at the Hotel del Coronado, with meals ranging $10 to $20. The Ocean Terrace is the outdoor dining area by the bay, a relaxed, casual, beautiful place to enjoy breakfast, lunch, or dinner while also enjoying the tranquil view. The Del has a

---

FOOD

Ⓐ Azzura Point
Ⓑ Beefeaters
Ⓒ Chart House
Ⓒ Chez Loma
Ⓓ Clayton's Coffee Shop
Ⓔ Coronado Brewing Company
Ⓔ Crown City Bistro
Ⓕ Island Pasta
Ⓕ McP's Irish Pub

FOOD (continued)

Ⓕ Miguel's Cocina Restaurante Mexicano
Ⓖ Ocean Terrace
Ⓗ Peohe's

LODGING

Ⓘ Best Western Suites
Ⓙ Coronado Island Inn
Ⓚ Coronado Village Inn
Ⓘ El Rancho Motel

LODGING (continued)

Ⓛ Glorietta Bay Inn
Ⓖ Hotel del Coronado
Ⓐ Loews Coronado Bay Resort
Ⓜ The Marriott at Coronado
Ⓝ Villa Capri

CAMPING

Ⓐ Silver Strand State Beach

Note: Items with the same letter are located in the same area.

Dining Adventure at Azzura Point

For fine dining of the highest quality in a setting that is casual yet elegant, you won't do better than **Azzura Point** at the Loews Coronado Bay Resort (619/424-4000). The chef has won all kinds of awards, but it's your taste buds that count, and the food here is delicious. The dinner menu includes appetizers like Peekytoe Crab Tortellini with sage, brown butter, shallots, and tomatoes; roasted calamari with cauliflower, olives, tomatoes, and garlic; and Lobster Risotto with porcini and white truffle essence. Salads include pan-roasted duck foie gras with date compote, banyuls, and brioche; and blue cheese and pine nut tartlet with mezuna, red grape preserves, and verjuice. Their main courses include Hawaiian onaga snapper with caramelized kumquats and Chino Farms vegetables; braised French turbot with Provençal vegetables, and herbed olive oil; saddle of rabbit stuffed with foie gras, grilled greens and nectarines, and oregano jus; and herb-crusted rack of lamb with chile-corn ragout, and black truffle essence. Most entrees start above $25.

But for the real adventure, there's the Chef's Menu, a six-course meal with an optional wine (three-ounce pour) for each course. The wine is specifically selected to match each course. One example of the Chef's Menu (it changes regularly) featured roasted Sonoma foie gras (with Perrin, Muscat de Beaumes-de-Venise, Rhone Valley, France); salad of Daurade Royale (with Villa Del Borgo, Pinot Grigio, Friuli, Italy), Atlantic monkfish Cordon Bleu (with Leroy D'Auvenay, Bourgogne Blanc, Burgundy, France), Harissa-marinated rack of lamb (with Alejandro Fernandez, Condado De Haza, Ribera Del Duero, Spain), cheese course (terrine of Gorgonzola with golden raisins and pine nuts, served with Allegrini, Palazozo Della Torre, Veneto, Italy), and (for the last course) caramelized orange tart and a chocolate sorbet, served with Banfi, Brachetto D'Acqui, Piedmont, Italy.

This culinary adventure (during which, if you like, they'll tell a bit about how the wine was selected) lasts about two hours, and is priced at $100; $65 without the wine. Each table in the room has a view of the bay with the Chocolate Mountains in the background.

reputation as a fantasyland and this large, pleasant deck contributes to that fanciful quality. Breakfast specialties include lox and bagel, Primavera Frittata (an open-faced three-egg omelette topped with peppers, mushrooms, zucchini, spinach, tomatoes, and mozzarella cheese that is as good as it sounds), shrimp omelette, breakfast burritos, and The Californian: seasonal fruit and berries, granola, and low-fat yogurt (isn't this what you eat *after* vacation?). Other meals feature fish and chicken, there are always items from the bakery, and there's a children's menu (including pancakes, French toast, hot dogs, ravioli, and milk).

For breakfast, try **Clayton's Coffee Shop**, 979 Orange Ave., 619/435-5425. Its '50s decor includes tabletop jukeboxes, and meals generally cost less than $10. Several restaurants offer Sunday brunches, including **Crown City Bistro**, 520 Orange Ave., 619/435-3678; **McP's Irish Pub**, 1107 Orange Ave., 619/435-5280; and Peohe's, Chez Loma, and the Coronado Brewing Company.

Crown City Bistro also offers delicious choices for breakfast (cinnamon apple French toast, bananas Foster French toast), lunch (grilled shrimp and avocado salad) and dinner (lamb shank au burgundy, calamari meunière) with prices generally under $10.

LODGING

Home to three resort hotels, Coronado offers a variety of lodging options, from locally owned and operated places to popular chain motels. **Coronado Village Inn**, 1017 Park Pl., 619/435-9318, is a quiet European-style hotel with 15 rooms, each decorated in its own style. It's one block from Orange Avenue and one block from the ocean. Rates start at $75 in winter and $86 in summer.

Coronado Island Inn, 301 Orange Ave., 619/435-0935, on the north end of Orange Avenue, has 12 rooms and is close to the Ferry Marketplace. Kitchen units are available, with winter rates starting at $55 and summer rates at $79 (more for the kitchen units). Nearby is **El Rancho Motel**, 370 Orange Ave., 619/435-2251, a quiet, six-unit Spanish-style building. Rooms include microwaves, mini-fridges, HBO, and air-conditioning, with rates ranging from $45 to $90. **Best Western Suites**, 275 Orange Ave., 800/528-1234, is farther north on Orange Avenue. Rates vary with the seasons, ranging from $89 to $130.

Looking for luxury? The **Hotel del Coronado**, 800/HOTEL-DEL or 619/435-6611; **Loews Coronado Bay Resort**, 800/81-LOEWS; and the **Marriott at Coronado**, 619/435-3000 or 800/228-4290, offer resort amenities at resort prices.

The centrally located Del's Pacific-view rooms start at $430, with other room rates ranging from $205 to $595. The Del offers history and a stunning architecture, the glamour of show business, and a fairy-tale atmosphere. Each room is unique (the architecture is such that there are few right angles) and includes a mini-bar, iron and ironing board, hair dryer, robes, and TV.

The Loews, farther south on the isle, overlooks both the bay and the ocean and is the true getaway spot in Coronado. It's a more modern resort featuring spacious rooms with balconies, a mini-bar, TV, and bathrooms with a tub and a separate shower (!) and numerous activities (chef's cooking classes, fitness classes, herb garden tour, kung fu and Tai Chi lessons, sailing lessons, a sunset sail, gondola rides, golf, tennis, and more). The Loews Kids Camp offers a super-vised series of activities for kids 4–12. The staff is friendly and helpful—first-rate. Rates are $185 and up.

You can enjoy views of the bay and San Diego from the Marriott, with rooms starting at $235—rooms with a view of Superior Bay (and San Diego) start at $285. The Marriott offers quiet elegance not far from the Coronado's activities and near the bridge to San Diego. The grounds are beautifully land-scaped, creating the effect that you are far away from it all when you're really close to everything. Each spacious room comes with a coffeemaker, mini-bar, in-room safe, iron and ironing board, separate tub and shower, robes, and a living-room area. The bar features a jazz duo every Friday and Saturday night.

The **Villa Capri**, 1417 Orange Ave., 800/231-3954, across from The Del, offers European style and design in its kitchen apartments, suites, and single accommodations. Rates range from $79.50 to $299.50, including a free conti-nental breakfast. Also across from the hotel is the **Glorietta Bay Inn**, 1630 Glorietta Blvd., 800/283-9383, the former mansion of sugar baron John Spreckels. Rates for this historic landmark, which is surrounded by lush gardens, range from $89 for "snug" rooms to $300 for suites in the mansion.

CAMPING

There's no tent camping in town, but **Silver Strand State Beach**, 619/435-5184, allows overnight RV camping for $16 a night; $14 for seniors ($4 less for off-season), $6 for each extra vehicle, and $1 per dog. Food service and pic-nicking facilities (at $4/table) are available; fishing and swimming allowed. It's four miles south of Coronado on Highway 75.

NIGHTLIFE

McP's Irish Pub, 1107 Orange Ave., 619/435-5280 features live entertain-ment, and the bar at the Marriott (above, Lodging) features a jazz duo every Friday and Saturday night.

3
SOUTHERN
COASTAL REGION

Stretching from Oceanside through Newport Beach, the southern coastal region is a beautiful 60-mile expanse of coastline hugging the wondrously blue Pacific, which can be seen from the highway. Heading north, take I-5; near San Juan Capistrano the interstate veers inland, but the Pacific Coast Highway (PCH) is easily accessed if you wish to continue up the coast.

While the coastal towns of Oceanside, San Juan Capistrano (which is not exactly on the coast, but Capistrano Beach is), Laguna Beach, and Newport Beach are each very distinct, they also have much in common. In each town you can expect stunning views, fine accommodations, ocean-side restaurants, and a variety of unique shops and boutiques.

At the same time, an elusive character and a distinct flavor distinguishes each of these coastal towns from the others. For example, Laguna Beach, sheltered by a bend in the coastline, feels like it could be an enclave on an island paradise. The nearby town of San Juan Capistrano offers a beautiful and interesting mission to explore. Newport Beach is a city on the move. Visitors can have fun here, but business is also being transacted and the community is not solely focused on tourists. The city of Oceanside, which is home to the San Luis Rey Mission, has the feel of a tranquil getaway.

A PERFECT DAY ALONG THE SOUTHERN COAST

Start your day with breakfast in Oceanside, take in the California Surf Museum and Buena Vista Lagoon, then head for the San Luis Rey Mission—a great way to appreciate the cultural spectrum from surfing to Spanish missionary settlement in this area. Next, head north to the Mission San Juan Capistrano, and spend part of the afternoon at Laguna Beach. Take in the Top of the World View, hike in Laguna Heights, or do some shopping at the oceanfront boutiques. Travel north to Newport Beach, arriving in plenty of time to see the sunset. Dine at one of Newport's many restaurants or on a dinner cruise, and enjoy dance music at Bob Burns or Woody's Wharf, or a concert at the Crazy Horse Steakhouse. It's a day of history, scenic landscape, ocean views, good food, and music.

SIGHTSEEING HIGHLIGHTS

★★★★ CALIFORNIA SURF MUSEUM
223 N. Coast Highway, Oceanside, 760/721-6876
It's a surf museum! Like, dude, you gotta check this out. It's, like, mandatory. I mean, this is Southern California. . . . This museum is dedicated to the history of surfing, going back to the 1920s and the days of 200-pound redwood boards (today they weigh two pounds and are made of foam or fiberglass). Check out the permanent exhibit on Duke Kahanamoku, who is considered to be the father of surfing. Also on display are different photos, boards, and revolving exhibits. One recent exhibit, Riders of the Sunset Seas, featured memorabilia about Tom Blake, the first man to patent a surfboard (in 1932) and the first to put a fin on a board (in 1935). This place is a trip, impressing even non-surfers, who comprise about 80 percent of its visitors.
Details: *Open daily 10–4. Admission is free. (1 hour)*

★★★★ MISSION SAN JUAN CAPISTRANO
Camino Capistrano and Ortega Highway
714/248-2049
This mission, known as the "Jewel of the Missions," truly lives up to its name. It's one of the largest and most architecturally elaborate of the missions in Southern California and features beautiful grounds, courtyards, and gardens. The mission was established in 1775, destroyed by an earthquake in 1812, secularized in 1833, sold in 1845, and returned to the church in 1865. The extensive museum offers displays depicting

SOUTHERN COASTAL REGION

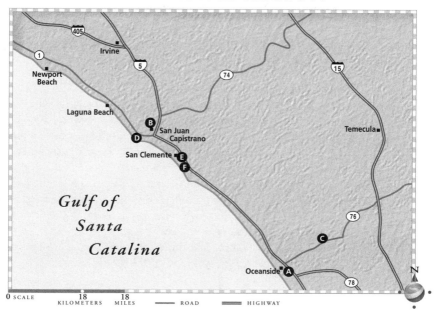

SIGHTS

Ⓐ Buena Vista Lagoon
Ⓐ California Surf Museum
Ⓑ Los Rios Historic District
Ⓑ Mission San Juan Capistrano

SIGHTS *(continued)*

Ⓒ Mission San Luis Rey de Francia
Ⓓ O'Neill Museum
Ⓓ Swallows of San Juan Capistrano

LODGING

Ⓐ Oceanside Marina Inn

CAMPING

Ⓓ Doheny State Beach
Ⓔ San Clemente State Beach
Ⓕ San Onofre State Beach

Note: Items with the same letter are located in the same town.

what life was like for the priests and Indians; the church, still active today, has a 300-year-old Baroque reredo imported from Barcelona. There is a cemetery near the church—it's a little spooky. And a current archaeological site and display shows that research is ongoing (they think they just found what was the hospital) and how this kind of painstaking investigation is done.

Details: Take I-5 to San Juan Capistrano and follow the signs. The mission is at the corner of Camino Capistrano and Ortega Highway. Open daily 8:30–5. Admission is $5; $4 seniors and children 3–12. (2 hours)

★★★★ MISSION SAN LUIS REY DE FRANCIA
4050 Mission Ave., Oceanside, 760/757-3651

Although not as profound as the mission in San Juan Capistrano, this mission, built circa 1798, named for Louis IX, and known as "King of the Missions," features a fairly comprehensive museum depicting the rigorous life led by missionaries and natives. The largest collection of 18th- and 19th-century Spanish vestments in the United States is displayed. Though it weathered a rocky past similar to the Capistrano mission, the building was rededicated in 1893. And while the mission in San Juan Capistrano has an active archaeological site, this mission is an active retreat. Gift shop on premises.

Details: From Oceanside, take State Highway 76 about five miles east. Open daily 10–4:30. Admission is $3 for a self-guided tour. (1 hour)

★★ BUENA VISTA LAGOON
2202 S. Coast Highway
Oceanside, 760/439-2473

This 200-acre ecological preserve provides a habitat for nearly 200 species of resident and visiting birds, including white pelicans, song sparrows, and blackbirds. There is an on-site nature center and museum.

Details: Open Tue–Sat 10–4; Sun 1–4. Admission is free. (30 minutes)

★★ LOS RIOS HISTORIC DISTRICT

This area in San Juan Capistrano offers another glimpse into the rich history of Southern California. Los Rios displays what a small Southern California town, complete with 31 adobe homes, looked like in the late nineteenth century. One historic house (the Montanez Adobe, 31745 Los Rios St., open 10–4) has a fascinating docent, Mary Snowbird, who is a born storyteller. It's important to note, however, that the houses are interspersed with "real" houses where people live . . . please respect the "No Trespassing" and "Private Residence" signs.

Details: *Located next to the Capistrano Depot, within walking distance of Mission San Juan Capistrano (see above). (1 hour)*

★★ O'NEILL MUSEUM
31831 Los Rios St., San Juan Capistrano, 714/493-8444
Housed in a small Victorian building constructed in the 1870s, this museum contains furniture and artifacts from the late 1800s.
Details: *Open Tue–Fri 9 a.m.–noon and 1–4; Sun noon–3; closed Sat and Mon. (30 minutes)*

★★ SWALLOWS OF SAN JUAN CAPISTRANO
The swallows return to the mission each spring on St. Joseph's Day (March 19), on their way from Mexico to their homes in the north. The Swallow's Day Festival is held the third Saturday in March at the mission.

★★ TOP OF THE WORLD VIEW
This spectacular overlook from Top of the World View Park takes in a curvaceous mountain-sloped coastline and Laguna Beach.
Details: *Take Park Avenue east from Pacific Coast Highway all the way up to Alta Laguna Boulevard, turn right, then turn left at Tree Top Lane, where you'll see the park. (30 minutes)*

★ NEWPORT HARBOR NAUTICAL MUSEUM
151 E. Coast Highway, Newport Beach, 714/673-3377
Located on the sternwheeler *Pride of Newport* (a replica of an antebellum boat), this museum is for the nautical enthusiast, featuring comprehensive displays of maritime and historical items.
Details: *Open Tue–Sun 10–5. Admission is $4 adults, $1 children. (1 hour)*

FITNESS AND RECREATION
Sportfishing and whale-watching from Oceanside are provided by **Helgren's Sportfishing Trips**, 760/722-2133. **Pacific Coast Sail Charters** offers sailing aboard a luxury yacht, 760/722-2963.

In Laguna Beach, the seven-mile scenic coastline offers more than 30 unique beaches. **Main Beach**, at the center of town, is a popular place for water sports of all kinds. Farther north, between the beach and the cliff, is **Heisler Park**, an excellent spot for picnicking, biking, swimming, and sunning.

NEWPORT BEACH

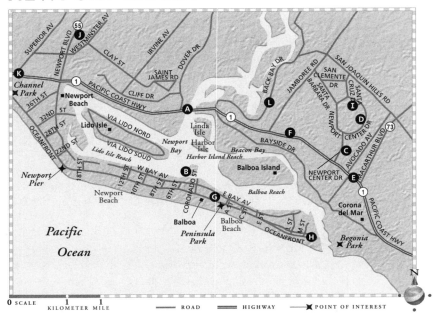

SIGHTS

A Newport Harbor
Nautical Museum

FOOD

B Newport Landing
C Tutto Mare
D Twin Palms
E Windows on the Bay

LODGING

F Balboa Bay Club
G Balboa Inn
H Doryman's Oceanfront Inn
I Four Seasons Hotel
J Little Inn on the Bay
K Newport Channel Inn

CAMPING

L Newport Dunes Resort

Note: Items with the same letter are located in the same area.

Crescent Bay, north of Heisler Park, offers great bodysurfing, while Sleepy Hollow, south of Main Beach, has excellent swimming. Beautiful, too, are Woods Cove and Victoria Beach, farther south of Sleepy Hollow. You can play volleyball at Victoria. Shaw's Cove and Divers Cove are said to be excellent for scuba divers. Aliso Creek County Beach, 31131 Pacific Coast Highway (south of Laguna), has picnic tables, barbecues, and fire pits; surf at **Thousand Steps Beach**, Pacific Coast Highway and Ninth Street, South Laguna. If you're north of Crescent Bay, relax at **Emerald Bay** and **Cameo Cove**; these are also beautiful beaches.

Hikers and bikers enjoy **Crystal Cove State Park**, which includes 3.5 miles of coastline between Laguna Beach and Corona del Mar (to the north). The park features **Reef Point** (an access point to a popular beach known for bodysurfing), **Pelican Point** (also an access point to the beach, it offers restrooms, outdoor showers, and a one-mile trail that parallels the coastline with a terrific view), and **Underwater Park** (a 1,000-acre underwater park featuring an abundance of aquatic life for snorkelers and divers). Check in at the park office at 8471 Pacific Coast Highway, 949/494-3539. (For camping in this park, see Camping, below.)

For more hiking, cycling, bird-watching, and reveling in nature, consider **Laguna Coast Wilderness Park**, 949/854-7108. Permits are required and cost $20. From Main Beach, take Laguna Canyon Road east toward I-405. On the right is **Laguna Heights**, open daily 7 a.m. to sunset. On the left is **Laurel Canyon**, open through docent-led tours only. Farther east on the right is the **Jim Dilley Greenbelt Preserve**, open the third Saturday of each month 10 a.m. to 4 p.m. The park is managed by Orange County; call the Laguna Coat Wilderness Park Access Line, 949/854-7108, for information. Adjacent to Greenbelt, the **Irvine Company Open Space Reserve**, 949/832-7478, is managed by the Nature Conservancy. It offers hiking, cycling, and equestrian tours. Tours are docent-led only, and reservations are a must. **Alta Laguna Park**, 949/497-0716, has hiking trails with views of the ocean and the countryside to the east. From PCH, take Park Avenue to Alta Laguna Boulevard, turn left, and drive to the end of the road. Reservations and guides are not necessary.

The **Upper Newport Bay Ecological Reserve** provides numerous hiking, biking, and horse trails through a 752-acre coastal wetland. Ask about canoe and kayak tours, twilight cruises, and family campfire programs at the Department of Fish and Game office, 949/640-6746, located on Shellmaker Island off Back Bay Drive. Admission is free but donations are welcome. Explore a 2.5-acre wildlife habitat at the **Environmental Nature Center** located at 1601 16th St., Newport Beach (between Irvine Avenue and Dover Drive), 949/645-8489. Trail guides and naturalists lead guided walking tours especially for children 5 and older. The center is open Monday through Friday 8 a.m. to 4 p.m., and Saturday 8 a.m. to 3 p.m. Admission is free but donations are welcome.

For sportfishing and whale-watching from Newport Beach, call **Newport Landing/Sportfishing and Whale Watching**, 949/675-0550, and **Davey's Locker/Sportfishing and Whale Watching**, 949/673-1434.

LAGUNA BEACH

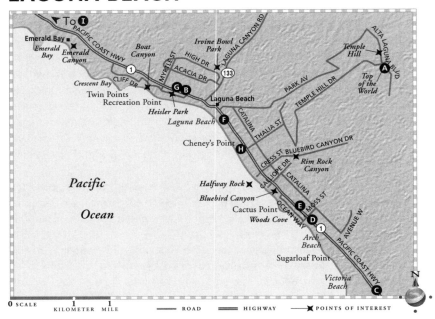

SIGHTS
A Top of the World View

FOOD
B The Cottage
C The Terrace

LODGING
D Bay View Laguna Inn
E Casa Laguna Inn
F Hotel Laguna
G Inn at Laguna Beach
H Laguna Riviera

CAMPING
I Crystal Cove State Park

(Remember, whale-watching is seasonal, roughly late December through March. Be sure to call first.)

Newport Beach's best golfing can be found at the **Hyatt Newporter**, 1107 Jamboree Road, 949/729-1234, with a nine-hole course; the **Newport Beach Golf Course**, 3100 Irvine Ave., 949/852-8681, with an 18-hole course (par 71, 3,450 yards), also open nightly; and the **Pelican Hill Golf Club**, 22651 Pelican Hill Road S., just off Pacific Coast Highway, 949/759-5190, with two 18-hole courses.

If you're interested in dinner cruises, Newport Beach's **Hornblower**

Dining Yachts, 949/631-2469, and the Cannery Restaurant, 949/675-5777, are among those providing elegant culinary experiences at sea. Also in Newport Beach, **Electra Cruises, Inc.**, 949/723-1069, offers cruises; and **Balboa Boat Rentals**, 949/673-7200, offers rentals. For other water sports, the following outfitters operate bayside in Newport Beach/Balboa: **Fun Zone Water Bikes**, 714/673-5002; **Walk on Water**, (Jet-Skis and Sea-Doos), 714/675-6800; and **Balboa Parasail**, 714/673-3372. The kids will love **Balboa Fun Zone**, 400 E. Bay St., Balboa Peninsula, 714/673-0408, with rides, video games, and more. Open noon to 8 p.m.

FOOD

In Laguna Beach enjoy home-style California cuisine on the patio at **The Cottage**, a Laguna landmark home, 308 N. Coast Highway (across PCH from the Laguna Art Museum), 714/494-3023. Entrees range from $12 to $20. **The Terrace**, 425 S. Coast Highway, Laguna Beach (at the Hotel Laguna), 714/494-1151, serves "California contemporary" (who makes up these labels?). The Terrace has a great view of Main Beach and is an excellent place either for breakfast or to enjoy the sunset. Entrees are generally less than $12.

In Newport Beach fine dining can be pricey. **Twin Palms**, 630 Newport Center Dr., 714/721-8288, prepares California coastal cuisine (a mix of a variety of influences). Entrees range from $10 (for pasta and salads) to $28 (for herb-crusted filet mignon). **Windows on the Bay**, 2241 W. Coast Highway, 714/722-1400, features contemporary California cuisine in an elegant setting complete with 25-foot ceilings, Moroccan archways, and floor-to-ceiling windows. And, yes, a great view of the bay. Meals range from $12 to $26. **Tutto Mare**, 545 Newport Center Dr., 714/640-6333, is known for its creative Northern Italian cuisine with an emphasis on seafood, served in a very happening place. Entrees range from $11 to $20.

Newport Landing, 503 E. Edgewater, Balboa, 714/675-2373, offers waterfront dining on fresh seafood or prime beef. Or dine at the casual upstairs lounge, with a patio deck and live entertainment. Restaurant entrees start at $14.95; oyster bar entrees start at $8.95.

LODGING

Nestled in the mouth of the harbor, **Oceanside Marina Inn**, 2008 Harbor Dr. N., Oceanside, 760/722-1561 or 800/252-2033, offers rooms with ocean and harbor views. Rates range between $120 and $260.

In Laguna and Newport Beaches your choices range from motels to resorts, several of which are on or overlooking the beach. **Casa Laguna Inn**, 2510 S. Coast Highway, 714/494-2996 or 800/233-0449, is a Spanish-style B&B overlooking the Pacific. Rates range from $69 to $225. At the oceanfront **Laguna Riviera**, 825 S. Coast Highway, 714/494-1196 or 800/999-2089, rates range from $60 to $176. Also on the beach are the **Inn at Laguna Beach**, 211 N. Coast Highway, 714/497-9722 or 800/544-4479, $99 to $449; and the **Hotel Laguna**, 425 S. Coast Highway, 714/497-2163 or 800/524-2927, $65 to $200. Finally, the **Bay View Laguna Inn**, 2020 S. Coast Highway, 714/494-5450, is one block from the beach with an ocean view. Rates range from $55 to $130.

The four-star **Balboa Bay Club**, 1221 W. Coast Highway, Newport Beach, 800/445-7153, offers panoramic bay views and virtually all the resort amenities. Rates range from $150 to $500. Another four-star option in Newport Beach, the **Four Seasons Hotel**, 690 Newport Center Dr., 800/332-3442, has suites above Newport Harbor and the Pacific. It supplies the usual four-star amenities with rates starting at $345.

The **Balboa Inn**, 105 Main St., Balboa Peninsula, 714/675-341, is a historical landmark B&B that offers both ocean and bay views, with a fireplace and spa in each of its suites. Winter rates start at $99, $139 in summer. **Doryman's Oceanfront Inn**, 2102 W. Oceanfront, Newport Beach, 800/634-3303, is a late-19th-century B&B with 10 rooms and suites. Pacific sunsets can be viewed from the rooftop deck. Rates start at $185. **Little Inn on the Bay**, 2627 Newport Blvd., Balboa Peninsula, 949/673-8800, has a beach ambiance and is only 300 steps from the sand. Bicycles are included in rates starting at $100. And the **Newport Channel Inn**, 6030 W. Coast Highway, Newport Beach, 800/255-8614, is a motel located just across from the beach. Winter rates start at $49, $59 in summer.

CAMPING

Between Oceanside and Laguna Beach, three state parks furnish facilities for tent campers, motor homes, and travel trailers. **Doheny State Beach**, 34320 Del Obispo, Dana Point, 714/496-6171, has picnicking, fishing, hiking, swimming, a nature trail, and exhibits, but no hookups. **San Clemente State Beach**, 225 Avenida Calafia, San Clemente, 714/492-3156, offers picnicking, fishing, hiking, swimming, and 75 hookups. **San Onofre State Beach**, 3030 Avenida de Presidente, San Onofre, 714/492-4872, provides primitive campsites, chemical toilets, and water for cooking only. The tent area runs on a first-come, first-served basis. Swimming, hiking, and some hookups are available.

Crystal Cove State Park offers environmental camping on 2,200 acres of backcountry, 714/494-3595 or 800/444-7275. Bring your own supplies. No shower facilities; open fires and pets are not allowed. From Pacific Coast Highway, take School–State Park Road and follow the signs. Register at the ranger station. Campsites are about a three- to four-mile hike in. Admission varies seasonally between $7 and $11 per car.

Newport Dunes Resort, 1131 Back Bay Dr., 714/729-DUNE or 800/288-0770, a 100-acre RV heaven adjacent to the beach, offers many amenities such as flush toilets, showers, and beach tables. Groceries, a Laundromat, and propane can be found within five miles of the resort; water-sport rentals are also available.

NIGHTLIFE

The fine restaurant **Bob Burns**, 881 Newport Center Dr., Newport Beach, 714/644-2030, has live entertainment Wednesday through Saturday.

For those who want to see nationally known entertainers like Waylon Jennings and Charlie Daniels, nearby Santa Ana hosts **Crazy Horse Steakhouse**, 1580 Brookhollow Dr., 714/549-1512. This nightclub/restaurant is designed to resemble an Old West saloon.

For those in search of a sports bar and live entertainment, there's **Knuckles at the Hyatt Newporter**, 1107 Jamboree Road, 714/729-1234; the blues band plays on Fridays and Saturdays.

Check out jazz and rock on Saturdays and a steel band on Sundays at the **Newport Landing Restaurant**, 503 E. Edgewater Ave., Balboa Peninsula, 714/675-2373. **Woody's Wharf**, 2318 W. Newport Blvd., Newport Beach, 714/675-0474, stages live rock 'n' roll Thursday through Saturday.

SHOPPING

The classy **Fashion Island**, Newport Beach, features numerous shops with designer fashions and more than 40 great choices for indoor or patio dining, including Twin Palms and Tutto Mare (listed above) and Bob Burns (also listed above). Open Monday through Friday 10 a.m. to 9 p.m., Saturday 10 a.m. to 7 p.m., Sunday, 11 a.m. to 6 p.m. Fashion Island is just off Pacific Coast Highway and west of I-405 between MacArthur Boulevard and Jamboree Road, 714/721-2000.

4
SANTA CATALINA
ISLAND

Santa Catalina is a beautiful mountaintop of an island that lies about an hour from the coast. It's just 21 miles long and eight miles wide, with its highest elevation at Mount Orizaba (2,069 feet). Inhabited by various Native American tribes for more than 7,000 years, the island was home to the Pimungans when explorers Juan Cabrillo, and later Sebastian Vizcaino, arrived. In the 1820s the Pimungans, decimated by disease and their trading economy disrupted by the Spanish mission system, moved to the mainland.

The island's recent history is that of a resort. Discovered by vacationers in the 1880s, it has been a popular getaway ever since. Its Avalon Tuna Club, the oldest fishing club in the United States, was founded in 1889. Early club members included Zane Grey, Cecil B. De Mille, and Winston Churchill. In 1975 the Santa Catalina Island Conservancy acquired 86 percent of the island to preserve and protect.

The center of activity on Catalina is the village of Avalon. Most boats land there, where the major restaurants and hotels are located, and from which most tours begin. On the other side of the island is Two Harbors, mostly consisting of a small lodging and camping site. A few main roads and hiking and biking trails are scattered throughout the island, but most of the island remains wilderness.

Though it's no longer exclusively a resort town, it is in some ways a natural Disneyland—in that virtually everything has a ticket price. Nonetheless, Catalina is a fantastic place to experience Southern California's wilderness and water.

SANTA CATALINA ISLAND

Boat to Newport Beach

Boat to Long Beach

Avalon Bay

East End Light

A

Avalon ■

Goat Harbor

C

D

Black Jack Mountain

E

Little Harbor

B

Two Harbors

Catalina Harbor

Emerald Bay

Parson's Landing

F

Land's End

Pacific Ocean

PLACE OF INTEREST

FERRY

ROAD

0 SCALE

4 KILOMETERS

4 MILES

A PERFECT DAY ON CATALINA

Since most of Catalina's sights combine well with recreational activity, the first thing to do after breakfasting at the Pancake Cottage is to start seeing the island. If you're a hiker staying in Avalon or camping at Hermit Gulch, you might want to get started on the nearest trails. Another option is to take one of the tours of the interior. Observe the buffalo by taking either a bus or jeep tour. (The tours don't guarantee you'll see them, but chances are you will.) After lunch, visit the museum and then spend some time in and around the water. Have a sunset dinner at Armstrong's overlooking the bay. After dinner, enjoy live music at one of the island's clubs.

GETTING TO CATALINA

To get to Catalina, take your own boat, rent a boat in Long Beach (all moorings are first-come, first-served), or take a cruise with either **Catalina Cruises**, 800/CATALINA, or **Catalina Express**, 800/464-4228. Catalina Express leaves from a dock right next to the *Queen Mary*. From Newport Beach take the **Catalina Flyer**, 714/673-5245. And you can fly from San Diego with **Island Hopper/Catalina Airlines**, 619/279-4595.

GETTING AROUND CATALINA

Once you're in Avalon, almost everything (lodgings, restaurants, tour and rental places, shops, casino) is within view and walking distance. Very few

---

SIGHTS

Ⓐ Underwater Wildlife and Plant Life in Lover's Cove

FOOD

Ⓑ Doug's Harbor Reef Saloon
Ⓑ Doug's Harbor Restaurant
Ⓑ Reef Grill

LODGING

Ⓑ Banning House Lodge
Ⓑ Two Harbors Cabins

CAMPING

Ⓒ Blackjack Campground
Ⓓ Catalina Yurt Cabins
Ⓔ Little Harbor Campground

CAMPING *(continued)*

Ⓕ Parson's Landing Campground
Ⓑ Two Harbors Campground

Note: Items with the same letter are located in the same town.

---

businesses list addresses—they're more likely to say "across from the Green Pier," "facing the harbor," or "in the Metropole Market Place." Things are easy to find because street signs include the names of shops, restaurants, and lodgings.

When calling listings with a 310 area code, dial all 10 digits, even if you're calling locally.

If you want to just roam around and hike or bike, be aware that biking requires a $50 permit. (Hiking permits are required, too, but they're free.) Tourists are not allowed to bring cars onto the island. Your only transport options are bikes, cabs, tour buses, and golf carts, which you can rent or hire. Rent or hire them, and note the restrictions.

SIGHTSEEING HIGHLIGHTS

★★★★ CATALINA ISLAND MUSEUM
1 Casino Way, 310/510-2414
This museum traces Catalina Island's 7,000-year history, from the artifacts of early occupants, through the Spanish discovery and the establishment of Union Army barracks, and on into the modern era. Here you can see exhibits on ranching and mining, and in the video theater you can view presentations about the island's archaeology, as well as the island fox, bison, and the celebrated pigeon mail service of the 1890s.

Details: Located in the Casino Building; open daily 10:30–4. Admission is $1.50. (1 hour)

★★★ BUFFALO ON CATALINA ISLAND
A fascinating sight. It's hard to believe that you're not on some Midwestern prairie but on an island off the coast of California. Twenty of these picturesque and historic animals were brought over in the early 1900s to be used in the filming of Zane Grey's *The Vanishing American*. But though their moment in the limelight ended up on the cutting-room floor, the buffalo were left on the island to multiply— and they did. By the late '60s more than 400 buffalo roamed Catalina; now they are managed. To see them, you must either take a tour or spot them while hiking or biking.

Details: See Fitness and Recreation, below. (1/2 day)

★★★ UNDERWATER WILDLIFE AND PLANT LIFE IN LOVER'S COVE

This underwater cove is out of this world. All sorts of fish (including the occasional barracuda and eel) swim amid swirling seaweed above the coral-pocked and sandy ocean floor. You can snorkel here for an up-close-and-personal view, or take the submerged boat or glass-bottom boat tour.

Details: See *Fitness and Recreation, below.* (1 day)

★★ CATALINA CASINO
1 Casino Way, 310/510-0179

This theater was the first theater designed for "talking pictures." It features art deco architecture, epic murals, and a very rare pipe organ. Tours are available only during the day; it's a regular movie theater at night.

Details: See *Fitness and Recreation, below, for tour information.* (2 hours)

FITNESS AND RECREATION

There is a lot to see and do here, most of it accessible only through tours. Depending on the season, many activities stop around 4 p.m. Be sure to check on first and last departure times.

Rafting and diving trips, kayaking, boat rentals, and fishing charters are offered by **Adventure Rafting**, 310/510-0211; **Joe's Rent-A-Boat**, 310/510-0455; **Argo Diving Service**, 310/510-2208; and **Catalina Diver's Supply**, 800/353-0330.

Among the outfits that rent "autos" (motorized carts) and bikes are **Catalina Auto and Bike Rental** (no phone, but located at the corner of Metropole and Crescent); **Brown's Bikes**, 310/510-0986; and **Island Rentals**, 310/510-1456. Brown's Bikes and Island Rentals are on Pebbly Beach Road, near the dock.

Note: Outside of the village of Avalon, biking and hiking permits are required. Hiking is free, biking is $50. Call **Catalina Island Conservancy**, 310/510-2595, for further information.

For golfers, there's the **Catalina Visitor Golf Course**, 310/510-0530, nine holes with a spectacular view of Avalon and the ocean below. The course is said to be the oldest west of the Rocky Mountains.

Water- and land-tour outfitters include **Catalina Adventure Tours**, 310/510-2888, which guides an Inside Adventure tour along the coastline and

AVALON

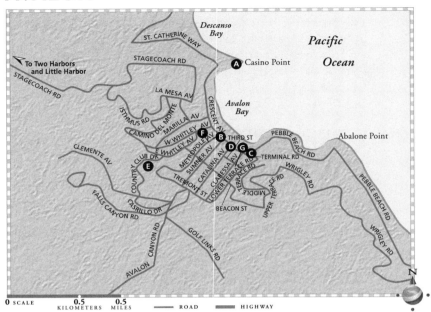

SIGHTS

Ⓐ Catalina Casino
Ⓐ Catalina Island
Museum

FOOD

Ⓑ Armstrong's
Ⓒ Blue Parrot
Ⓐ Catalina Cantina–
Topless Tacos and
Burgers

FOOD (continued)

Ⓒ Channel House
Ⓓ Coyote Joe's
Ⓓ Eric's on the Pier
Ⓓ Pancake Cottage
Ⓒ Ristorante Villa
Portofino

LODGING

Ⓔ Catalina Canyon
Resort
Ⓕ Catalina Cottages and
Hermosa Hotel

LODGING (continued)

Ⓖ Catalina Island
Seacrest Inn
Ⓒ Hotel Metropole
Ⓐ Zane Grey Pueblo
Hotel

CAMPING

Ⓐ Hermit Gulch

Note: Items with the same letter are located in the same area.

into the interior to see the wildlife, including the buffalo, from an air-conditioned bus. This two-hour tour costs $19 for adults, $10 for children under 12; children under 3 are free. They also offer water taxis and harbor cruises, a tour of the city and the botanical garden, and a glass-bottom boat tour. **Discovery Tours**, 310/510-TOUR, has similar tours, plus a Seal Rocks Cruise to see the migratory seals in their natural habitat (55 minutes; $8 adults, $4.25 children), a casino tour (50 minutes; $8 adults, $4.25 children), and an undersea tour in which you travel submerged in a specially designed boat to view orange garibaldi, spotted calico bass, opaleyes, sheepshead, and more (40 minutes; $19.50 adults, $13 children).

FOOD

Tourist-oriented Catalina has a variety of restaurants for a variety of tastes, both culinary and visual. Many restaurants have ocean views. **Armstrong's**, 310/510-0113, 306 Crescent (two blocks from Green Pier), Avalon, serves tasty, fresh seafood indoors and on the deck, with a front-seat view of the bay. Entrees average around $14. The **Blue Parrot**, located at the entrance to Metropole Market Place, 205 Crescent Ave., 310/510-2465, has a tropical atmosphere and a view of the bay from its second-story location. The American-cuisine entrees average around $12, and there is live entertainment most weekends. **Channel House**, on Crescent, 310/510-1617, offers fine dining with continental cuisine and an ocean view. Entrees range from $16 to $24. **Ristorante Villa Portofino**, on Crescent, facing the bay, 310/510-0508, serves Italian cuisine in that classically Californian atmosphere of informality and elegance. Dinners average $16.

Catalina Cantina–Topless Tacos and Burgers, on Crescent, facing the bay, 310/510-0100, feels like the only "it's not restricted here and you don't need a ticket to get in" place on the island. The food's ordinary, the music might be too loud, the game's on, and in any other place in Southern California it wouldn't be worth mentioning. But it's a great place to sit and people-watch in an atmosphere different from the rest of the island's.

Coyote Joe's, about a half-block up from the Green Pier on Catalina Ave., 310/510-1176, serves Mexican and American dishes; most meals are less than $10. Almost across the street, the **Pancake Cottage**, 310/510-0726, is the place for breakfast, serving omelets and, of course, pancakes. Most meals are less than $10. Open from 6:30 a.m., **Eric's on the Pier** is a small counter-service outdoor restaurant serving tacos, fries, eggs, and very tasty buffalo burgers. It's a place for a quick lunch in the middle of a busy day, where you can enjoy the beautiful weather.

QUEEN MARY, LONG BEACH

Launched in 1934, this famous luxury liner once carried almost 2,000 passengers and more than 1,100 crew on each of its many trips across the Atlantic. It sailed into Long Beach in 1967 and now anchors the 55-acre **Queen Mary Seaport**. The complex, made up mostly of the liner, includes the shipboard **Hotel Queen Mary**, with 365 rooms and a shopping/dining area called the **Queen's Marketplace**. Hotel rates start at $65 for inside cabins and range up to $550 for parlor suites.

On-board restaurants include the casual **Promenade Cafe** (entrees starting at $9.95); **Sir Winston's**, with a menu starting at $19.95 and featuring venison and swordfish; and **The Chelsea**, featuring seafood specialties and free-range chicken, starting at $13.50. Also check out the art deco **Observation Bar**, which was once the first-class lounge.

Tours of the ship include a video presentation of the Queen Mary story, plus engine and stateroom exhibits, a maritime heritage hall featuring ship models, and an exhibit called **Ships of Destiny**, which tells the story of famous ships. Walk through the promenade deck, officers' quarters, the radio room, dining rooms, a World War II display, and more. Open daily 10 a.m. to 6 p.m. (with extended summer hours). Admission is $13 adults, $11 seniors and military, $8 children 4–11; free for children under 4.

The Queen Mary is located at the south end of I-710; follow the signs. For hotel reservations call 562/432-6964; for tour information, call 562/435-3511.

In Two Harbors your options are few. If you're not camping and cooking your own food, try **Doug's Harbor Restaurant**, **Doug's Harbor Reef Saloon**, or for quick lunches or snacks, the **Reef Grill**. Both can be reached at 310/510-2800.

LODGING

Catalina offers lodgers B&Bs, hotels, and resorts, many with views of the harbor. The AAA-rated **Catalina Island Seacrest Inn**, on Third and Clarrisa, a block from the beach, 310/510-0800, has a Victorian decor but modern amenities including a double-whirlpool or tub for two in most of its suites. Rates range from $76 (per person) to $130, with special romance and honeymoon packages available. The **Hotel Metropole**, in the Metropole Market Place, two blocks from the Green Pier, 310/510-1884, is about a block from the beach, but many of its rooms have ocean views, fireplaces, Jacuzzis, and private balconies. Rates range from $76 (per person) to $130. Less pricey and not as close to the water (but still within walking distance) is the **Catalina Cottages and Hermosa Hotel**, 131 Metropole Ave., 310/510-1010, where rates also start under $75. The **Catalina Canyon Resort**, 888 Country Club Drive, 800/253-9361, is in the foothills above Avalon (about a mile from the beach). A courtesy shuttle to boat terminals near the beach is provided. Rates start at $69. The mountaintop **Zane Grey Pueblo Hotel**, 199 Chimes Tower Road, 310/510-0966, features a garden and free shuttle service for rates starting around $85.

At the other side of the island, in Two Harbors, **Two Harbors Cabins** are waterfront cabins that sleep two, have small refrigerators, a heater, and closet. They also offer detached restrooms and showers and a covered outdoor cooking area. Guests need to bring their own bedding and towels, unless they opt to rent the linen package available at the cabins. Also in Two Harbors, **Banning House Lodge** is an 11-room historic inn with a view of the isthmus; phone both at 310/510-2800. Rates vary seasonally.

Many of the lodgings offer transportation packages, and Catalina Express (see Getting to Catalina, page 61) offers transportation/lodging packages.

CAMPING

While there are several camping sites on the island, the only one near Avalon is **Hermit Gulch**, 310/510-TENT. It's about a mile from town, and near the hiking trails and the Wrigley Memorial and Botanical Garden. Facilities include fresh water, picnic tables, charcoal grills, lighted restrooms, flush toilets, tent and equipment rentals, indoor hot showers, and a ranger on-site. No electrical hookups; no pets or wood fires allowed. Hiking permits and shuttle service available. Rates run $7.50 per day per person; discount packages available for large groups. Reservations are required in July and August, but are suggested year-round.

Two Harbors Campground, about a quarter-mile from town, offers three options near the beach: private, semiprivate, and shared campsites; tent cabins that sleep six (cots, camp stove, lantern, picnic table, barbecue, fire ring, and sunshade included); and teepee tents that sleep 8 to 10 (foam pads, lantern, camp stove, barbecue, and fire ring included).

Parson's Landing Campground offers beach camping on a remote tip

AVALON HARBOR, CATALINA ISLAND

Catalina Island Visitors Center

of the island accessible by trail or shore boat. You can fish, swim, and dive here, but campers should pack in all supplies except firewood and bottled water.

Little Harbor Campground, one of the island's most beautiful coves, is nestled six miles from Two Harbors and 16 miles from Avalon. You can sun, swim, dive, boogie-board, and fish here. Accessible by shuttle.

Surrounded by the island's two highest peaks, **Blackjack Campground** still has great vistas. On clear days you can see the mainland of California and the other Channel Islands to the north. Hiking is the main activity here. Access by shuttle or trail.

There are also some primitive boat-in campsites and the boat-in deluxe **Catalina Yurt Cabins** at Goat Harbor.

Two Harbors General Store stocks supplies for campers. For information and reservations for any of the sites listed above, call Catalina Island Camping, 800/446-0271.

NIGHTLIFE

The **Catalina Cantina**, the **Blue Parrot**, and **Coyote Joe's** often have live music in the evenings. The **Channel House** has a piano bar on the weekends. **Catalina Comedy Club**, 310/510-1700, features nationally known and unknown comics. Show times and covers vary.

5
LOS ANGELES BEACHES

Marina del Rey, Venice, and Santa Monica are here for the fun of it—for the ocean, beach, boardwalk, shopping, eating, and nightlife. The climate is wonderful, averaging 328 sunny days a year, with an average high of 70°F and a low of 53°F.

Marina del Rey began as a dream more than 100 years ago, when citizens first envisioned a large commercial harbor on this slip of coast. In 1963 the final breakwater was built, creating the largest manmade, shallow-draft harbor exclusively devoted to pleasure boating. The town offers numerous restaurants and shops, boat-launch ramps for more than 100,000 trailer-class boats annually, public fishing docks, view piers, and a promenade. Don't miss the beautiful sunsets.

Just north is Venice and world-famous Venice Beach. Named for the Italian city, Venice was developed with 16 miles of canals, most of which no longer exist. Founder/developer Abbot Kinney envisioned Venice as an environment that would foster a cultural renaissance in America. For some, Venice represents just that; for others perhaps more cynical, Venice is "stuck in the '60s."

Santa Monica is probably best known for its popular bay and pier. Wide white beaches, continual sunshine, and casual ambiance make it one of Southern California's best beachside destinations.

LOS ANGELES BEACHES

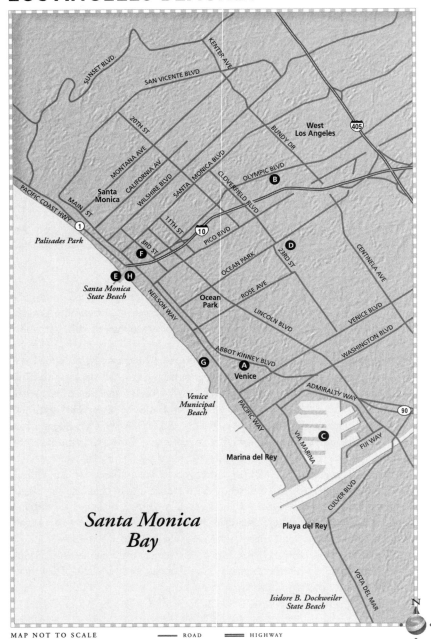

MAP NOT TO SCALE   ROAD   HIGHWAY

A PERFECT DAY AT THE BEACHES

No matter which town you're in, start your day with a stroll along the beach. If you decide to leave the beaches at all and wander into town, you'll find a wide array of amusements from which to choose. In Venice, breakfast at the Firehouse Restaurant, then explore the sights and entertainers along the Venice Boardwalk. In Santa Monica, visit the Bergamot Art Complex or stroll Main Street to Edgemar, the stunning shopping mall designed by the famous architect Frank O. Gehry; after lunch head over to the Third Street Promenade and check out the shops and entertainers. Complete your day by watching the sunset from the Santa Monica Pier, Venice Beach, or Marina del Rey. For dinner, the choices are endless. Dine in the Marina overlooking the harbor or outside on a patio at one of several restaurants. And after dinner, take in a music or comedy club, or just enjoy the sidewalk entertainers at the promenade.

SIGHTSEEING HIGHLIGHTS

★★★★ SANTA MONICA PIER AND CAROUSEL
310/458-8900, www.santamonicapier.org

Walk out on this huge wooden pier in the daytime and you can see the beautiful coastal views north to Malibu and south to Marina Del Ray. And you can look back at the pier and marvel at the engineering, and enjoy the rides (such as the solar-powered Ferris wheel and the world-famous Santa Monica carousel), ice cream, and hot dogs almost as if this were a seaside county fair. At night, the oldest West Coast pleasure pier becomes a carnival, with the sounds of the rides and games mixing with the smells of food from the restaurants and the sounds of live music from Rusty's Surf Ranch. Every Thursday night during summer there's a free outdoor concert—previous acts

SIGHTS

A Abbot Kinney Boulevard
B Bergamot Art Complex
C The Marina
D Museum of Flying
E Santa Monica Pier and Carousel
F Third Street Promenade
G Venice Boardwalk
H Wind Harp Chairs

have included John Mayall, Bo Diddley, Maynard Ferguson, Ozomatli, swing bands, Latin bands, and more.

Details: *West end of Colorado Avenue at Ocean Avenue. Pier open year-round; carousel open 10 a.m.–9 p.m. in summer, 10 a.m.–5 p.m. in winter. Admission to pier is free and carousel rides are still just 25 cents. Park on the pier, on a nearby street, or in a public garage. (1 hour)*

★★★★ VENICE BOARDWALK

Alongside Venice Beach, this strip of land less than two miles long is bounded by restaurants, stores, and apartments on one side and a bike path and the beach on the other. The asphalt and concrete boardwalk features a circus-like variety of entertainment and a colorful selection of arts and crafts, many representing the multiple tastes, styles, and trends of California culture. On any weekend, and many weekdays between March and November, this pedestrian walkway is the stage for a multitude of artists and performers of almost every kind: jugglers, magicians, singers, dancers, comics, puppeteers, portrait painters, hair weavers, fortune-tellers, clowns, one-person bands, Michael Jackson and Madonna impersonators, and more. All seek to amuse and entertain, selling wares for tips or modest prices. Here you'll find Charlie Chaplin's red-brick studio (now a collection of shops), and see various movie locations (for instance, the parking lot used for the basketball court in the movie *White Men Can't Jump*). You can dine on California cuisine at outdoor cafés, shop at clothing and jewelry boutiques and numerous sidewalk stands, or bike or rollerblade on the bike path that runs from Marina del Rey to Malibu. Views include the Santa Monica Mountains to the north and Santa Catalina Island to the west.

When calling listings with a 310 area code, dial all 10 digits, even if you're calling locally.

Details: *Venice Boardwalk extends from Rose to Washington. If you're not in Venice, take I-10 west to Lincoln Boulevard, go south to Rose and head west, and you're there; public parking is right in front of you. There's additional public parking south of Rose on the (one-way south) Speedway. (2 hours)*

★★★ ABBOT KINNEY BOULEVARD

A palm-lined lane (Kinney imported the palms in the early 1900s) featuring boutiques, art galleries, and restaurants, this strip is as funky and diverse as Santa Monica's Third Street Promenade is slick. It's more than just a shopping area, it's a lifestyle center. This and the boardwalk (see above) are the two quintessential Venice experiences.

Details: *Abbott Kinney Boulevard runs southeast from Brooks to Washington. If you're in Santa Monica or Venice, take Main Street to Brooks, then head southeast—you're on Abbott Kinney. If you're in (or south of) Marina del Rey, take Washington to Abbott Kinney and head northwest. Park on the street or in parking lots (marked) behind some of the stores on the east side of the street. (1 hour)*

★★★ BERGAMOT ART COMPLEX
2525 Michigan Ave., Santa Monica, 310/829-5854

You may be used to a block of art galleries, maybe even a street that has several galleries—but how about a five-acre complex that houses over 29 galleries and the city's Museum of Modern Art? That's Bergamot Station, a.k.a. Bergamot Art Complex. Housing some of the West's most renowned art galleries (such as Shoshana Wayne Gallery, Robert Berman Gallery, Sherry Frumkin Gallery, Patricia Faure Gallery, Craig Krull Gallery, Flowers West, Taka-Ishii Gallery, and the Gallery of Functional Art) and the Santa Monica Museum of Modern Art, this complex offers an exciting array of what's happening in the world of modern art, featuring unknowns, break-outs, and nationally known artists in mid-career. There's also a café serving lunch and dinner (Buffalo burgers run around $6) with outdoor dining. Art, of course, is in the eye of the beholder, so this experience may be cutting-edge or pedestrian, but it presents an incredible variety, all around one free parking lot, and only the museum charges (a modest) admission.

Details: *Open Tue–Sat. (2 hours)*

★★★ THIRD STREET PROMENADE

This pedestrian promenade in Santa Monica runs three very long blocks from Broadway to Wilshire, and features hundreds of shops, restaurants, art galleries, and street performers. This, too, is not only a shopping area but also a lifestyle and entertainment center, especially at night.

Details: *Runs north-south from Wilshire to Broadway on what would be Third Street if it were a street and not a pedestrian promenade (hence the name). There are several public parking structures along Fourth and*

Second Streets; hourly rates are charged during the day, and after 6 p.m. it's a flat $3. (2 hours)

★★★ WIND HARP CHAIRS

Two steel and aluminum lifeguard chairs, made by Douglas Hollis in 1987, become instruments when the wind blows through them. Sit in one and listen to the magical melodies.

Details: *This free exhibit is located on the beach off Ocean Front Walk, just north of Pica Boulevard in Santa Monica. (30 minutes)*

★★ THE MARINA

The largest manmade, shallow-draft harbor that is exclusively devoted to pleasure boating, the Marina also features many shops and restaurants, generally located along Admiralty Way and at Fisherman's Wharf.

Details: *Enter off Washington Avenue at Via Marina or off Lincoln Road at Fiji Way, Marina del Rey. (30 minutes)*

★★ MUSEUM OF FLYING

2772 Donald Douglas Loop North, Santa Monica, 310/392-8822

This aviation museum, located at the Santa Monica Airport, features vintage aircraft and exhibitions as well as a children's interactive area. Although a bit disorganized and not nearly as thorough as the Air & Space museum in San Diego, here you'll see old biplanes and World War II–era fighters and read about the history of flight and transatlantic and global air travel. The exhibit on the famous Tuskegee Airmen is outstanding: They were the first black pilots allowed in the U.S. armed forces during WWII, and flew with spectacular distinction. On Saturdays Tuskegee Airman and decorated pilot Frank Jackson is there to tell their story. The children's interactive area features games, rides, and a helicopter that the kids can play in.

Details: *Open Wed–Sun 10–5. Admission is $7 adults, $5 seniors, $3 ages 3–17. (1 hour)*

★ MURAL AND PUBLIC ART TOURS

More than 100 murals adorn the Santa Monica/Venice/Marina del Rey area, many on the Venice Boardwalk. Don't miss the one on Ocean Park Boulevard between Lincoln Avenue and Sixth Street.

Details: For a brochure listing Los Angeles–area murals, contact the Social and Public Art Resource Center, 685 Venice Blvd. (two blocks west of Lincoln), Venice, 310/822-9560. The resource center also sells a book called Street Gallery, *with photos of many area murals. (1 hour)*

FITNESS AND RECREATION

In addition to the 26-mile bike (and inline skating) path that runs from north of Santa Monica south to Marina del Rey and the local public beaches, Venice Beach offers paddle tennis, basketball, and handball courts (no fee, no reservations required). Venice's outdoor gym and play area entertains kids with slides, swings, and climbing toys, and adults with adjacent sand volleyball courts.

If you're looking for a more serious gym, Venice also hosts the original world-famous **Gold's Gym**, 360 Hampton Dr., 310/392-6004. For a day rate of $15 you can use any of its equipment and facilities. Open Monday through Friday 4 a.m. to midnight, Saturday and Sunday 5 a.m. to midnight.

Marina del Rey's 8.2-acre **Admiralty Park** has a bike path, jogging path, and views of the boats and main channel. **Aubrey E. Austin Jr. Park** is known for its spectacular views of the main channel and passing boats; fishing is allowed off the rock jetty. You can barbecue, picnic, bike, fish, or simply appreciate the views and extensive grassy hills at 10-acre **Burton W. Chace Park**.

Looking for a peaceful day of sailing? Sailboats may be chartered with or without a captain. For the novice, lessons are also offered. Among the outfitters renting boats are **Marina Boat Rentals**, 13719 Fiji Way, in the Fisherman's Village in the Marina, 310/574-2822. Their eight-person electric boats (with canopies and picnic tables) start at $45/hour. The marina also rents powerboats, Wave Runners, and kayaks, some for in-harbor use, some for going out to sea. Also renting and chartering boats is **California Yachting Services**, 2532 Lincoln Blvd., Suite 164, Marina del Rey, 310/391-2630. Individually chartered sailboats with a captain can start at $350; other boats and charters can range from several hundred to several thousand dollars, depending on how long you'll be gone. California Yachting Services serves as a clearinghouse of information about rentals and charters from the Marina. And if the beauty and romance of the area spark your passions, they can legally perform marriages at sea.

Santa Monica's **Palisades Park** runs parallel to and overlooks the beach, from Montana Avenue south to Colorado Avenue. Here you can walk, jog, sit on the benches, and enjoy!

LOS ANGELES BEACHES

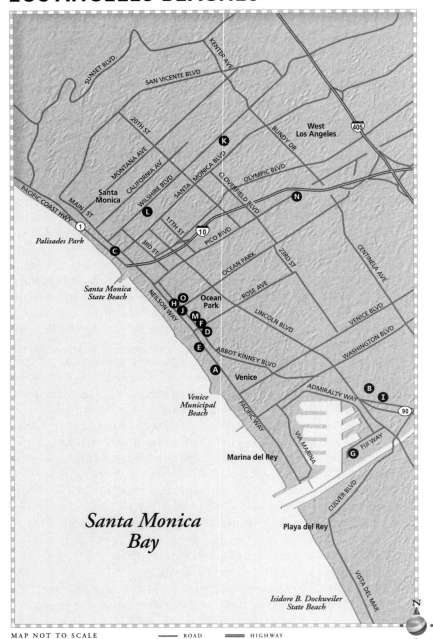

MAP NOT TO SCALE ▬▬ ROAD ▬▬ HIGHWAY

FOOD

Dining out is a local pastime, and whatever your taste, there's a restaurant to match. Many have outdoor decks or patios that are heated when the temperature drops. What follows is by no means a complete listing, but each of these restaurants should please both the palate and the pocketbook.

Since Venice is known for its bodybuilders, why not eat where they do? Try the **Firehouse Restaurant**, 213 Rose Ave., 310/396-6810, featuring steak and eggs, and buffalo burgers. Breakfast, lunch, and dinner are served, patio dining is always available, and meals start at $6. (It was at this intersection that Keanu Reeves saw the bus blow up and then got the phone call on the pay phone from Dennis Hopper in the movie *Speed*.)

For a fine dinner overlooking the harbor in the Marina, try **The Fishmarket** on Fisherman's Wharf, 310/823-8444, serving seafood, steak, and pasta. Entrees start at less than $10.

If you're looking for fine Southern cooking, **Aunt Kizzy's Back Porch**, 4325 Glencoe Ave., Marina del Rey, 310/578-1005, is the best. Meals average $14; the only credit card they take is American Express.

For steak and seafood with a 1940s ambiance and a piano bar straight out of every great Hollywood detective movie, there's **Bob Burns**, 202 Wilshire Blvd., Santa Monica, 310/393-6777, with entrees ranging from $18 to $45 and nightly piano bar entertainment.

Mediterranean-style pasta, seafood, and steak are offered in a relaxing open-air environment at **Chaya Venice**, 110 Navy St., Venice, 310/396-1179. Entrees begin at $12 for pasta, $20 and up for steak and seafood.

The Figtree, 429 Ocean Front Walk, Venice Boardwalk, 310/392-4937, offers indoor/outdoor dining on health-conscious California cuisine. Entrees start at $8, and all desserts are made on the premises.

In Santa Monica, **The Galley**, 2442 Main St., 310/452-1934, serves

---

FOOD

- Ⓐ 72 Market Street
- Ⓑ Aunt Kizzy's Back Porch
- Ⓒ Bob Burns
- Ⓓ Chaya Venice
- Ⓔ The Figtree
- Ⓕ Firehouse Restaurant

FOOD *(continued)*

- Ⓖ The Fishmarket
- Ⓗ The Galley
- Ⓘ Jerry's Famous Deli
- Ⓙ Ocean Park Omelette Parlor
- Ⓓ Schatzi on Main
- Ⓚ Thai Dishes

COFFEEHOUSES

- Ⓛ Anastasia's Asylum
- Ⓜ Novel Cafe
- Ⓝ Unurban Cafe
- Ⓞ Wednesdays House

Note: Items with the same letter are located in the same place.

American steak and seafood. The restaurant features a full bar, several indoor dining rooms, and a relaxing heated patio under the stars. Seafood entrees start at $16, steak entrees at $18.50. And you must try their house salad dressing! (As the story goes, Captain Ron bought the place because it was the only way he could get the salad-dressing recipe.)

For 24-hour deli connoisseurs, there's **Jerry's Famous Deli**, 13181 Mindanao Way, Marina del Rey, 310/821-6626. Jerry's is the home of great bagels, knockwurst, and brisket—the whole schmeer. Sandwiches start at $8, dinners run $10 to $20. Sample the rich desserts, pastries, and fresh-baked breads.

For a delicious breakfast or lunch inside or on the patio, try **Ocean Park Omelette Parlor**, 2732 Main St., Santa Monica, 310/399-7892. Meals run $3 to $8. Popular dishes include the eggs Benedict and the Showcase West Salad. Open 6 a.m. to 2 p.m. weekdays, until 4 p.m. on weekends.

For fine Thai food at reasonable prices, visit **Thai Dishes**, 1910 Wilshire Blvd., Santa Monica, 310/828-5634. Be sure to try the coconut chicken soup! Meals start at $7.

If food served at restaurants owned by movie stars whets your appetite, try **Schatzi on Main**, 110 Main St., Santa Monica, 310/399-4800, which used to be owned by Arnold Schwarzenegger. Wiener schnitzel, Kaiserschmaren, the Zwiebelrostbraten (Arnold's favorite), and international cuisine entrees range from $10 to $25. Dudley Moore sometimes plays piano at his **72 Market Street** restaurant, 72 Market St., Venice, 310/392-8720. Known for its oyster bar and its American fare prepared by a French chef, entrees start at $14. Both celebrity restaurants are within two blocks of the beach.

COFFEEHOUSES

You've seen these Santa Monica java shops on TV, now experience the real deal, without commercials. The **Unurban Cafe**, 3301 Pico Blvd., 310/315-0056, has wonderful meals and desserts and features excellent live acoustic music on the weekends. There's a music open mike on Mondays and a comedy open mike on Wednesdays. **Wednesdays House**, 2409 Main St., 310/452-4486, has poetry and music nights, excellent chili, and—in addition to being a fine coffeehouse and comfortable hangout—also has some clothes for sale. **Anastasia's Asylum**, 1028 Wilshire Blvd., 310/394-7113, has live folk/acoustic entertainment. The **Novel Cafe**, 212 Pier Ave., 310/396-8566, is the hangout, day or night, for many slackers, writers, and hippies. It's also a fine used-book store, with live entertainment (comedy, poetry, music) many evenings during the week.

LODGING

Three hundred feet from the beach, and just steps away from the Venice Boardwalk, is the **Marina Pacific Hotel and Suites**, 1697 Pacific Ave., Venice, 310/452-1111 or 800/421-8151. Featuring a rooftop sundeck with ocean and city views, it offers intimate singles, doubles, and suites. Many of the rooms and suites have ocean views and balconies. Room rates range from $80 to $120, and suites from $165 to $225. Also near the beach, the **Venice Beach House**, 15 30th Ave., Venice, 310/823-1966, is a bed-and-breakfast built in 1911. The four rooms with shared baths cost $95. They also have three rooms with private baths for $120 to $130. Suites, one with a fireplace and one with a Jacuzzi, are $145 to $165. Both of these lodgings are five minutes from Main Street (Santa Monica's own Restaurant Row) and 10 minutes from the Third Street Promenade.

In Marina del Rey the **Marina International Hotel**, 4200 Admiralty Way, 310/301-2000, has rooms starting at $99; separate bungalows start at $150.

For a more European-style architecture and a generous continental breakfast only a few blocks from the beach, try the **Mansion Inn**, 327 Washington Blvd., 310/821-2557. Rooms are $85 to $95 (single or double); suites are $125 to $135.

Santa Monica offers choices in deluxe, tourist, and budget hotels, many at or near the beach. Among the deluxe hotels at the beach are the **Georgian Hotel**, 1415 Ocean Ave., 310/395-9945, www.georgianhotel.com; **Loews Santa Monica Beach Hotel**, 1700 Ocean Ave., 310/458-6700, with rates from $175 to $195; and **Shutters on the Beach**, One Pico Boulevard, 310/458-0030, where rates begin at $305.

The Georgian is an escape to the past, a historic art deco hotel with 84 unique rooms decorated from that period, each with an honor bar, personal robe, hair dryer, complimentary coffee and coffeemaker, and daily delivery of *USA Today*. Departing from the art deco decor, rooms are equipped with dataport telephones. The alfresco veranda overlooks Santa Monica Bay, offering a spectacular view and a fine place to eat breakfast.

Loews Santa Monica Beach Hotel, a huge hotel with a beautiful view of the waterfront, offers many of the amenities (including mini-bars) and has a new spa and fitness center. Their Lavande restaurant serves California Provencal, the more casual Cafe has an outdoor dining deck, and the lobby bar and lounge has live entertainment nightly.

Shutters on the Beach is the romantic getaway. A large hotel (though not as big as the Loews), it has the feel of a beach cottage with its white picket fencing and white-and-blue color scheme. There's a beautiful pool deck with ocean

LOS ANGELES BEACHES

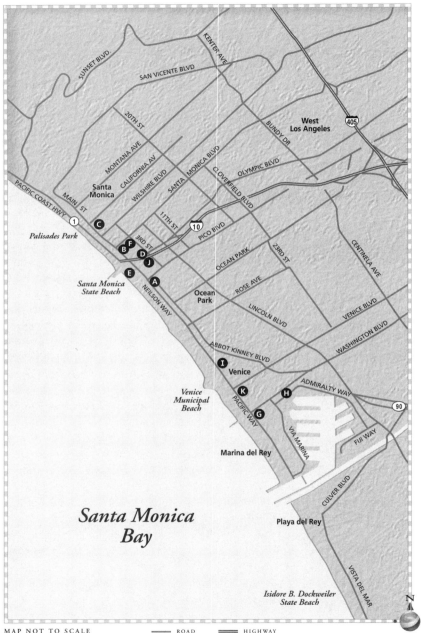

MAP NOT TO SCALE · ROAD · HIGHWAY

view, and the rooms have balconies large enough for two people to have an intimate breakfast with the ocean and coastline as their canvas.

Among the deluxe hotels close to the beach and closer to Santa Monica's Third Street Promenade is the **Holiday Inn Santa Monica Beach Area**, 120 Colorado Ave., 310/451-0676, where rates range from $105 to $120. Located adjacent to the Santa Monica Place Mall, it's closer to the shopping than the beach (although it's just two blocks from the pier and three from the beach itself). The rooms offer mini-bars, coffeemakers, hair dryers, irons and boards; there's a heated pool, and the restaurant is open for breakfast and dinner. Rooms range from $149 to $229.

Among the moderately priced hotels on the Santa Monica beach is the **Hotel California**, 1670 Ocean Ave., 310/393-2363. The hotel has recently been remodeled: rooms are spacious, their hardwood floors are stunning, and if you're inclined to prefer a smaller place with a motel feel but with a resort quality, this is the place. The rooms include mini-bars, TVs, and VCRs; oceanside rooms start at $145, suites at $225. The **Best Western Ocean View Hotel**, 1447 Ocean Ave., 310/458-4888, is a stately place with comfortable rooms offering TV and data-port telephones; ocean-view rooms include coffeemakers and mini-fridges. This hotel near the beach and Third Street offers some of the best rates at $99 to $169 in winter and $129 to $219 in summer. It's not the Loews or Shutters, but for travelers who know they're going to be out and about most of the time and just need a comfortable room at an affordable price to spend the night, this is the place. The **Travelodge Santa Monica Beach**, 1525 Ocean Ave., 310/451-0761, across the street from the beach and easy walking distance from the Third Street Promenade, offers basic rooms (many overlooking the ocean) with rates between $85 and $230. You pull in, you park, you're steps away from your room. The fancy hotels can't say that.

LODGING

- **A** Bayside Hotel
- **B** Best Western Ocean View Hotel
- **C** Cal Mar Hotel Suites
- **D** Georgian Hotel
- **D** Holiday Inn Santa Monica Beach Area
- **E** Hotel California
- **F** Hotel Carmel
- **B** Loews Santa Monica Beach Hotel
- **G** Mansion Inn
- **H** Marina International Hotel
- **I** Marina Pacific Hotel and Suites
- **J** Ocean Lodge Beach Hotel
- **B** Shutters on the Beach
- **C** Travelodge Santa Monica Beach
- **K** Venice Beach House

Note: Items with the same letter are located in the same area.

Two blocks from the beach and next to the Third Street Promenade is **Hotel Carmel**, 201 Broadway, Santa Monica, 310/451-2469. Room rates run $90 to $149.

Also two blocks from the beach, near the Montana shopping area, is the **Cal Mar Hotel Suites**, 220 California Ave., 310/395-5555, offering efficiency, standard, and master suites in a garden setting with a self-service laundry and a heated swimming pool, with rates ranging from $89 to $109.

Among the budget hotels on the beach is the **Bayside Hotel**, 2001 Ocean Ave., Santa Monica, 310/396-6000, where rates for economy rooms start at $74. The Bayside offers a choice of one king, one queen, or two double beds, and rooms come with cable TV and a direct-dial phone with data port. They also offer courtyard, deluxe, and ocean-view rooms with rates ranging from $79 to $119. Another budget beachfront hotel is the **Ocean Lodge Beach Hotel**, 1667 Ocean Ave., Santa Monica, 310/451-4146, with rates starting at $45 for a single.

NIGHTLIFE

Blues is king at **Harvelle's Blues Club**, 1432 Fourth St., Santa Monica, 310/395-1676. Cover varies. **McCabe's**, 3101 Pico Blvd., Santa Monica, 310/828-4403, is an intimate concert hall located behind a guitar and music shop; they serve coffee, tea, sweets, and no alcohol. Performers have included Loudon Wainwright III, Bruce Cockburn, Steve Forbert, John Jorgenson, Gil Scott-Heron, and T-Bone Burnett. Tickets average $17.50.

In addition to its shopping and dining, the **Third Street Promenade**, Third Street between Broadway and Wilshire, also has nightlife. Many sidewalk performers, all working for donations, play music (classical, folk, country, blues) and perform a variety of acts.

Also on the promenade is **Gotham Hall**, 1431 Third Street Promenade 310/394-8865, featuring upscale pool and dancing to live DJs. (And they have some great food specials during happy hour.)

The **Santa Monica Pier** (west end of Colorado Avenue) has restaurants, bars (like **Rusty's Surf House**—catch the Red Elvises if they're there!) featuring live music, an arcade, the carousel, a Ferris wheel, and other rides. During summer there are free concerts every Thursday night at 7:30.

For rock 'n' roll music and dancing, visit **Brennan's**, 4089 Lincoln Blvd., Marina del Rey, 310/821-6622. Every Thursday night around 9:30 you can catch Brennan's popular turtle races. See for yourself what they're all about! Cover varies.

Also featuring rock music (Thursday through Saturday) is **O'Brien's**

SOUTH BAY BEACHES
(MANHATTAN BEACH, HERMOSA BEACH, REDONDO BEACH)

Three other coastal towns south of Marina del Rey each boast fine beaches, restaurants, and nightlife. They're similar to Santa Monica and Venice in lifestyle, but more village-like, with the extra value of being farther away from the crush of Los Angeles.

Manhattan Beach dining options include **Talia's**, 1148 Manhattan Ave., 310/545-6884, serving southern Italian cuisine with meals ranging from $9 to $14; **The Kettle**, 1138 Manhattan Ave., 310/545-8511, serving all-American cuisine with meals ranging from $6 to $16; and **Hennessey's Tavern**, 313 Manhattan Beach Blvd., 310/546-4813, serving salads, burgers, chicken, and fish, with meals from $6 to $12.

In **Hermosa Beach, Ragin' Cajun**, 422 Pier Ave., 310/376-7878, offers Cajun entrees starting at $8 and is closed Monday. The **Bottle Inn**, 26 22nd St., 310/376-9595, serves Italian dishes amid a decor of hundreds of miniature liquor bottles, and meals are generally less than $20. Healthy vegetarian food can be found at **The Spot**, 110 Second St., 310/376-2355.

A good choice in **Redondo Beach** is **Chez Melange**, 1716 Pacific Coast Highway, 310/540-1222, featuring meals ranging from homemade sausage to sushi. Most entrees cost under $20.

Among the many clubs presenting music, comedy, and dancing are: **Sangria**, 68 Pier Ave., Hermosa Beach, 310/376-4412, good for dancing; **The Lighthouse**, 30 Pier Ave., Hermosa Beach, 310/376-9833, for live rock 'n' roll, jazz, blues, funk, and alternative music—they suggest you call 'cause it's "a different thing" every night; and the **Comedy and Magic Club**, 1018 Hermosa Ave., Hermosa Beach, 310/372-1193, for name comics. Jay Leno's been known to show up here and work on material for "The Tonight Show."

2941 Main St., Santa Monica, 310/396-4725, a cozy bar with an outdoor patio in front.

And remember those coffeehouses (see above): they're even more interesting at night.

SHOPPING

The **Third Street Promenade**, Santa Monica, between Broadway and Wilshire, is a pedestrian walkway with more than 100 retail stores, 75 restaurants, a few art galleries, and three theaters. And although it's an entertaining place at night, the shopping there has become ordinary since its increasing domination by chain stores (the **Midnight Special** bookstore being a prominent exception). The promenade is anchored on the southern end by **Santa Monica Place**, a huge indoor mall with adjacent parking.

Main Street (between Marine and Pico) **Santa Monica** is more representative of the area's uniqueness. Encompassing everything from funk to fashionable, from down-home to trend du jour, it features clothing boutiques, unique gift shops (like **Raintree**), surf wear, designer furniture, handcrafted jewelry, and more, in all kinds of stores and several art galleries and restaurants.

Also in Santa Monica, between Seventh and Seventeenth Streets, **Montana Avenue** offers upscale boutiques, art galleries, and restaurants.

Venice's **Abbot Kinney Boulevard**, a beautiful palm-lined street between Venice Avenue and Brooks, features more boutiques, art galleries, restaurants, and many antique furniture shops.

6
LOS ANGELES
AND HOLLYWOOD

If Southern California is the land of imagination, then Los Angeles and Hollywood are certainly the epicenter. Where else is storytelling the number-one industry? (And that's what it's called, as in: "Are you in The Industry?" "Yes, here's my card.")

Remember, earthquakes are more than just reality here; they're also a metaphor for the constantly shifting landscape of the mind. To paraphrase Rod Serling, there's a signpost up ahead and it says you've just entered Los Angeles.

Prior to 1781, a tribe of Indians called the Yangna lived in this area. In 1781 a group of Spaniards, Indians, Blacks, and mestizos made their way from Sonora and Sinaloa in Mexico and founded El Pueblo de Nuestra Señora la Reina de Los Angeles (or "The Village of Our Lady Queen of the Angels"). The town was officially declared a city under the Mexican government in 1835, and 12 years later the American flag was raised over the city. The site of the original settlement is downtown, at 125 Paseo de la Plaza; the Avila Adobe, the first house in Los Angeles, still stands.

Hollywood wasn't much of anything until the Nestor Film Company rented an old tavern and barn in 1911 and started making movies. Now, of course, it's synonymous with the film industry, even though much of it isn't in Hollywood anymore and most of that old, supposedly real, soft-focus glamour is gone.

Welcome to the "city of angels," the heartbeat of Southern California.

LOS ANGELES AND HOLLYWOOD

N

CENTRAL AVE

GRAND AVE

To Anaheim

E

5

110

VERMONT AVE

LOS FELIZ BLVD

Griffith Park

A

Los Angeles

H

WESTERN AVE

134

Universal City

101

D

I

BEVERLY BLVD

WILSHIRE BLVD

B

SANTA MONICA FREEWAY

JEFFERSON BLVD

LA BREA AVE

Hollywood

HOLLYWOOD BLVD

SUNSET BLVD

SANTA MONICA BLVD

MELROSE AV

OLYMPIC BLVD

LA CIENEGA BLVD

LAUREL CANYON BLVD

North Hollywood

170

West Hollywood

F

Culver City

COLDWATER CANYON

CULVER BLVD

BEVERLY GLEN BLVD

Beverly Hills

10

G

Sherman Oaks

VENICE BLVD

405

C

Encino

MULHOLLAND DR

WILSHIRE BLVD

LINCOLN BLVD

HIGHWAY

VENTURA BLVD

Santa Monica Mountains
National Recreation Area

SAN VINCENTE BLVD

SUNSET BLVD

Santa Monica

ROAD

Tarzana

Santa Monica Bay

TOPANGA BLVD

1

MILES

Woodland Hills

Topanga

PACIFIC COAST HWY

0 SCALE   4   KILOMETERS   4   MILES

101

A PERFECT DAY IN LOS ANGELES AND HOLLYWOOD

Begin with breakfast at Duke's, then head over to the George C. Page Museum and La Brea Tar Pits. After you've seen the 40,000-year-old bones and other exhibits, step across the street to the Petersen Automotive Museum and check out the historic automobiles. Then take in the Hollywood Entertainment Museum or the Paramount Studio tour. Now you're familiar with the basics of Los Angeles and it's time for lunch. Have lunch at Jerry's Famous Deli. If you're closer to West Hollywood, have lunch at Ed Debevic's. Spend the afternoon at Universal Studios in "the Valley" (as locals call the nearby San Fernando Valley), or in Griffith Park at the observatory and the Autry Museum of Western Heritage. Enjoy a relaxing dinner at the Cat and Fiddle, Orso, or Kass Bah, then check out the House of Blues and the Comedy Store. That leaves the Getty and the other art museums, the homes of famous people, the Dodgers, and Disneyland for another day.

SIGHTSEEING HIGHLIGHTS

★★★★ AUTRY MUSEUM OF WESTERN HERITAGE
4700 Western Heritage Way, Hollywood, 323/667-2000,
www.autry-museum.org

If you love the West, real (as in historical) or imagined (as in the movies and on TV), this museum should figure prominently in your plans. Built by the late great singing cowboy who loved both Wests, this museum features art, artifacts, and other special exhibits. The exhibits on the settlement of the West rival similar exhibits at the Institute of Texan Cultures and the Smithsonian, with the spotlight not only on what the

SIGHTS

- **A** Autry Museum of Western Heritage
- **B** George C. Page Museum of La Brea Discoveries and La Brea Tar Pits
- **C** The Getty Center
- **D** Hollywood Entertainment Museum
- **D** Hollywood Walk of Fame
- **B** Los Angeles County Museum of Art
- **D** Mann's Chinese Theatre
- **E** Museum of Contemporary Art
- **F** Museum of Television and Radio
- **G** Museum of Tolerance
- **H** Natural History Museum of Los Angeles County
- **I** Paramount Studios
- **B** Petersen Automotive Museum

Note: Items with the same letter are located in the same area.

settlers did, what they wore, how they traveled and what tools they used, but also on who they were: Irish, Mormon, black, and the rest. There are detailed displays on Native Americans and on the Mexican vaqueros, the original cowboys; it's a history lesson for young and old. Of course, exhibits on gunfighters, lawmen, and outlaws are also here, with an exceptional collection of revolvers and rifles used by Pat Garret, Billy the Kid, and many other real-life heroes and villains. There's also a large collection of movie posters and memorabilia that extends far beyond Autry's own career (this is not a vanity museum that simply celebrates its namesake) to include Tom Mix, Gary Cooper, Clint Eastwood, and virtually every other movie gunman who rode across the silver screen. The art collection, too, is extravagant and includes the famous Remington sculptures of cowboys and Indians. Vintage Western movies are shown and special events programs are held in the Wells Fargo theater.

When calling listings with a 310 area code, dial all 10 digits, even if you're calling locally.

Details: *In Griffith Park, at the junction of the 5 and 134 freeways. From the 5 north, exit at Zoo Drive; from the 5 south, exit at Western; from the 134 east, exit at Victory; and from the 134 west, exit at Zoo Drive. Open Tue–Sun 10–5. Admission is $7.50 adults, $5 students and seniors, $3 children 2–12. (1 1/2 hours)*

★★★★ **GEORGE C. PAGE MUSEUM OF LA BREA DISCOVERIES AND LA BREA TAR PITS**
5801 Curson Ave., Los Angeles, 323/934-PAGE, www.tarpits.org
This museum, located next to the famous tar pits that hid ancient skeletons for thousands of years, represents the only active paleontological excavation site in the United States. It displays Ice Age fossils, recovered from the sticky asphalt, of animals that are 10,000 to 40,000 years old, and graphically depicts what the territory was like during the last Ice Age, 40,000 years ago. Many of the exhibits are designed with children in mind. During summer, visitors can watch the excavation from Pit 91 of fossils that include bones of saber-toothed cats and dire wolves.

Details: *On Museum Row, the site is open Tue–Fri 9:30–5, Sat and Sun 10–5. Admission is $6 adults, $3.50 students and seniors, $2 children 5–12, and free for children under 5. (2 hours)*

★★★★ PETERSEN AUTOMOTIVE MUSEUM
6060 Wilshire Blvd., Los Angeles, 323/930-CARS,
www.petersen.org
Located on Museum Row and created by the founder of several auto-mobile and hot-rod magazines, this museum has one of the largest (and coolest) collections of cars anywhere. Covering four floors, it features displays on the history of the automobile in the twentieth century: exhibits and dioramas that visitors can walk through to experience settings of early Los Angeles, where the world's first shopping district was designed. Interactive multilingual computers (available in five languages) allow international visitors to participate in the exhibits. The second floor is devoted to race cars, classic cars, vintage motorcycles, concept cars, celebrity and movie cars, and automotive design and technology.

Details: *Open Tue–Sun 10–6 p.m., Fri until 9 p.m. Admission is $7 adults, $5 students and seniors, $3 children 5–12, and free for children under 5. All-day museum parking is available for $4. (1 hour)*

★★★ THE GETTY CENTER
1200 Getty Center Dr., Los Angeles, 310/440-7300,
www.getty.edu
This is a controversial museum. Supporters praise the architecture, the gardens, the views, and . . . the collection. Critics cite the architecture, the location, the lack of planning that can make it inconvenient to attend without advance reservations and . . . the collection. I went on a beautiful day as part of a tour, so I didn't have to deal with advance parking reservations; the views are spectacular, the collection is—well, I'm not an art critic. I enjoyed the Dutch paintings. And I thought van Gogh's *Irises* was worth the trip. If you've never seen a van Gogh in person . . . well, you should see at least one van Gogh in person.

The Getty Center, comprised of six buildings on a 110-acre "campus" perched in the Santa Monica mountains, is also the home of the J. Paul Getty Trust, a private foundation dedicated to the visual arts and the humanities. Designed by architect Richard Meier, the center houses European paintings, drawings, illuminated manuscripts, sculpture, decorative arts, and American and European photographs. The open-air campus offers beautiful views of downtown Los Angeles and the Pacific Ocean. Visitors can enjoy the art, the views and concerts, gallery talks, lectures, film screenings, and leisurely strolls through beautiful gardens. There are restaurants and snack stands on-site.

Details: Advance parking reservations are required; call 310/440-7300. If driving, take the Getty Center Drive exit off the 405. Visitors can also come by public bus, taxi, and shuttle. Open Tue and Wed 11–7, Thu and Fri 11–9, Sat and Sun 10–6. Free admission. (4–5 hours)

★★★ LOS ANGELES COUNTY MUSEUM OF ART (LACMA)
5905 Wilshire Blvd., Los Angeles, 323/857-6552, www.lacma.org

This museum houses one of the world's largest collections of art—not just modern art, not just nineteenth-century art, not just Himalayan art—all kinds of art from all over the globe from virtually any time period that may interest you. Now, I'm no art critic, but the folks I know who are celebrate this museum. The collections are varied and extensive. There's weird sculpture, classical portraits, a presentational piece where you walk through what seems to be a cluttered garage (actually I think it really *was* a cluttered garage). And there's a fantastic Pavilion for Japanese Art that features not only beautiful sculpture and screens and delicate carvings, but also radical architecture: the building itself is designed in the style of a Japanese building surrounded by Japanese gardens. The standing collection is compelling, the special collections are also dynamic: recent shows included Picasso and an acclaimed van Gogh exhibit.

Details: On Museum Row; open Tue–Thu 10–5, Fri 10–9, Sat and Sun 11–6. Admission is $6 adults, $4 students 18 and older and seniors, $1 children, free for children under 5. (1 hour)

★★★ MUSEUM OF CONTEMPORARY ART (MOCA)
250 S. Grand Ave., Los Angeles, 213/626-6222

Located downtown, this museum features modern art. What is modern art? I can't say for sure. I think it's the kind of art that inspires you to say things to the person you're with like "Is that art?" or "Why is that art?" or "What comes after postmodern?" This museum, celebrated by critics and patrons, offers the visitor a challenge: this is what's happening in the world of art. What do you think? If you want to be challenged, here it is.

Details: Open Tue–Sun 11–5. Admission is $6 adults, $4 students and seniors, free for kids under 12, and free to all Thu 5–8 p.m. (1 hour)

★★★ MUSEUM OF TELEVISION AND RADIO
465 N. Beverly Dr., Beverly Hills, 310/786-1000, www.mtr.org

LOS ANGELES SKYLINE

Los Angeles CVB/Michele & Tom Grimm

Located in Beverly Hills, this museum offers a fascinating collection of over 95,000 historical and contemporary television and radio programs and advertisements. (And watching old TV commercials is a kick!) Visitors can view or hear selected programming at individual consoles or attend special screenings in one of the museum's two theaters. Recent screenings included early TV appearances by Woody Allen and Richard Pryor. Often during the year special panel programs, open to the public, are presented, featuring the casts of historic and popular TV shows (*Cheers, Fernwood 2Night, ER*, etc.); call ahead or check local papers when you're in town.

 Details: *Open Wed–Sun noon–5; Thu until 9. Admission is $6 adults, $4 students and seniors, $3 children under 13. (And there's two hours' free parking with validation.) (2 hours)*

★★★ **MUSEUM OF TOLERANCE**
9786 W. Pico Blvd., Los Angeles, 310/553-8403
The Simon Wiesenthal Center presents interactive exhibits depicting the history of racism and prejudice in America and the history of the Holocaust. It's a chilling remembrance of the horrors of the past and an inspirational monument to idealism for the future. There are also special programs for adults and children.

Details: Open Mon–Thu 10–6:30, Fri 10–3:30, Sun 10–7:30. Final admission time is 2¹/₂ hours before closing. Admission is $8 adults, $6 seniors, $5 students, $3 children 3–10. (1 hour)

★★★ NATURAL HISTORY MUSEUM OF LOS ANGELES COUNTY
900 Exposition Blvd., Exposition Park, Los Angeles, 213/763-DINO, www.nhm.org

Founded in 1913, this is one of the preeminent natural and cultural history museums in the United States. By size it is the third largest, with more than 33 million specimens and artifacts. There's a kid-friendly Discovery Center that welcomes children and families with hands-on interactive education. The accompanying Insect Zoo, the largest in the western United States, presents live insects from around the world. (Okay, I wasn't really thrilled about that many live bugs, but some people find it moving.) Permanent exhibit halls include dramatic collections of fossils and dinosaurs, exquisite gems and minerals, and grand animal dioramas.

Details: Open Tue–Fri 9:30–5, Sat and Sun 10–5. Admission is $8 adults, $5.50 seniors and students, $2 kids 5–12. (half–full day)

★★ HOLLYWOOD ENTERTAINMENT MUSEUM
7021 Hollywood Blvd., Hollywood, 323/465-7900

This new museum is about the history and evolution of the "magic" of moviemaking. Exhibits explain special effects, makeup, props, animation, editing, and all the other essential behind-the-scenes activities. There are even props from various movies and TV shows, including the captain's chair from *Star Trek*. (Fade in music . . . "Space, the final frontier . . .")

Details: In the Hollywood Galaxy Complex, downstairs from General Cinema Theatres. Open daily 10–6. Admission is $7.50 adults, $4.50 seniors and students, $4 children 5–12, free for children under 5. (2 hours)

★★ PARAMOUNT STUDIOS
5555 Melrose Ave., Hollywood, 323/956-1777

"The only major studio still located in Hollywood" offers a two-hour tour that features its history and its current productions.

Details: Open Mon–Fri 9–2. Last tour begins at 2 p.m. For the tour, enter through the walk-in entrance at 5555 Melrose. Because this is a working environment, children under 10 are not allowed. Tour price is $15. (2 hours)

★ HOLLYWOOD WALK OF FAME

In the pavement you can spot the stars belonging to your favorite entertainers on this self-guided tour of show-biz honorees.

Details: *Along Hollywood Boulevard from La Brea to Gower Street and on Vine Street between Yucca Street and Sunset Boulevard. (1 hour)*

★ HOMES OF FAMOUS PEOPLE

Vendors along Sunset Boulevard (especially in Beverly Hills and Brentwood) and at many newsstands around the city sell maps identifying the locations of celebrities' homes.

Details: *Many companies offer tours—see Fitness and Recreation, below. (2 hours)*

★ MANN'S CHINESE THEATRE

6925 Hollywood Blvd., Hollywood, 323/464-8111

This theater, still active, is famous for the hand- and footprints of more than 150 screen legends (past and present) in the cement of its forecourt. (30 minutes, unless you're also seeing a movie)

FITNESS AND RECREATION

At **Griffith Park** more than 4,000 acres of hills, canyons, and flatlands offer hiking and horseback-riding trails, an 18-hole golf course, and playground and sports facilities. There are live-pony and wagon rides, a miniature train, an old-fashioned carousel, and many hiking trails. The **Griffith Park Ranger Station and Visitor's Center**, 323/665-5188, is open from 6 a.m. to 10 p.m. and offers free hiking maps. **Griffith Observatory**, 323/664-1191, offers planetarium and Laserium shows and (on clear days) a view all the way to the ocean.

For additional personal fitness activities, you can talk about dieting over a lite lunch, visit one of many gyms and spas, or take a **Los Angeles Conservancy Walking Tour**, 213/623-CITY.

Many outfits offer special-interest tours of Los Angeles: **Hollywood Fantasy Tours**, 323/469-8184; **Oskar Sightseeing Tours**, 818/501-7590; **Limousine Tours & Services**, 310/475-5708; and **Ultra Limousine Tours**, 310/274-1303 and 818/755-3982, all offer tours of movie stars' homes. **Ultra** allows you to customize your own private tour at competitive rates. And **Grave Line Tours**, 323/469-4149, offers a tour of celebrity death sites.

The Los Angeles area teems with professional spectator sports. Among them are the NBA **Los Angeles Lakers**, 213/480-3232, and **Los Angeles**

LOS ANGELES AND HOLLYWOOD

N

To Anaheim

GRAND AVE

CENTRAL AVE

Griffith Park

LOS FELIZ BLVD

Los Angeles

VERMONT AVE

WESTERN AVE

WILSHIRE BLVD

SANTA MONICA FREEWAY

JEFFERSON BLVD

LA BREA AVE

LA CIENEGA BLVD

BEVERLY BLVD

MELROSE AV

SUNSET BLVD

HOLLYWOOD BLVD

SANTA MONICA BLVD

OLYMPIC BLVD

Universal City

Hollywood

North Hollywood

LAUREL CANYON BLVD

COLDWATER CANYON

West Hollywood

Beverly Hills

Culver City

CULVER BLVD

BEVERLY GLEN BLVD

Sherman Oaks

VENICE BLVD

Encino

MULHOLLAND DR

Santa Monica Mountains
National Recreation Area

WILSHIRE BLVD

LINCOLN BLVD

HIGHWAY

VENTURA BLVD

SAN VINCENTE BLVD

SUNSET BLVD

Santa Monica

ROAD

Tarzana

Santa Monica Bay

Woodland Hills

Topanga

TOPANGA BLVD

PACIFIC COAST HWY

MILES

KILOMETERS

SCALE

Clippers, 213/748-6131; the NHL's **Los Angeles Kings**, 310/419-3182, and **The Mighty Ducks** (in Anaheim), 714/704-2700; and baseball's **Los Angeles Dodgers**, 323/224-1500, and **Anaheim Angels** (in Anaheim), 714/634-2000.

FOOD

Los Angeles and Hollywood are eating towns. They have to be: Business is done at lunch (and breakfast and dinner), and people just breaking into show-biz have to support themselves—without restaurants, where would they work?

Serving breakfast (the most important meal of the day) is **S & W Country Diner**, 9748 Washington Blvd., Culver City, 310/204-1233. It's a bit off the beaten track, but the diner atmosphere and the taste and portions are worth it. Most breakfasts are less than $7; lunch and dinner are also served. **Café Latte**, 6254 Wilshire Blvd., Los Angeles, 323/936-5213, serves breakfast, lunch, and dinner, but it's best for breakfast, featuring eggs-and-pasta and pancakes. Breakfasts are less than $10, most meals less than $15, and there's live entertainment on some nights. Also good for breakfast is **Duke's**, 8909 W. Sunset Blvd., West Hollywood, 310/652-9411; its menu is basic but the portions are generous and the food is good. Breakfasts are less than $10.

Ed Debevic's, 134 N. La Cienega Blvd., Beverly Hills, 310/659-1952, is a fun, '50s-style diner where everything on the menu is under $8. **Spago**,

FOOD
- Ⓐ Café Latte
- Ⓑ Cat and Fiddle
- Ⓒ Duke's
- Ⓓ Ed Debevic's
- Ⓔ Engine Co. No. 28
- Ⓕ Georgia
- Ⓖ Jerry's Famous Deli
- Ⓗ Jino's Beverly Hills
- Ⓘ Kass Bah
- Ⓙ Maria's Italian Kitchen
- Ⓚ Nate & Al's Delicatessen
- Ⓚ Orso
- Ⓛ S & W Country Diner
- Ⓜ Spago

FOOD (continued)
- Ⓝ Versailles
- Ⓞ Water Grill

LODGING
- Ⓞ Best Western Hollywood Plaza Inn
- Ⓒ Best Western Sunset Plaza Hotel
- Ⓑ Biltmore
- Ⓒ Chateau Marmont
- Ⓞ Days Inn
- Ⓟ Holiday Inn Hollywood

LODGING (continued)
- Ⓠ Hollywood Best Inn
- Ⓡ Hollywood Metropolitan Hotel
- Ⓞ Hollywood Roosevelt Hotel
- Ⓔ Hotel Figueroa
- Ⓢ Hotel Nikko at Beverly Hills
- Ⓜ Hyatt West Hollywood
- Ⓔ The Mayfair
- Ⓣ Ramada Inn
- Ⓤ San Vicente Inn
- Ⓥ Travelodge
- Ⓔ Westin Bonaventure

Note: Items with the same letter are located in the same area.

8795 Sunset Blvd., West Hollywood, 310/652-4025, the famous spot that always hosts an exclusive post–Academy Awards party, was Wolfgang Puck's first restaurant. It serves California cuisine with meals under $35; reservations are absolutely required, unless you're a Somebody. (Another Spago is in Beverly Hills at 176 N. Canon, 310/385-0880). Also in the West Hollywood area is **Orso**, 8706 W. Third St., West Hollywood, 310/274-7144. It serves Italian cuisine with a continental flair, has a wonderfully secluded patio, and makes excellent desserts. Meals are $25 and up. **Kass Bah**, 9010 Melrose Ave., West Hollywood, 310/274-7664, is an upscale bistro with a full bar. It's casual and centrally located, serving California cuisine. Entrees average $17.

If you crave deli and you're near the Museum of Radio and TV or elsewhere in Beverly Hills, visit famous **Nate & Al's Delicatessen**, 414 Beverly Dr., Beverly Hills, 310/274-0101. This is a classic deli with professional waitresses and waiters. They serve pickles and cole slaw while you wait for your meal; it's delicious, casual, and for those who remember what delis really used to be, nostalgic. They serve Matzo Brei for breakfast not just during Passover but all year 'round! (They might be the only place west of New York City that has it on the menu.) A good sandwich might be $8, but it's a *good* sandwich. Meals are generally less that $20. Also in the Beverly Hills area is **Jino's Beverly Hills**, 9010 Wilshire Blvd., 310/859-1111; this cozy dining spot around the corner from the Writer's Guild serves tasty Italian dishes like *penne di calamari*, homemade lasagna (of course), and chicken piccata (it's great!). Meals are generally less than $10.

Located downtown and also serving American fare is **Engine Co. No. 28**, 644 S. Figueroa St., Los Angeles, 213/624-6996. It's not as casual and a little pricier: meals can run over $30. Also downtown and even fancier is **Water Grill**, 544 S. Grand Ave., Los Angeles, 213/891-0900. It specializes in seafood, features a massive oyster bar, and takes pride in its ahi tuna, salmon, mahi-mahi, swordfish, and creative sauces. Entrees range from $16 to $24.

Serving wonderful Cuban dinners is **Versailles**, 1415 S. La Cienega Blvd., Culver City, 310/289-0392. Although it has a variety of dishes, the roast chicken dinner with rice and fried plantains is the popular choice. The place is very casual and meals are generally less than $15; most are less than $10.

One of the best places to eat under the stars is the **Cat and Fiddle**, 6530 Sunset Blvd., Hollywood, 213/468-3800. Set in the style of an English pub, it serves fresh fish and chips, bangers and mash, shepherd's pie, and fine lamb and pasta dishes. Entrees range from $7 to $16. There's live jazz on Sunday afternoons. You can eat indoors, if you like, but the appealing things about the place are the courtyard and the service. On a clear Southern California night it's the right place to be.

One of the newest restaurants is **Georgia**, 7250 Melrose Ave., Los Angeles, 323/933-8420, offering real Southern cooking, including crab cakes, ribs, and scrumptious fried chicken served with great corn bread, fried green tomatoes, and black-eyed peas. Full meals run less than $30.

In the Valley, **Jerry's Famous Deli**, 12655 Ventura Blvd. Studio City, 818/980-4245, open 24 hours, serves great corned-beef sandwiches, bagels, knockwurst, and brisket—the whole schmeer. Sandwiches start at $8, dinners run $10 to $20. Sample the rich desserts, pastries, and fresh-baked breads. And keep an eye out for TV and movie actors and comics—there's even a booth with a plaque declaring it the Jerry Seinfeld table. Also on Ventura Boulevard is **Maria's Italian Kitchen**, 13353 Ventura Blvd., Sherman Oaks, 818/906-0783, a tasty family restaurant with the motto "Where an Italian Woman Prepares Italian Food." Most entrees are well under $15. Other Maria's locations include Encino, Woodland Hills, and Northridge.

LODGING

The Los Angeles/Hollywood area has hundreds of motels and hotels, covering almost all ranges of style, price, and use. Among the chain motels in Hollywood are a **Travelodge**, 1401 N. Vermont Ave., Hollywood, 213/665-5735, with rates starting at $39.95; a **Ramada Inn**, 1160 N. Vermont Ave., Hollywood, 800/272-6232, with rates starting at $69; a **Best Western Hollywood Plaza Inn**, 2011 N. Highland Ave., Hollywood, 800/232-4353, with rates starting at $59; and a **Days Inn**, 7023 Sunset Blvd., Hollywood, 800/346-7723, with rates starting at $45.

The recently renovated **Hollywood Roosevelt Hotel**, 7000 Hollywood Blvd., Hollywood, 323/466-7000, across from Mann's Chinese Theatre, was built in 1927 and is one of L.A.'s most historic hotels, with rates starting at $99. The Blossom Room was the site of the first Academy Awards. The Cinegrill room was a haven for movie stars and for writers like Hemingway and Fitzgerald, and still offers quality entertainment. The rooms offer hair dryers, coffeemakers, irons and boards, and mini-bars. But one of its best features, besides the fact that its centrally located in the heart of Hollywood, is its lobby. It's an extremely restful place to sit, relax, enjoy a drink, and toast past glamour and present comfort.

The **Holiday Inn Hollywood**, 1755 N. Highland Ave., Hollywood, 213/462-7181, doesn't feel like a Holiday Inn. It feels more like a fine hotel in a busy, exciting urban area. There's a fully equipped exercise facility, outdoor

THE VALLEY

Over the mountains, north of Los Angeles and Hollywood, lies the San Fernando Valley, known to Angelenos simply as "the Valley." According to one story, if you drive north over the 405 at night, the lights you see in the Valley inspired Steven Spielberg to make the movie Close Encounters of the Third Kind. Another story says those same lights gave George Lucas his vision of the underside of a spacecraft for Star Wars. In any case, the Valley is a vast expanse of populated settlement that includes movie and television studios and theme parks.

Among the attractions is **Warner Brothers Studios**, 4000 Warner Blvd., Burbank, 818/954-1744, which offers a VIP tour explaining how movies and TV shows are made and displaying some of its history (such as Bogart's Maltese falcon, James Dean's motorcycle, and Sam's piano from Casablanca). The two-hour tours are given weekdays between 9 a.m. and 3 p.m. and take no more than 12 people at a time. The studio suggests reservations and also states that, because the tour visits working areas, children under 10 are not allowed. Enter at Gate 4 at Hollywood Way and Olive Avenue. Tour price is $29.

NBC Studios, 3000 W. Alameda Ave., Burbank, 818/840-3537, "the only network that opens its doors to you!" offers a 70-minute walking tour of its broadcast complex. (From the 134 headed east, take the Bob Hope Drive exit, turn left onto Bob Hope Drive, then left on Alameda; from the 134 west, take the Buena Vista exit, turn right on Buena Vista, and left on Alameda.) The studio suggests calling for current schedule. No cameras allowed. Admission is $7 adults, $6.25 seniors, $3.75 children ages 5–12, and free for children under 5.

Universal Studios (the studio and theme park), 100 Universal

heated pool and sundeck, a revolving rooftop restaurant and lounge (the views of Hollywood, the Sunset Strip, and the Hills are terrific), and light jazz entertainment Tuesday through Saturday, 7 to 11 p.m. Rates start at $129.

Among the Hollywood-area non-chain lodgings is the **Hollywood Best Inn**, 1822 N. Cahuenga Blvd., Hollywood, 213/467-2252, with rates starting at $30. Despite a less-than-resort–like appearance, this motel is clean, comfortable, and conveniently located. Also try **Hollywood Metropolitan Hotel**, 5825 Sunset Blvd., Hollywood, 213/962-5800, with rates starting at $69.

City Plaza, Universal City, 818/508-9600, offers tours and numerous movie-themed rides, including its new Terminator II ride, Jurassic Park—The Ride, Waterworld, Back to the Future—The Ride, an E.T. bicycle ride, and several shows, including Wild West and a Nickelodeon show. The tram tour runs throughout the day until 4:15 p.m. The park is open daily 10 to 6, 9 to 6 on Saturdays and Sundays; and open until 10 p.m. seasonally. Admission is $38 adults, $28 children 3–11, and $33 seniors. Parking is $7. Universal CityWalk is also here.

Six Flags Magic Mountain, 26101 Magic Mountain Parkway, Valencia, 805/255-4111 or 818/367-5965, about 30 minutes north of Los Angeles on I-5, features dozens of rides and attractions, including The Riddler's Revenge (billed as the world's tallest and fastest stand-up roller coaster), Superman The Escape, and Batman The Ride, as well as Bugs Bunny World, the Batman & Robin Live Action Show, and the Looney Tunes characters. Open 10 a.m. weekends and holidays year 'round, daily March 27–Sept 12. Closing hours vary. Admission is $36, children under 48" in height $18, seniors $20. Children two years and younger are admitted free.

Six Flags Hurricane Harbor, next door (and with a separate admission), is a theme water park featuring 22 water slides, including high-speed body slides and tube slides. There's also a lazy river, a wave pool, and the pirate-themed Castaway Cove. Open 10 a.m. weekends beginning May 15, daily May 29–Sept 6, and weekends through Sept 26. For specific dates and times (closing hours vary) call 805/255-4100. Admission is $19, children under 48" in height and seniors $12. Children two years and younger are admitted free.

All of the above hotels and motels are not far from Mann's Chinese Theatre, the Greek Theatre, Universal Studios and Universal CityWalk, the Hollywood Walk of Fame, NBC, Griffith Park, and Paramount. They're also convenient to the restaurants and nightlife in West Hollywood, on the Sunset Strip, in Beverly Hills, and downtown.

In West Hollywood, the **San Vicente Inn**, 837 N. San Vicente Blvd., West Hollywood, 310/854-6915, is a B&B with nine cottages; rates start at $69. On Sunset Boulevard, near the Comedy Store and the House of Blues, the **Best Western Sunset Plaza Hotel**, 8400 Sunset Blvd., West Hollywood, 213/654-0750, has rates starting at $109 and one of the best lounges in the area. You can watch sports, hear comics from the Comedy Store reenact and critique their shows ("I waited too long." "You waited too long." "I shoulda said the line, just given it a moment, then, bam!"), or sit quietly in the corner with your agent discussing how you're going to fix the second act of your screenplay. Across the street, the **Hyatt West Hollywood** (formerly the Hyatt on Sunset), 8401 Sunset Blvd., West Hollywood, 323/656-1234, was recently renovated and has rates starting at $109.

Nearby is the **Chateau Marmont**, 8221 Sunset Blvd., Hollywood, 323/656-1010, where Howard Hughes and Greta Garbo didn't die and John Belushi did; rates start at $210. Adjacent to Beverly Hills is **Hotel Nikko at Beverly Hills**, 465 S. La Cienega Blvd., West Hollywood, 310/247-0400, with rates starting at $290; this hotel was built by whomever invented the word "posh."

In the downtown Los Angeles area are **The Mayfair**, 1256 W. Seventh St., Los Angeles, 213/484-9789, a Best Western hotel with a rooftop sundeck and rates starting at $80; **Hotel Figueroa**, 939 S. Figueroa St., Los Angeles, 213/627-8971, built in 1926 in the Mediterranean style, with rates starting at $78; the **Westin Bonaventure**, 404 S. Figueroa St., Los Angeles, 213/624-1000, with outside-of-the-building elevators and rates starting at $179; and the historic, recently renovated **Biltmore**, 506 S. Grand Ave., Los Angeles, 213/624-1011, where rates start at $165.

NIGHTLIFE

Los Angeles and Hollywood offer nightlife for virtually every taste in music, comedy, theater, and dance. On the Sunset Strip in West Hollywood is the **House of Blues**, 8430 Sunset Blvd., West Hollywood, 323/848-5700, www.hob.com, home to big-name musicians. Across the street, at 8433 Sunset Blvd., is the **Comedy Store**, 323/656-6225, featuring both famous and up-and-coming comics. Farther west on the strip are **The Roxy**, 9009 Sunset Blvd., West Hollywood, 310/276-2222; and Johnny Depp's **Viper Room**, 8852 Sunset Blvd., West Hollywood, 310/358-1880, presenting a variety of rock acts.

Also in West Hollywood, Doug Weston's **Troubadour**, 9081 Santa Monica Blvd., 310/276-1158, www.iuma.com/troubadour, showcases alternative bands (and was the place where what later became the Eagles formed as Linda Ronstadt's backup band). **LunaPark**, 665 N. Robertson Blvd., West Hollywood, 310/652-0611, has recently become one of the hottest venues in town for up-and-coming music groups and for alternative comedy. (It's so happening the maitre d', hostesses, and other staff personnel wear headset communicators.) It features three full bars, a high-energy nightclub upstairs, a Cabaret room downstairs, and what they call a Cal-Euro-Asian fusion restaurant. Valet parking is available, and cover varies.

For an offbeat evening, check out Marty and Elayne playing and singing show tunes, jazz and big-band era music at the **Dresden Room**, 1760 N. Vermont Ave., Hollywood, 323/665-4294—they've been there for over 15 years. (And this is the place featured in the movies *Swingers*.)

Among the newest clubs is the **Coconut Club Swing**, located in the Beverly Hilton, corner of Santa Monica and Wilshire Boulevards, Beverly Hills 310/285-1358; this is Merv Griffin's new supper club, featuring swing dance music.

For more comedy, visit the **Laugh Factory**, 8001 Sunset Blvd., West Hollywood, 213/656-1336; and **The Improv**, 8162 Melrose Ave., West Hollywood, 213/651-2583; both feature famous and up-and-coming comics. **The Groundlings Theatre**, 7307 Melrose Ave., West Hollywood, 213/934-4747, featuring sketch comedy and improvised bits, launched several *Saturday Night Live* stars.

Among the really fine concert halls are the **Greek Theatre** (outdoor amphitheater inside Griffith Park), 2700 N. Vermont Ave., Hollywood, 213/665-1927; **The Wiltern**, 3790 Wilshire Blvd., Los Angeles, 213/380-5005; and **The Pantages**, 6233 Hollywood Blvd., Hollywood, 213/480-3232, a beautiful theater with elaborate art deco motifs; in these halls, every seat's a good one. If one of your favorites is playing at one of these venues while you're in town, don't miss it—especially if it's at the Greek (which is closed in winter). There's something about music outdoors under the stars on a balmy Southern California night . . .

In the Valley, **Universal CityWalk** (1000 Universal Center Dr., Universal City) is a two-block-long pedestrian walk between Universal Studios and Universal City Cinemas. It's like a theme mall, lit by colored neon and featuring oversized signs, with many stores, restaurants, and nightclubs, including **B.B. King's Blues Club**, 818/6-BB-KING.

The theater scene in Los Angeles is often criticized for being merely a show-case for actors looking for sitcom roles and writers looking for movie deals. However, you can definitely find good theater in Los Angeles, too. One-person shows are also popular here. **The Tiffany Theater** (on Sunset Boulevard near the Strip), **Theater/Theater** in Hollywood, the **Odyssey Theater**, **The Tamarind**, and **The Complex** are among the many theaters offering well-known and cutting-edge plays. The Complex is located on what is known as Theatre Row, on Santa Monica Boulevard between Highland and Cahuenga. For concise information about what's playing, check the Sunday Calendar section of the *Los Angeles Times*.

Of course, Los Angeles is the center of so much live entertainment, this is hardly a complete listing. For further information about venues and schedules, pick up a free copy of the *L.A. Weekly*; it's the most complete listing you'll find.

SHOPPING

The famous **Rodeo Drive** and the **Golden Triangle** (bordered by Crescent Drive and Wilshire and Little Santa Monica Boulevards) in Beverly Hills offer world-class boutiques and several area parking structures. In nearby Century City is the **Century City Shopping Center and Marketplace** at Santa Monica Boulevard and Avenue of the Stars, with more than 140 stores under one roof. And close to that is the **Westside Pavilion** (10800 W. Pico Blvd., Los Angeles), a three-story shopping complex housed in a postmodern building. The upscale grocery store has valet parking. **Sunset Plaza**, between La Cienega and San Vicente Boulevards on Sunset Boulevard is a very chic retail strip; there are also several restaurants with sidewalk dining, and plenty of free parking behind the strip. **Melrose Avenue**, from San Vicente to La Brea, is a strip of funky boutiques, offbeat shops, and trendy restaurants and coffeehouses. While some of the stores are fun, this strip reveals what goes wrong when "hip" becomes institutionalized. Nearby, at La Cienega and Beverly, is the **Beverly Center**, a huge mall with over 180 shops (unhip institutionalized). Also nearby, at Fairfax and Third, is the famous **Farmers Market**, with over 150 shops and restaurants and, of course, vegetable and fruit stands.

Downtown's **Olvera Street**, an open-air marketplace in the historic district, features vendors selling mostly Mexican goods from stalls as strolling mariachis play their tunes. Nearby **Chinatown**, on Hill Street north of Sunset, has shops featuring Chinese products.

HELPFUL HINTS

Note that the term "Los Angeles" applies to a large area that encompasses numerous smaller communities. Despite the size, it's not difficult to get around in Los Angeles, except for the traffic. Morning rush hour in many places does not end until at least 9 a.m.; evening rush hour can begin as early as 3 p.m., especially on Friday. Saturday and Sunday traffic generally runs smoothly, except on

ANAHEIM

Anaheim is just an hour south of Los Angeles; you can take the 5 out of the downtown area or, if you're closer to the west side, take the 405 south to the 105 east to the 5, then head south. Anaheim is home to Disneyland and Knott's Berry Farm.

Disneyland is Disneyland; recently the park has added Animazement and the Mulan Parade. It's at 1313 Harbor Blvd., Anaheim, 714/781-4565. Hours vary seasonally, and Hunchback shows are only on weekends. Tickets are $38 for adults, $28 for children 3–11.

Knott's Berry Farm, 88030 Beach Blvd., Buena Park, 714/220-5200, which bills itself as "America's First Theme Park," is on Beach Boulevard (exit at Beach Boulevard from the 5, 91, 22, or 405 freeways). It features the thrill ride Hammerhead, an 1880s ghost town, the multi-sensory Mystery Lodge, Wild Water Wilderness, Indian Trails, Fiesta Village, The Boardwalk, and Camp Snoopy. Open every day except Christmas, but hours vary, so be sure to call ahead. Admission is $29.95 adults, $19.95 children 3–11 and seniors. Free for children under two.

If you decide to spend the night instead of returning to Los Angeles, there are numerous chain motels near both parks.

Sunday evenings, when everyone is returning at the same time from their weekend trips. Freeway accidents at any hour can cause unanticipated delays. Plan ahead and have an alternate route in mind, just in case. If you're driving from the west side to the Valley or to Hollywood, figure at least a half-hour without traffic, 1 1/2 hours with. Tune in to KNX 1070 AM radio for traffic reports every six minutes. (Listening to traffic reports is not an idle suggestion. Recently when I was driving back from Temecula, going north on I-15, I heard on KNX there was an accident on the 105. A truck carrying portable toilets had gone out of control and flipped some of its cargo onto the freeway, covering the highway with what the chopper pilot called "liquid" and tying up traffic for hours. Because I heard the report well enough ahead of time, I was able to take the 91 west to the 405 instead of the usual route of the 91 to the 605 to the 105. As I turned off the 405 and into Marina del Rey they were still cleaning up the mess on the 105.)

This, perhaps, is a different kind of scenic drive from the ones you encounter in other books, and it's different from the other drives mentioned in this volume: This is an urban scenic drive. From a small, relatively insignificant intersection just north of downtown; through a modest residential and commercial area; through now-seedy, now-glamorous Hollywood; past the mansions and to the Pacific; this scenic drive is more than a route: It's a cross-section of what Los Angeles is and was.

Sunset Boulevard (and its offspring, the Sunset Strip) presents a smorgasbord of the people and architecture and activities that make up much of Los Angeles. Beginning just north of downtown at Figueroa and Sunset, Sunset Boulevard will take you all the way through Hollywood, West Hollywood, Beverly Hills, Bel Air, Westwood, Brentwood, and Pacific Palisades, leaving you at the blue Pacific Ocean in Pacific Palisades, south of Malibu. The drive is 24 miles and will take approximately 90 minutes in non–rush-hour traffic.

For the first few miles, as you drive through **Echo Park**, you'll see urban commercial and residential buildings and murals depicting the exciting cultural mix of Los Angeles life (a mix that may be quite different from your own experience, depending

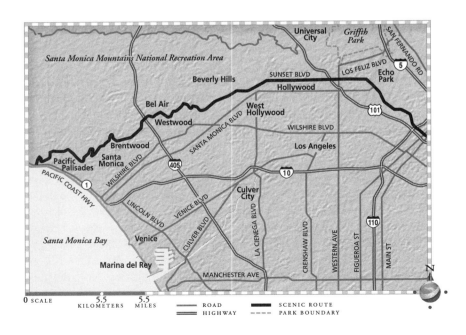

on where you're from). As you cross the 101 you can see **Griffith Park** off to your right, and as you enter **Hollywood** you begin to pass various entertainment offices and historic sites: **KTLA** (where one of the first talkies, The Jazz Singer, was filmed in 1927), **Fox Television Center**, and the **Sunset-Gower Studios**, where TV sitcoms and other shows are shot. At 6121, **KCBS** sits on the site of the Nestor Film Company, the first Hollywood motion picture studio. At 6212, the **Hollywood Palladium** has hosted the Golden Globe, Grammy, and Emmy Awards ceremonies. At 6230, the **Sunset Theater** housed many of Jerry Lewis' muscular dystrophy telethons and television's Queen for a Day. And at 6360, on your left, is the **Cinerama Dome**, built exclusively for Cinerama movies and still an active movie theater.

Next you'll enter **West Hollywood**, known for the famous **Sunset Strip**, with its huge vanity billboards advertising movies and record albums, its clubs and landmarks. At 8001 is the **Laugh Factory**; 8024 is the site of the former **Schwab's**, the pharmacy where Lana Turner wasn't discovered; at 8221 is the infamous **Chateau Marmont**, hideaway home-away-from-home-of-the-stars where John Belushi OD'd; at 8225 is the VIP club **The Roxbury**; and at 8358 is **The Argyle**, where Gable, Flynn, and others used to stay. Parts of Pretty Women and The Player were shot here. At 8401 is the **Hyatt West Hollywood** (formerly the Hyatt on Sunset), where Led Zeppelin allegedly had orgies (and they may not be the only ones).

Continuing along the Strip, at 8418 is **Sunset Strip Tattoo**, where many rock and movie stars have been 'tooed; at 8430 is the **House of Blues**; at 8433 is the **Comedy Store** (this was once Ciro's, a popular nightclub in the 1940s and '50s— you can picture Bogart saying "Ciro's" but not "the Comedy Store"); at 8440 is the **Mondrian Hotel**, a favorite of rock and movie stars; at 8852 is the **Viper Room** music club, owned by Johnny Depp, in front of which River Phoenix died; at 8901 is **The Whisky** (a rock club, allegedly where "Go-Go" dancing was born); at 9009 is **The Roxy**, a showcase for up-and-coming music talent; and at 9015 is the **Rainbow Grill** (the story is that Marilyn Monroe met Joe DiMaggio here on a blind date when it was the Villa Nova Restaurant).

Then you're out of the Strip and into plush and very green **Beverly Hills**. Numerous movie, TV, and music stars live off Sunset between here and Malibu, and many of the houses have been used for movies and TV shows.

The entrance to Beverly Hills is marked by hawkers selling maps to the stars' homes. Huge, fine mansions with immaculate lawns behind locked gates and iron fences line this stretch. On your right, at 9641, is the **Beverly Hills Hotel and Polo Lounge** (enough movie-star stories there to fill volumes), and 10100 was once

Jayne Mansfield's **Pink Palace**. *Farther along, on the left, there's* **UCLA***; on the right* **Bel Air***. The road winds quite a bit between the end of Beverly Hills and the beginning of* **Brentwood***, and you may just imagine you're James Dean in your Porsche Spyder. As a matter of fact, it's this curving area north of UCLA that inspired Jan and Dean's 1964 hit song "Dead Man's Curve."*

Brentwood is also upscale, and you'll pass some street names that may sound familiar, like **Bundy Drive***. You're not far from O.J. Simpson's former house. (Hmm. Richard Nixon wrote Six Crises while living on Bundy, and Marilyn Monroe lived and died just off Bundy: All right, conspiracy buffs, what do you make of that?)*

The scenery becomes greener and the city is left far behind as you move farther west. From Brentwood you enter **Pacific Palisades***, another upscale community, and within minutes you have a gorgeous view of the Pacific Ocean.*

Mullholland Drive

As an option to the urban scenic drive along Sunset Boulevard, try cruising along **Mulholland Drive**. North of Sunset Boulevard, Mulholland Drive winds its way from east to west (or west to east, if you want to start north of Malibu and end up near the Hollywood Bowl).

Starting on the 101 near the Hollywood Bowl exit (follow the signs for Mulholland Drive), the mostly two-lane road winds for 30 miles across the tops of the **Santa Monica Mountains**, through residential areas, canyons mostly free of development, ranchland, and sparsely settled coastal areas. And with a slight detour in the Valley, you can drive all the way from just north of downtown to the Pacific Coast Highway north of Malibu near the Ventura County line.

After you turn onto Mulholland you'll begin to ascend. Within minutes you'll be near the crest of the mountains that separate L.A. from the Valley. To your right you'll see the **Universal Studio complex** and the famous **Black Tower** (used in Die Hard), and for the next 10 miles you'll see spectacular views to the north and northwest of the Valley, and spectacular views to the south of the sprawling city. You'll pass several overlooks, and a few parks, including the popular **Runyon Canyon**

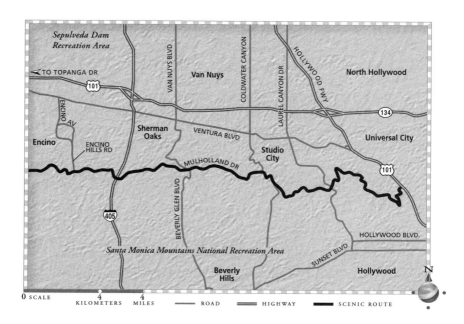

park; at times you'll be able to see views to the north and south at the same time; it's as if you're on a tightrope high above all of the greater L.A. area: fall to the right and you end up in the Valley; fall to the left and you're in Beverly Hills. Don't fall.

As you wind westward, you'll cross **Laurel Canyon Drive**, then **Coldwater Canyon Drive**, then Beverly Glen Boulevard. As you ascend higher, the views are broader—but remember to keep your eyes on the road! About 45 minutes after you started you'll cross the 405, and soon after, you'll reach a dead end where you can park, hike, or drive down **Encino Hills Road** into the Valley to take the detour. At this point you can either turn around, go back to the 405, go south, pick up Sunset Boulevard and take it west to the Coast, or you can take Encino Hills Road to Ventura Blvd., turn left, take Ventura to **Topanga**, turn left, then take Topanga to Mulholland, turn right, and you're back on Mulholland Drive, headed west.

Here the homes are fewer and farther apart. You'll climb into and drive through **Mulholland Canyon**, catch glimpses then rich views of the coast, then you'll descend through ranchland that feels (and is) very far away from L.A., on a very windy path to the Coast.

Compared to the Sunset Boulevard Scenic Drive, this is more on the order of a beautiful drive, and you may recognize parts of it—this road contains the hairpin turns where so many TV cops and private eyes and innocent victims seemed to always lose their brakes during nerve-racking car chases. But it's no TV show; it's another thrilling drive that gives you an overall view and feel of many of the fascinating facets that make up L.A.

7
PASADENA

Pasadena is home to more than just the Rose Bowl, although that's certainly the town's number-one claim to fame and, for many football fans, its sole reason to exist. Located northeast of Los Angeles, accessed by the 110 freeway out of downtown Los Angeles or the 210 east of the 134 (Ventura) freeway, Pasadena is bordered by the San Gabriel Mountains. In addition to the Rose Bowl game and the Tournament of Roses Parade, Pasadena has much to offer visitors in the way of culture, the arts, and history.

Modern Pasadena was founded in 1873 and was officially incorporated in 1886. The name of the town comes from the Chippewa for "crown of the valley." Soon wealthy easterners began to build grand mansions and hotels in Pasadena as an escape from the vicious winters back home.

If you have time, visit some of the historic sites to experience Pasadena's past. Visit the mission and the extraordinary museums, especially the Southwest Museum (in nearby Highland Park) and the Pacific Asia Museum, to experience the rich cultural mix of Pasadena and much of Southern California.

A PERFECT DAY IN PASADENA
Begin with breakfast at Marston's, then take in some of the area's history with Heritage Square, at least two of the historic houses, and the Pacific Asia Museum. Have lunch at Wok 'n' Roll, Sorriso Trattoria, or Clearwater

PASADENA

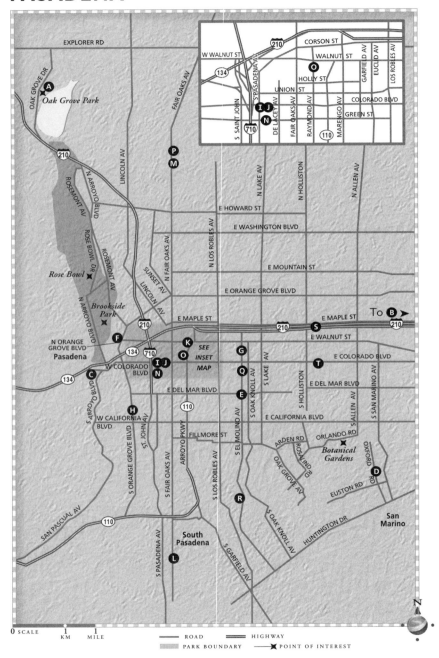

EXPLORER RD

OAK GROVE DR

A
Oak Grove Park

FAIR OAKS AV

210

LINCOLN AV

N ARROYO BLVD

ROSEMONT AV

ROSE BOWL DR

ROSEMONT AV

Rose Bowl ✗

SUNSET AV

N FAIR OAKS AV

LINCOLN AV

Brookside Park ✗

N ARROYO BLVD

210

E MAPLE ST

N ORANGE GROVE BLVD
F
Pasadena
134 710
K
O
SEE INSET MAP
W COLORADO BLVD
I J
N
134
C
S ARROYO BLVD

H
W CALIFORNIA BLVD
ST. JOHN AV
110

ARROYO PKWY
FILLMORE ST

S ORANGE GROVE BLVD
S FAIR OAKS AV
S JOHN AV

R

SAN PASCUAL AV
110

S PASADENA AV
South Pasadena
L
S GARFIELD AV

E HOWARD ST
N LAKE AV
N HOLLISTON
N ALLEN AV

N LOS ROBLES AV

E WASHINGTON BLVD

E MOUNTAIN ST

E ORANGE GROVE BLVD

E MAPLE ST
210 **S**
To **B** ➤
210

E WALNUT ST
G
S LAKE AV
E COLORADO BLVD
T
Q
S OAK KNOLL AV
S HOLLISTON
E DEL MAR BLVD
S SAN MARINO AV

E DEL MAR BLVD
E
E CALIFORNIA BLVD
S ALLEN AV

S EL MOLINO AV
ARDEN RD
ROSALIND RD
ORLANDO RD
OXFORD

Botanical Gardens ✗
OAK GROVE AV
D
EUSTON RD

S OAK KNOLL AV
HUNTINGTON DR
San Marino

Inset Map

210
CORSON ST
W WALNUT ST
WALNUT ST
GARFIELD AV
EUCLID AV
LOS ROBLES AV
134
S PASADENA AV
O
HOLLY ST
UNION ST
S SAINT JOHN
S 710
I J
N
DE LACEY AV
FAIR OAKS AV
RAYMOND AV
110
MARENGO AV
COLORADO BLVD
GREEN ST

N

0 SCALE   1 KM   1 MILE
▬▬▬ ROAD   ▭▭▭ HIGHWAY
▨▨▨ PARK BOUNDARY   ✗ POINT OF INTEREST

Seafood, then ponder your choices: Do you tour Cal Tech's Jet Propulsion Lab (if you made arrangements in advance) or see the incredible art and gardens at the Huntington? Take a hike or play a round of golf? Whatever you choose, one of those will fill up most of the afternoon, after which you might check out the Southwest Museum or the Norton Simon Museum. Then stroll around Old Pasadena, have dinner at JJ Steakhouse and take in a play at the world-famous Pasadena Playhouse, see a comedy show at the equally famous Ice House, or check out some jazz or R&B at one of the local clubs.

SIGHTSEEING HIGHLIGHTS

★★★★ HUNTINGTON MUSEUM AND GARDENS
1151 Oxford Road, San Marino, 626/405-2141

Also known as the Huntington Library, Art Collections and Botanical Gardens, the Huntington is located in nearby San Marino. This "home" sits on a 207-acre estate with botanical gardens containing more than 14,000 kinds of plants from around the world. The museum features one of the most comprehensive collections of eighteenth- and nineteenth-century British and French art, including the world-famous paintings Gainsborough's *Blue Boy* and Thomas Lawrence's *Pinkie*. The Virginia Steele Scott Gallery features American works from the 1730s through the 1940s. The library contains more than 600,000 rare books and 4 million manuscripts,

SIGHTS
A Cal Tech's Jet Propulsion Laboratory
B Fenyes Mansion
C Gamble House
D Huntington Museum and Gardens
E Kidspace
F Norton Simon Museum of Art
G Pacific Asia Museum
H Tournament House and Wrigley Gardens

FOOD
I Clearwater Seafood
J JJ Steakhouse
K Marston's Restaurant
L Old Town Bakery
L Raymond Restaurant
M Russell's
J Sorriso Trattoria
N Twin Palms
J Wok 'n' Roll
O Xiomara

LODGING
G DoubleTree Hotel at Plaza Las Fuentes
P Pasadena Bed and Breakfast
Q Pasadena Hilton
R Ritz-Carlton Huntington Hotel
S Saga Motor Hotel
T Vagabond Inn

Note: Items with the same letter are located in the same area.

including a fifteenth-century manuscript of Chaucer's *The Canterbury Tales* and a Gutenberg Bible (c. 1455).

Details: *Open Tue–Fri noon–4:30, Sat and Sun 10:30–4:30. Admission is $8.50 adults, $7 seniors, $5 students; children under 12 are free. Admission is free the first Thursday of every month. (1¹/₂ hours)*

★★★★ **NORTON SIMON MUSEUM OF ART**
411 W. Colorado Blvd., 626/796-4978
This museum displays collections of Renaissance to mid-twentieth-century European, Indian, and South Asian art, showcasing such artists as Raphael, Botticelli, Rubens, Rembrandt, Goya, Renoir, Monet, Degas, van Gogh, Cézanne, Picasso, Matisse—the list is endless!

Reputed to be one of the best collections west of the Mississippi—better than the Getty, some say—the collection includes the "seen before in books" pieces like Gustave Courbet's *Apples, Pears and Primroses on a Table* still life; luxuriant still lifes by Ambrosius Bosschaert the Elder; Rembrandt's penetrating *Portrait of a Bearded Man in a Widebrimmed Hat*; the grim work of Magnasco; art from the "What Is That?" school by Paul Klee and Wassily Kandinsky; and several Picasso paintings and sculptures, including his unusual *Bust of a Woman*.

The van Goghs include *Portrait of a Peasant, The Mulberry Tree*, and *Portrait of the Artist's Mother*. And Degas, lest you forget, is the one who did all the ballerina paintings your sister had on her wall, and many paintings of women preparing to bathe or combing their hair.

Although my personal favorites are van Gogh and the seventeenth-century Dutch painters, my favorite title is on an Italian Rococo painting called *The Triumph of Virtue and Nobility Over Ignorance*. Both Virtue/Nobility and Ignorance are depicted as women with bare breasts; Virtue/Nobility wears white, floats proudly in the sky, chest out, and is surrounded by admirers; Ignorance, wearing dark blue, tumbles downward through the sky.

Details: *Open Thu–Sun noon–6. Call for current admission fees; children under 12 are admitted free. (1¹/₂ hours)*

★★★★ **PACIFIC ASIA MUSEUM**
46 N. Los Robles Ave., 626/449-2742
This museum houses a fascinating and often-breathtaking collection of pottery, china, sculpture, and other artifacts from Asian civilizations over the centuries. The building is a replica of a Chinese imperial

palace, complete with green-tiled roof and dragons. This is the only museum in the southwestern United States dedicated to the preservation and understanding of the arts and culture of Asia and the Pacific.

Details: Open Wed–Sun 10–5. Admission is $4 adults, $2 seniors and students, free for children under 12. (1 1/2 hours)

★★★★ SOUTHWEST MUSEUM
234 Museum St., Highland Park, 323/221-2164

Located south of Pasadena in nearby Highland Park, the Southwest Museum is the oldest one in Los Angeles, founded in 1907. It exhibits Indian pottery, basketry, artifacts, and stone effigies. It's interesting to compare what Native American cultures were doing at the same time as Asian cultures (see exhibits at the Pacific Asia Museum, above). A visit to the History of Man Museum in San Diego provides even more information for your cultural time-line comparisons. The Southwest has special programs and a museum store.

Details: Open Tue–Sun 11–5. Admission is $5 adults, $3 seniors and students, $2 ages 7–18, free for children 6 and under. (1 hour)

★★★ CAL TECH'S JET PROPULSION LABORATORY (JPL)
4800 Oak Grove Dr., 818/354-9314

This lab, created during World War II, is managed for NASA by the California Institute of Technology (Cal Tech). JPL is the leading U.S. center for robotic exploration of the solar system, and its spacecraft have visited all known planets except Pluto (a Pluto mission is currently scheduled for around 2004; known as the Pluto-Kuiper Express, it will fly past Pluto to explore Kuipers—they're icy leftovers from our solar system's formation). In addition to its work for NASA, JPL conducts tasks for a variety of other federal agencies.

JPL offers family and self-selected group tours (up to nine persons), but they have to be arranged well in advance. The tours occur twice each month, generally during the first and third weeks. Group tours are also available; however, dates are generally booked about six months in advance. Advance reservations are required for all tours.

The tours include a multimedia presentation titled "Welcome to Outer Space" (which provides an overview of the lab's activities and accomplishments) and visits to the Spacecraft Museum, the Space Flight Operations Facility (the mission control area), and the Spacecraft Assembly Facility. Tours last two hours and involve considerable walking and stair-climbing. Cameras are welcome. Wheelchairs can be accommodated with advance notice. Tours are conducted from 10 a.m. to noon and from 1 to 3 p.m., weekdays only. Call four to six weeks ahead to reserve a place.

Details: *To arrange tours, contact Kay Ferrari, Mail Stop 186-113, Jet Propulsion Laboratory, 4800 Oak Grove Dr., Pasadena, CA 91109; 818/354-9314. (2 hours)*

★★★ MOUNT WILSON OBSERVATORY
626/793-3100

Located in the San Gabriel Mountains north of Pasadena, Mount Wilson is the observatory with the famous 100-inch telescope with which Hubble discovered the expanding universe and the Big Bang. Under construction is the world's most powerful visible-light interferometer. (Okay, I didn't know what it was 'til I read about it—that's what books and trips are for!) This instrument produces images so sharp that it can see an astronaut's footprint on the moon.

The views are fantastic. On a clear day you can see Glendale and Los Angeles all the way to the Pacific Ocean. The grounds also hold a museum, built in 1909 and updated in 1997. Exhibits' original captions appear along with the updated captions, giving visitors not only a history of astronomy, but a history of the history of astronomy.

Details: *Follow Route 2 (Angeles Crest Highway) out of La Cañada/Flintridge into the San Gabriel Mountains for 14 miles to Mount Wilson Road (Red Box Ranger Station), turn right and go another five miles to the observatory gate. Parking is available in the large main lot only. Picnic facilities are available; however, drinking water is not always available, so visitors are strongly advised to bring their own. An on-site walking tour begins at 1 p.m. at the pavilion on Sat, Sun, and holidays during the Daylight Savings Time period. The grounds are open to the public Sat–Sun only, 10–4, weather permitting. Admission is free. (1 hour)*

★★★ SAN GABRIEL ARCÁNGEL MISSION
428 S. Mission St., San Gabriel, 626/457-3048

Located just east of Pasadena, this mission was the fourth-established of California's chain of 21 missions. Founded in 1771, the mission includes Campo Santo Cemetery, the oldest cemetery in Los Angeles County. The mission church, built with cut stone and mortar, is the oldest structure of its kind south of Monterey and is considered architecturally unique among the California missions. The site includes many artifacts, such as the 300-year-old painting *Our Lady of Sorrows* and aboriginal paintings thought to be the oldest "Indian sacred pictorial art" in California. The five-foot-thick walls, the vats for wine-making, and the water cistern are all original. The restoration was completed in 1996. There is a museum and gift shop.

Details: *Open 9–4:30 daily. Closed most major holidays. Admission is $4 adults, $1 children. (1 hour)*

★★ HERITAGE SQUARE
3800 Homer St., Highland Park, 626/449-0193
This museum-village contains significant nineteenth-century buildings organized to preserve, restore, and interpret Southern California's history and culture between 1865 and 1914. If you don't have time to see the historic homes (see below), Heritage Square offers you a way to capture the feeling of the era in one place.

Details: *Open Fri–Sun noon–4. Admission is $5 adults, $4 seniors and ages 13–17, $2 children 7–12, and free for children 6 and under. (1 hour)*

★★ HISTORIC HOUSES
Founded in the late 1800s, Pasadena has taken pride in its history, and

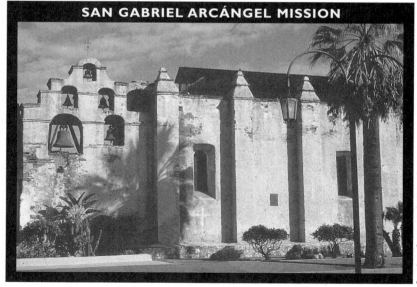

SAN GABRIEL ARCÁNGEL MISSION

Pasadena Convention & Visitors Bureau

taken pains to preserve some of that history. So for those who want to enjoy that history, there are—in addition to Heritage Square—several historic houses that can be viewed, and visited, toured, all within very quick driving distance from the center of Old Town. The **Fenyes Mansion** (470 W. Walnut St., 626/577-1660), built in 1905, doubles as the headquarters of the Pasadena Historical Museum. An example of Beaux Arts style, it contains original furnishings and artwork from turn-of-the-century Pasadena. A pop-culture note: Scenes from *Being There*, with Peter Sellers and Shirley MacLaine, were shot here. Built for David and Mary Gamble, of Proctor & Gamble fame, in 1908, the **Gamble House** (4 Westmoreland Pl., 626/793-3334) features hand-rubbed teakwood, original furnishings, multicolored glass windows, and cross-ventilation. It's considered a masterpiece of the Arts and Crafts era. Another pop-culture note: This was Christopher Lloyd's (a.k.a. Doc's) house in *Back to the Future*. The Italian Renaissance–style **Tournament House and Wrigley Gardens** (391 S. Orange Grove Blvd., 626/449-4100), built between 1908 and 1914 and purchased by chewing-gum magnate William Wrigley, is the headquarters for the Tournament of Roses Association. The garden (this should be no surprise) contains hundreds of varieties of roses, camellias, and annuals.

Details: *Fenyes Mansion is open Thu–Sun 1–4; admission is $4 adults, $3 students and seniors. The Gamble House is open Thu–Sun noon–3; admission is $5 adults, $4 seniors, $3 full-time students with ID, free for children 12 and under. Hours for the Tournament House and Wrigley Gardens vary; admission is free. (30 minutes per house)*

★★ KIDSPACE
390 S. El Molino Ave., 626/449-9143
This participatory museum for kids features hands-on exhibits including a TV studio, the Mouse House Computer Room, Critter Caverns, Toddler Territory, Ecology Beach, a fire station, and a grocery store.

Details: Open weekends year 'round 12:30–5; summer Tue–Fri 1–5; school-year Wed 2–5. Admission is $5. (1 1/2 hours)

★ SANTA ANITA PARK/RACE TRACK
285 W. Huntington St., Arcadia, 626/574-6400
Known worldwide for thoroughbred racing, the track offers guided tram tours through the stable areas.

Details: Tours available weekend mornings during racing seasons (October–mid-November and December–April). Admission is free. (1 hour)

PASADENA REGION

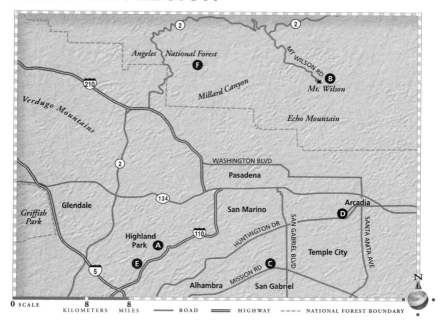

SIGHTS
Ⓐ Heritage Square
Ⓑ Mount Wilson Observatory
Ⓒ San Gabriel Arcángel Mission
Ⓓ Santa Anita Park/Race Track
Ⓔ Southwest Museum

CAMPING
Ⓕ Angeles National Forest

FITNESS AND RECREATION

For hikers, the Los Angeles River Ranger District in the **Angeles National Forest** maintains 160-plus miles of trails offering spectacular views, solitude, and beautiful scenery in a mountain wilderness that starts just a few miles from Pasadena. Seven self-guided nature trails are located here; three of these are short loops out of the **Chilao Visitor Center**. **Switzer's Picnic Area, Charlton Flat Picnic Area**, and **Bandido Group Campground** each have a short nature trail, and the **Mount Lowe Historic Hiking Trail**, over four miles long, traces the pathway of the old Mount Lowe Railway. Contact the Ranger District office, 4600 Oak Grove St., Flintridge, 818/790-1151; open 8 a.m. to 4:30 p.m., Monday through Friday; closed weekends.

Brookside Park, 360 N. Arroyo Blvd. (in Arroyo Seco right next to the Rose Bowl), Pasadena, 626/794-0581, has picnic tables, lighted tennis courts, badminton courts, handball courts, horseshoe courts, a golf course, and archery targets. The **AAF Rose Bowl Aquatics Center**, 626/564-0330, also in Brookside Park, has two 50-meter-by-25-yard pools.

Besides the 18-hole golf course at Brookside Park, you can tee off at two nine-hole courses: **Eaton Canyon Golf Course**, 1150 Sierra Madre Villa, 626/794-6773; and **Altadena Golf Course**, 1456 E. Mendocino, Altadena, 626/797-3821.

FOOD

Pasadena is also a dining center, with hundreds of restaurants: chains as well as locally owned and operated establishments.

For fine dining at its best, **JJ Steakhouse**, 88 W. Colorado Blvd., 626/844-8889, offers that rare combination of elegant atmosphere, comfort, a relaxing eating space, a fascinating decor, magnificent indirect lighting, a friendly and very professional staff, a wonderfully talented pianist who knows how to add to your evening without intruding, an owner who cares, and best of all, great food. Entrees (which average $26) feature swordfish, lobster, New York strip, rack of lamb, and free range chicken. Reservations are strongly suggested.

Also in the Old Pasadena area you'll find **Clearwater Seafood**, 168 W. Colorado Blvd., 626/356-0959, located at the edge of Old Town with a beautiful tree-shaded dining patio; entrees include sautéed king salmon, seared rare ahi tuna, Sake-Kasu Chilean sea bass, Idaho trout, and more, with prices starting at $14. **Old Town Bakery**, 166 W. Colorado Blvd., 626/793-2993, is a family-style restaurant with meals generally less than $10. **Russell's**, 30 N. Fair Oaks Ave., 626/578-1404, is another family-style restaurant featuring mountainous desserts and meals at generally less than $10. **Sorriso Trattoria**, 46 E. Colorado Blvd., 626/793-2233, offers indoor Italian dining in a casually elegant setting and outdoor sidewalk dining for those who enjoy watching the hustle and bustle of Old Town; meals are generally less than $15.

Xiomara, 69 N. Raymond Ave., 626/796-2520, features a menu emphasizing mixes of Cuban and other Latin favorites with a certain California touch. And the pricey **Raymond Restaurant**, 1250 S. Fair

Oaks Ave., 626/441-4470, serves California French cuisine; it's open Thursday through Sunday. At the edge of the area, **Twin Palms**, 101 W. Green St., 626/577-2567, formerly owned by Kevin Costner, has the ambiance of an expensive restaurant but falls more into the moderate price range; its meals are generally less than $20.

Wok 'n' Roll, 55 E. Colorado Blvd., 626/304-1000, features indoor and sidewalk dining, a sushi bar, and wonderfully creative sushi dishes (the Jerry Garcia Roll includes mushrooms, and the Elvis Presley Roll has deep-fried banana) as well as a fine choice of Japanese meals for generally less than $20. And the breakfast spot of choice is **Marston's Restaurant**, 151 E. Walnut St., 626/796-2459. Located northwest of the Old Pasadena area, it serves meals (breakfast and lunch only) for generally less than $7. Try the French toast.

LODGING

On the luxury list is the huge **DoubleTree Hotel at Plaza Las Fuentes**, 191 N. Los Robles Ave., 626/792-2727 or 800/222-8733, a 12-story, 350-room extravaganza with graceful fountains, a Spanish-Mediterranean court-yard, and rates ranging from $100 to $170. The **Pasadena Hilton**, 150 S. Los Robles Ave., 626/577-1000 or 800/445-8667, features Portuguese marble, skylights, a fully equipped fitness center, and rates that vary seasonally (they suggest you call). The **Ritz-Carlton Huntington Hotel**, 1401 S. Oak Knoll Ave., 626/568-3900 or 800/22-1777, situated on 23 acres, has gardens, lighted tennis courts, and California's first Olympic-sized swimming pool. Ritz rates range from $140 to $400.

On a more moderate scale are the **Vagabond Inn**, 1203 E. Colorado Blvd., 626/449-3170, with rates starting at $50; the **Saga Motor Hotel**, 1633 E. Colorado Blvd., 626/795-0431, where rates start at $60; and many other chain motels and hotels. The **Pasadena Bed and Breakfast**, 76 N. Fair Oaks Ave., between Union and Holly, 800/653-8886 or 626/568-8172 was built at the turn of the century. Each guest room is uniquely decorated with furnishings evoking the Old Pasadena setting; skylights let the daylight in. All 12 rooms have color TVs and central air-conditioning, and each has a private sink; there are five shared baths. No pets are allowed, and smoking is permitted in the courtyard only. Rates range between $65 and $195.

CAMPING

The **Angeles National Forest** offers camping in the Big Santa Anita Canyon area. Camps have picnic tables, grills, and pit toilets. Campfire permits are required year-round. The big attraction of Big Santa Anita is the 55-foot-high Sturtevant Falls, a two-mile hike from Chantry Flats and a very popular day hike. In addition to the falls hike, there are over 30 miles of trails in the area. (See Fitness and Recreation for information.)

NIGHTLIFE

Pasadena is home to two nationally known and important performance venues. The **Ice House**, 24 N. Mentor Ave., 626/577-1894, is one of the nation's oldest and most famous comedy clubs, established in 1960 as a folk-music club. Many of today's comedy stars got their start here. There are two rooms with shows nightly. The **Pasadena Playhouse**, 39 S. El Molino Ave., 626/356-PLAY, is nationally known as a training ground for America's theatrical, film, and television talent.

Old Pasadena has a variety of music clubs, including **Old Towne Pub**, 66 N. Fair Oaks Ave., 626/577-6583, for rock and R&B; and **McMurphy's**, 72 N. Fair Oaks Ave., 626/666-1445, featuring rock. Nearby music clubs include **Beckham Place**, 77 W. Walnut, 626/796-3399, offering country/folk music; and **John Bull Pub**, 958 S. Fair Oaks Ave., 626/441-4353, with R&B, world beat, and rock, depending on the night.

To find out what's happening pick up a free copy of *Pasadena Weekly*.

SHOPPING

Unlike indoor malls or shopping areas that feel more like theme parks, **Old Pasadena** is not sealed off or homogenized and therefore has the feel of a real old-time downtown shopping area—perhaps because it *is* an old-time downtown shopping area, only with modern-day products at modern-day prices. The district offers more than 130 retail shops, art galleries, boutiques, nightspots, and antiques shops. You can shop along tree-lined boulevards and soak up a little history as you soak in the California sun.

Tree-lined **Green Street Antique Row**, situated between 985 and 1005 E. Green St., beckons shoppers and browsers with numerous antiques shops. **South Lake Avenue**, running from Colorado Boulevard to California Boulevard, is another well-treed street that features a variety of upscale specialty stores and boutiques as well as restaurants with outdoor patios.

8
MALIBU

In what is now an upscale residential area and a mecca for surfers, sun-worshippers, and campers, the Chumash Indians once dwelled. Humaliwo was the name they gave to the beach at the mouth of Malibu Creek; it means "the surf sounds loudly." The first claim to land in Malibu after Spanish conquistadors had destroyed the Chumash was made in 1802 by Spanish settler Jose Bartoleme Tapia. This property became known as the "Rancho Topanga Malibu Simi Sequit" and was passed down through family inheritance until 1891, when it was sold (reportedly) for $300,000, thus creating the basis for the old joke: "If I had owned land in California in 1891 . . ."

The state had to battle with these new owners for the right to build a road and a railroad through the property. It wasn't victorious until 1929, when the Roosevelt Highway (now the Pacific Coast Highway) opened, allowing public transportation and commerce between Santa Monica and Oxnard. Shortly after that, May Rindge, the head of the family who owned the land, began leasing parcels to movie stars. One area became known as the Malibu Colony, and as gorgeous homes were built, the Rindges (the owners of the land) sold the lots.

Malibu is still home to many in the entertainment industry, with hundreds of beautiful homes on the coast and hillsides. It also features many beaches and parks that provide outdoor recreation opportunities. It's beautiful, it's romantic, the sunsets are breathtaking, and whether your interest is architecture, fine dining, surfing, sunning, hiking, or camping, Malibu has something for you.

MALIBU

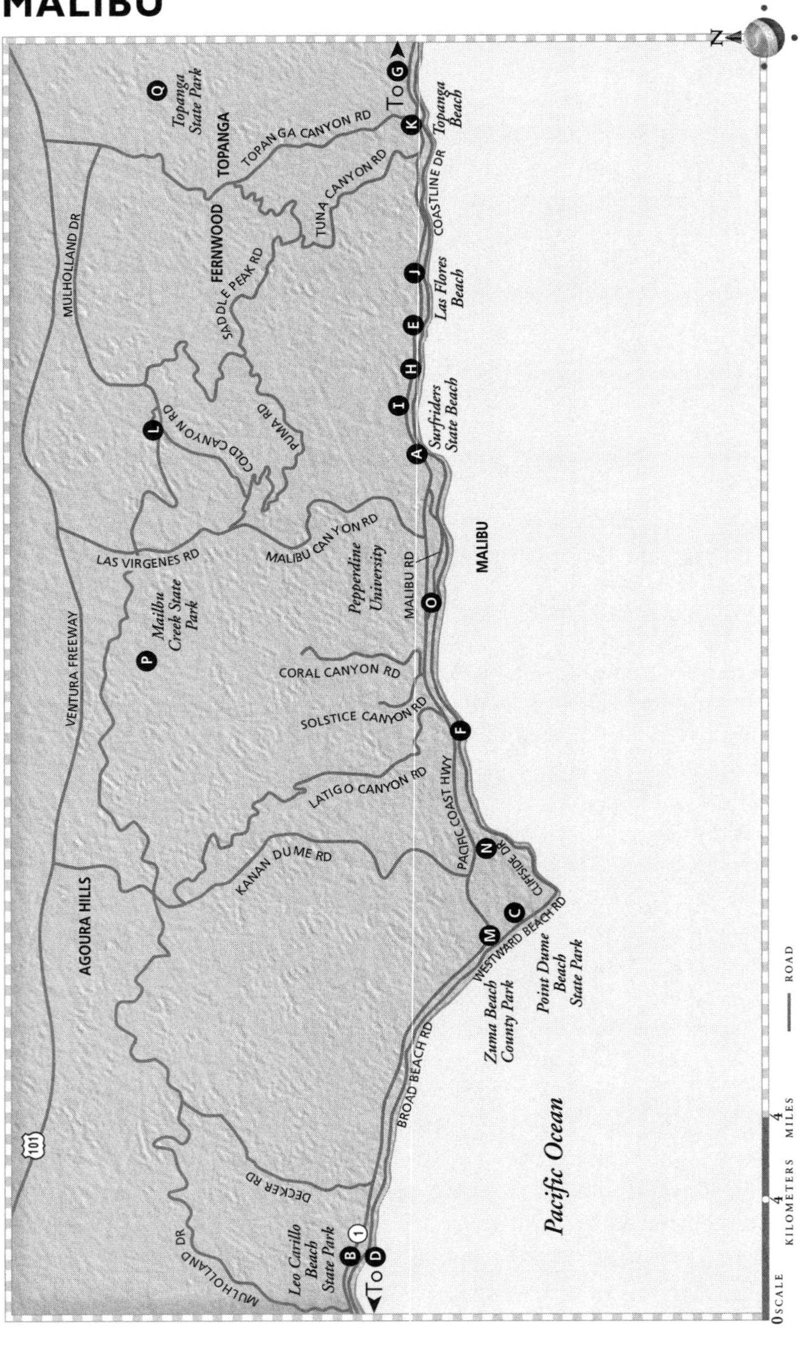

N
To G
To D
Topanga State Park
TOPANGA
TOPANGA CANYON RD
Topanga Beach
TUNA CANYON RD
COASTLINE DR
FERNWOOD
SADDLE PEAK RD
MULHOLLAND DR
Las Flores Beach
Surfriders State Beach
COLD CANYON RD
PUMA RD
MALIBU CANYON RD
LAS VIRGENES RD
Pepperdine University
MALIBU RD
MALIBU
Mailbu Creek State Park
VENTURA FREEWAY
CORAL CANYON RD
SOLSTICE CANYON RD
LATIGO CANYON RD
PACIFIC COAST HWY
CLIFFSIDE DR
KANAN DUME RD
AGOURA HILLS
WESTWARD BEACH RD
Zuma Beach County Park
Point Dume Beach State Park
BROAD BEACH RD
101
DECKER RD
MULHOLLAND DR
1
Leo Carillo Beach State Park
Pacific Ocean
0 SCALE
4 KILOMETERS
4 MILES
ROAD
A
B
C
D
E
F
H
I
J
K
L
M
N
O
P
Q

A PERFECT DAY IN MALIBU

Have breakfast at the Malibu Inn, then remind yourself that there's no rush. Check out the Adamson House and the Malibu Lagoon Museum, or spend your day outdoors. You can surf Topanga State Beach or Surfriders Beach at Malibu Lagoon State Beach, scuba dive at Las Flores Beach, kayak at Dan Blocker State Beach, bicycle at Point Dume or Zuma Beach, and when and if you're done with that, you can hike to see wildflowers and creeks at Topanga State Park. For dinner, if you're in the mood for fine dining, try Geoffrey's. If you want to dine by the sea, head for Moonshadows. At night you can find blues, jazz, or rock 'n' roll at the Malibu Inn. Or you can take in a local theater production.

SIGHTSEEING HIGHLIGHTS

★★★ ADAMSON HOUSE
23200 Pacific Coast Highway, 310/456-8432
This 1929 Moorish/Spanish Colonial–style residence features Malibu tile made by the Malibu Potteries between 1926 and 1932. The house also contains hand-carved teakwood doors, murals, handwrought ironwork, and lead-framed bottle-glass windows. The tile is extravagant, with designs specific to each room, and is used throughout the house. There's even tile styled after Persian rugs with tiles featuring rug fringes—it's a tile carpet. The house was built for the daughter and

SIGHTS
A Adamson House
B Leo Carrillo State Park and State Beach
A Malibu Lagoon Museum
C Point Dume State Beach
D Point Mugu State Park

FOOD
E Duke's
F Geoffrey's

FOOD (continued)
G Gladstone's
H Johnnie's New York Cafe-Pizzeria
I Malibu Inn
J Moonshadows
K Reel Inn
L Saddle Peak Lodge

LODGING
I Casa Malibu Inn on the Beach

LODGING (continued)
I Malibu Beach Inn
M Malibu Country Inn
N Malibu Riviera Motel

CAMPING
B Leo Carrillo State Park
O Malibu Beach RV Park
P Malibu Creek State Park
Q Topanga State Park

Note: Items with the same letter are located in the same area.

son-in-law of the last owners of the Malibu Spanish Land Grant. An extensively decorated pool and several fountains also feature Malibu tile. The restored grounds encompass elaborate gardens that include trees from Africa and Australia, and a gift shop.

Details: Open Wed–Sat 11–3. (The last house tour is at 2 p.m.) Admission is $2 adults, $1 children over 6; children under 6 are free. (1 hour)

★★ LEO CARRILLO STATE PARK
35600 Pacific Coast Highway, 818/880-0350
Located 14 miles northwest of Malibu on the Pacific Coast Highway, this beach and park is a quiet getaway, a place to walk and enjoy a rocky beach at the foot of the lush Santa Monica Mountains. It offers the water enthusiast 1.5 miles of beach for swimming, surfing, windsurfing, and walking.

Details: Open year-round, weather permitting. Parking is $6 if you park in the lot, but you can park legally along the highway for free. (1 day)

★★ MALIBU LAGOON MUSEUM
23200 Pacific Coast Highway, 310/456-8432
The museum adjoins the Adamson House and features artifacts, photos, maps, documents, and out-of-print publications on the history of Malibu, the Malibu Railroad, the legal battle over the Malibu Highway, the Malibu Movie Colony, and more. The museum display raises the question of whether this was the Chumash village that Cabrillo sighted and visited on his way up the coast—it doesn't answer the question because the historical record just isn't there.

Details: Open Wed–Sat 11–3. Free. (30 minutes)

★★ POINT DUME STATE BEACH
6800 Westward Dr., 818/880-0350
This beach park is tucked away off the beaten path, a beautiful stretch where you can walk, play, swim, and hike. But it is popular and, depending on the season, it can get very crowded. Within the park is a 34-acre nature preserve that's a wonderful vantage point for whale-watching. The park is also home to some unique and endangered plants.

Details: Take Westward Drive off the Pacific Coast Highway (follow the signs) and you'll see the beach and park. There is a parking fee of $6 unless you park on Westward Drive. (1 day)

★★ POINT MUGU STATE PARK

**19 miles northwest of Malibu, on Pacific Coast Highway,
818/880-0350**

This 13,300-acre park includes the Boney Mountain State
Wilderness Area, with open meadows, canyons, a beach, and a
curving, windy drive along the coast that culminates in a gorgeous
view of the ocean and a huge boulder (similar to but not as large
as the Morro Bay Rock). The drive from Malibu to Point Mugu is
one of the most scenic sections of the Pacific Coast Highway. The
beach is secluded from civilization, but it is popular and usually
crowded.

Details: *There are two entrances to the state park: at Sycamore
Canyon and at Thornhill Broome Beach. Parking fees at each entrance vary
seasonally. Open year-round. (1 day)*

FITNESS AND RECREATION

Malibu and the vicinity offer abundant opportunities for hiking, picnicking, fishing, horseback riding, mountain biking, and exploring nature trails in search of
wildflowers and creeks. The town is also the gateway to many of the area's
rugged parks. The beaches are all along the Pacific Coast Highway; most of the
parks are accessed off the Pacific Coast Highway.

For surfing, hit **Topanga State Beach**; for scuba diving and tide pools,
it's **Las Flores Beach**; for surfing, kayaking, hiking, bird-watching, and tide
pools, visit **Malibu Lagoon State Beach/Surfriders Beach** (a quarter-
mile west of Malibu Pier, on the Pacific Coast Highway). For kayaking, scuba
diving, hiking, and bird-watching, try **Dan Blocker State Beach (Corral
Beach)**; for surfing, kayaking, windsurfing, bicycling, and beach volleyball, go
to **Zuma Beach County Park**; for surfing and hiking, visit **Nicholas
Canyon State Beach**; and for surfing (but no lifeguards), there's **County
Line State Beach**.

On land, for hiking, picnicking, horseback riding, mountain biking, and seeing wildflowers and creeks, try **Topanga State Park** (Entrada Road off
Topanga Canyon Boulevard off the Pacific Coast Highway). For hiking, picnicking, fishing, horseback riding, mountain biking, and seeing wildflowers (and the
site where TV's *M*A*S*H* was shot), visit **Malibu Creek State Park** (Malibu
Canyon Road off the Pacific Coast Highway). For hiking and picnicking, there's
Tapia Park (Malibu Canyon Road off the Pacific Coast Highway); go hiking and
mountain biking at **Castro Crest** (Corral Canyon Road off the Pacific Coast
Highway); and if you want all three, head for **Solstice Canyon** (Corral Canyon

Road off the Pacific Coast Highway), **Rocky Oaks** (Mulholland Highway off Kanan Dume Road off the Pacific Coast Highway), and **Zuma Canyon** (Busch Drive off the Pacific Coast Highway).

For more information on any of these parks and beaches, contact **Malibu Parks and Recreation**, 310/317-1364, or the **National Park Service**, 818/597-9192.

FOOD

Duke's, 21150 Pacific Coast Highway, 310/ 317-0777, on the ocean with a wonderful view, serves a tasty variety of fish, ribs, and steak dishes along with delicious appetizers and huge, rich desserts. Their Mac Nut and Crab Wonton "starter" (crab, cream cheese, and macadamia nuts) is choice, as are the salad bar and Hawaiian Seafood Gumbo. Entrees start at $11.95. **Moonshadows**, 20356 Pacific Coast Highway, 310/456-3010, serving American fare with an excellent salad bar, also features ocean-view dining. Entrees start around $15. South of Malibu proper but with an excellent ocean view is **Gladstone's**, 17300 W. Pacific Coast Highway, 310/459-3822. It serves American fare and seafood, and features clam chowder, fresh salmon, lobster, oysters, and prime steaks. Meals average $15, but the main attraction is the view.

Also serving seafood is the **Reel Inn**, 18661 Pacific Coast Highway, 310/456-8221. The blackboard outside usually has a fishy pun on some fairly recent movie ("Mr. Holland's Octopus"), and the atmosphere is the opposite of fine dining. The food is good and inexpensive, with most meals less than $13. Another inexpensive spot is **Johnnie's New York Cafe-Pizzeria**, 22333 Pacific Coast Highway, 310/456-1717, which serves excellent New York–style pizza. Most meals run under $15.

For the best in very expensive fine dining, **Geoffrey's**, 27400 Pacific Coast Highway, 310/457-1519, features California cuisine. Meals run $30 and up. Nearby, in Calabasas, the **Saddle Peak Lodge**, 419 Cold Canyon Dr., 818/222-3888, has a view of the mountains and serves exquisitely prepared wild game and American favorites in a rustic yet elegant setting. Meals start at around $50.

For the best breakfast in Malibu, try the **Malibu Inn**, 22969 Pacific Coast Highway, 310/456-6106. This popular, spacious, historic restaurant, located on the east side of the highway but with a fine ocean view from several tables, also serves lunch and dinner. Its walls are filled with signed photos of stars and historic photos of the place, some dating back to the 1940s. The inn serves American fare, with most meals under $15.

WILL ROGERS STATE HISTORIC PARK

Located in Pacific Palisades, at 14253 Sunset Blvd. (between Santa Monica and Malibu), this was once Will Rogers' home and ranch. Okay, maybe you don't remember who Will Rogers is. Humorist, writer, actor, he was the Mark Twain of the first half of this century. And this 186 acres he used to own is now a state park. The site offers hiking trails and picnic areas, and also features exhibits inside Rogers' house, maintained as it was when he lived there in the 1920s and 1930s, including Rogers' memorabilia and his art collection. The house has 31 rooms including 11 baths and seven fireplaces. But the park is more than just a historic site; it's also a working ranch featuring a roping and training area where visitors can watch horses being put through their paces. Weather permitting, polo games are held Saturday afternoons and Sunday mornings. Free guided tours of the home last 30 minutes and start every half-hour, 10:30 to 4:30. Visitors are advised to call the park, 310/454-8212 or 818/706-1310, for details; open daily 10–5. Parking is $6.

LODGING

Malibu offers fine lodging, but none of it is inexpensive. The **Malibu Beach Inn**, 22878 Pacific Coast Highway, 310/456-6445, is a beautiful resort designed to create the feeling that each room is a private beach cottage (even though it isn't). Guests at the inn enjoy using the tennis facilities at Malibu Racquet Club, the golf facilities at Malibu Country Club, and the fitness facilities at Malibu Health Spa. Room rates start at $150; rooms with Jacuzzi start at $225. **Casa Malibu Inn on the Beach**, 22752 Pacific Coast Highway, 310/456-2219, has ocean- and garden-view rooms, and each room has a refrigerator. Garden-view rooms start at $99, ocean-view rooms at $159, and beach-front rooms and suites at $189. The **Malibu Country Inn**, 6506 Westward Beach Road, 310/457-9622, is Malibu's only B&B. Built in 1943, it's a Cape Cod near the beach featuring 16 unique rooms. Rates start at $155.

Farther north, close to Zuma Beach, is the **Malibu Riviera Motel**, 28920 Pacific Coast Highway, 310/457-9503, featuring a spa, a short walk to the beach, and lower year-round rates: $50 and $60 during the week, $70 and $80 on weekends.

CAMPING

Malibu Beach RV Park, 25801 Pacific Coast Highway, 310/456-6052, has ocean- and mountain-view campsites, with the beach only a few yards away. The park has restrooms and complete laundry facilities. Rates range from $35.84 (electric and water without a view) to $39.20 (full hookups with a view).

For tent camping, **Leo Carrillo State Beach**, (800) 444-7275, has 138 developed sites with 50 sites near the beach; tent camping is not allowed on the beach. **Malibu Creek State Park**, 818/880-0367 or 800/533-7275, has 60 tent camping sites, but no wood fires are allowed. **Topanga State Park**, 310/455- 2465, has tent camping, water, toilets, hitching rails, and water troughs.

NIGHTLIFE

The **Malibu Inn**, 310/456-6106, features a bar with live rock 'n' roll, blues, and jazz, and billiards. The **Malibu Stage Company**, 29243 Pacific Coast Highway, 310/456-8226, is a professional theater company supported by, among others, Ed Asner, Robert Altman, Charles Bronson, Johnny Carson, Jack Lemmon, George C. Scott, and Martin Sheen. And the **Center for the Arts/Smothers Theatre** at Pepperdine University, 24255 Pacific Coast Highway, 310/456-4522, is a beautiful theater offering nationally known performers and touring companies. Tickets usually start at $30. The season is announced each fall, so if you know you're going to be traveling through, you may want to contact them well in advance. During summer, in nearby Topanga Canyon, the **Will Geer Theatricum Botanicum**, 1419 N. Topanga Canyon, Topanga, 310/455-2322, presents Shakespeare and a variety of other theater works in matinees and evening shows only on weekends. Tickets are $15 adults, $8.50 seniors and students, $4 children 6–12, and children under 6 are free.

9
SANTA BARBARA

Less than two hours north of Los Angeles along Highway 101, on the coast between the Santa Ynez Mountains and the Pacific, is the city of Santa Barbara, often referred to as "California's Riviera." Whether or not Santa Barbara merits that comparison, it certainly is a beautiful jewel in the coastline crown.

Several thousand years ago the Chumash Indians settled here. In the 1500s the Spanish explored the region, but they didn't settle until 1782. Forty years later this land became part of Mexico when it won independence from Spain. The 1848 discovery of gold in California brought thousands of settlers, and by 1850 the American flag flew over Santa Barbara. In the 1870s Santa Barbara became a haven for health-seekers and tourists.

Santa Barbara offers escape and relaxation, along with opportunities to contemplate the ocean, mountains, and engaging vistas, and to explore a bit of history and humankind's relationship to coastal ecology. The area offers a multitude of activities for active and passive vacationers: everything from swimming, boating, hiking, and sportfishing to the more exotic helicopter rides, jet-boating, kayaking, whale-watching, windsurfing, horseback riding, and more. Or you can select your beach lounge chair, watch the scenery, and think great thoughts.

Santa Barbara enjoys a pleasant Mediterranean climate that is generally mild and sunny all 12 months of the year, with relatively stable temperatures; there is no real "off-season."

SANTA BARBARA

Pacific Ocean

Santa Barbara Harbor

Lauro Reservoir

Laguna Blanca

To San Marcos

EAST VALLEY ROAD

HOT SPRINGS RD

HILL RD

EUCALYPTUS

CANYON RD

SYCAMORE

SIERRA

OLD COAST HWY

SALINAS ST

CABRILLO BLVD

ALAMEDA PADRE

MONTECITO ST

MILPAS

DE LA GUERRA ST

MONTECITO ST

SHORELINE DR

STANWOOD DR

MOUNTAIN DR

MISSION CANYON RD

LAGUNA ST

SANTA BARBARA ST

ANAPAMU ST

ARRELLAGA

MISSION ST

LOS OLIVOS ST

CONSTANCE AVE

BATH ST

CASTILLO ST

STATE ST

CARRILLO ST

MEIGS RD

CLIFF DR

SAN ROQUE RD

LAS POSITAS RD

FOOTHILL RD

STATE ST

LA CUMBRE RD

SAN MARCOS PASS RD

LAS PALMAS DR

MARINA DR

192

101

154

0 SCALE

1.2 KILOMETERS

1.2 MILES

HIGHWAY

ROAD

A PERFECT DAY IN SANTA BARBARA

Start your day with breakfast at one of the restaurants on the beach or at Stearns Wharf, overlooking the ocean. Visit the Sea Center, then rent a bike or rollerblades or just take a stroll along the waterfront. You can visit the zoo or stop in at the historic Biltmore (now the Four Seasons Biltmore). Walk or take the trolley along State Street, browsing the shops, restaurants, and historic buildings at the Santa Barbara Historical Museum, El Presidio de Santa Barbara State Historic Park, and the Courthouse. After lunch, visit the natural history museum and the Old Mission, then travel on up to the Botanical Garden. Return to Stearns Wharf in time for sunset, then spend the evening dining, enjoying live music, or taking another stroll along the beach in the beautiful night air.

SIGHTSEEING HIGHLIGHTS

★★★★ MISSION SANTA BARBARA
Laguna Street at Los Olivos, 805/682-4713
The cornerstone of historic Santa Barbara, the Old Mission was built in 1786. It was the 10th of California's religious outposts founded by Spanish Franciscans, and was for many years a home to Chumash Indians who lived in the area. This mission is architecturally unique, based on designs made by a Roman architect and published in 27 B.C., 1,800 years before the mission was built. Its beautiful setting, unique

SIGHTS
A El Presidio de Santa Barbara State Historic Park
B Mission Santa Barbara
C Santa Barbara Botanical Garden
D Santa Barbara Historical Museum
E Santa Barbara Museum of Natural History
F Santa Barbara Zoo
G Sea Center
G Stearns Wharf

FOOD
H Eliado's
G Harbor Restaurant
I Julian's
G Longboard's Grill
J Natural Cafe
K Roy
A Sojourner Cafe
J Something's Fishy

LODGING
L Casa Del Mar
M Harbor View Inn
N Hotel State Street
O Ivanhoe Inn
P The Radisson
Q Santa Barbara City Center Travelodge

CAMPING
R Santa Barbara Sunrise RV Park

Note: Items with the same letter are located in the same area.

Santa Barbara Conference & Visitors Bureau and Film Commission

SANTA BARBARA COURTHOUSE

twin bell towers, and lovely but formidable facade have earned it the title "Queen of the Missions." Take the self-guided tours of the museum, garden, chapel, and cemetery, and visit the gift shop.

Details: *At the upper end of Laguna Street. Open daily 9–5. Admission is $3 adults, free for children under 12. (1 hour)*

★★★★ **SANTA BARBARA BOTANICAL GARDEN**
1212 Mission Canyon Road, 805/682-4726

This garden's 65 acres feature over 1,000 species of native California plants and offer visitors a wonderful place for a quiet, peaceful, meditative, and (if you want) educational stroll. Organized in sections connected by over three miles of walking trails, visitors can stroll past native trees, shrubs, and wildflower cacti, all in a natural setting. The Desert Section features plants that thrive (obviously) in the desert; the lush Canyon Section includes Western sycamore and white alder; and the Redwood Section features massive redwoods planted in the 1930s. Guided tours for those who want in-depth information and commentary are offered daily at 2 p.m. and also at 10:30 a.m. on Saturday, Sunday, and Thursday; but for those who decide not to take the tour, there's still plenty to see, learn, and enjoy, and there's more solitude. Near the main entrance (and the end of the walk described above) is a nursery with plants for sale, and a gift shop. **Details:** *Located 1.5 miles north of the mission. Open Nov 1–Feb 28, 9–4 weekdays, 9–5 weekends; Mar 1–Oct 31, 9–5 weekdays, 9–6 weekends. Admission is $3 adults, $2 seniors and teens, $1 children 5–12, and free for children under 5. (2 hours)*

★★★★ SANTA BARBARA MUSEUM OF NATURAL HISTORY
2559 Puesta del Sol Road, 805/682-4711

This museum presents a wide array of exhibits, including some on lizards and snakes (in the Lizard Lounge), Chumash life, the pygmy mammoth, fossils and geology, marine life, bird diversity, plants and insects, mammals, and bird habitats. There is a blue-whale skeleton out front and a gift shop and antique natural-history art gallery inside. The exhibit on Chumash life is the most complete and historically accurate in the city, far surpassing that at the Santa Barbara Historical Museum. **Details:** *Open Mon–Sat 9–5; Sun and holidays 10–5. Admission is $5. (1 hour)*

★★★ SANTA BARBARA ZOO
500 Niños Dr., 805/962-5339

Set on 30 acres overlooking East Beach, this zoo features 600 "ambassadors of the wild" from around the world. There are lions and leopards, no bears, many birds, some reptiles, elephants and giraffes, many members of the simian family, and a few unusual animals such as the caracal, which looks like it was created by the folks at *Star Trek*—it's a lynx-sized cat that looks like a small deer, with disproportionately large pointed ears (maybe it originates on Vulcan). The layout provides for a comfortable walk, and at the center on the crest of the hill there's a great view of the hillside and the ocean. And there's a play area for the kids, uh, children, next to the area with the goats, uh, kids. Signs suggest that afternoon visits are better than morning in that the monkeys are more likely to be active as the day draws to a close. **Details:** *Open daily 10–5. (except Thanksgiving and Christmas). Admission is $6 adults, $4 seniors and children 2–12, children under 2 are free. Tickets sold until 4 p.m. (1 hour)*

★★★ SEA CENTER
211 Stearns Wharf, 805/962-0885

This branch of the Natural History Museum is especially designed for kids, and features a "touch tank" with live sea creatures, aquariums, archaeology exhibits, life-size models of dolphins and whales, many interactive computer booths, shipwreck artifacts, and more. Its location on the pier adds to the feel that it's not really just a stuffy museum, but an integral part of the immediate environment of the ocean, channel, and coastal areas.

Details: *Open daily 10–5; Sun 11–5. Admission is $3 adults, $2 seniors, $2 ages 13–17, $1.50 children 5–12, and free for children under 5. (1 hour)*

★★★ STEARNS WHARF

This is the oldest working pier on the West Coast, and houses the Sea Center (see above), the Nature Conservancy, numerous restaurants, shops, marine-related businesses, and the Santa Ynez Winery, which features tastings and spectacular views on its second-story tasting deck. It's a beautiful place to visit, walk, and dine. Come at sunset, or later at night, and enjoy the city lights.

Details: *Visible as you drive along Cabrillo Blvd. or Shoreline Dr., the pier is located at the foot of State Street; open daily 7 a.m.–midnight. Admission is free. (1 hour)*

★★ EL PRESIDIO DE SANTA BARBARA STATE HISTORIC PARK
East Cañon Perdido Street 805/966-9719

This is an ongoing restoration and reconstruction of the eighteenth-century Spanish fort that served as the religious and military headquarters for the territory stretching from San Luis Obispo to Los Angeles. And although there are a few pieces of the original, most of it is a reconstruction, using modern materials fashioned to look like old construction to show what once was. For history buffs, this project gives an excellent portrayal of the magnitude and style of the Spanish military presence; for strict buffs, however, it's not like the missions or other fortresses around the state and country that still contain mostly original construction materials.

Details: *In the 100 block of East Cañon Perdido Street; open daily 10:30–4:30. Donation requested. (1 hour)*

★ SANTA BARBARA HISTORICAL MUSEUM
136 E. De la Guerra St., 805/966-1601

This museum presents documents, paintings, and costumes from the area's Spanish, Mexican, and American past. Perhaps of more interest are the historic buildings behind the museum.

Details: *Open Tue–Sat 10–5; Sun noon–5. Closed Mon. Donation requested. (1 hour)*

FITNESS AND RECREATION

Biking, hiking, horseback riding, jet-boating—Santa Barbara is a fitness and recreation town. Although this is not a complete list, the following will get you started.

For biking, **Cycles 4 Rent**, 805/966-3804, offers all kinds of cycles, rollerblades, electric mopeds, and jogging strollers. **Rent A Bike!**, 805/966-6733, offers blades, skates, all kinds of cycles, and four-wheel surreys. Rates vary.

For boating, fishing, hiking, and wildlife tours, try **Cachuma Lake Recreation Area**, Star Route, Highway 154, 805/686-5054. Less than 45 minutes from Stearns Wharf, it has tent and RV camping, boating, fishing, naturalist programs, wildlife tours and cruises, campground services, and accessible facilities. (To find out how the fish are biting each week, call Cachuma Fishwatch at 805/686-5054 and press 4.) For boat rental at Cachuma, call **Cachuma Lake Boat Rentals**, 805/688-4040.

Rancho Oso, 805/683-5686, offers horseback riding on 310 acres with access to Los Padres National Forest. They also provide horse boarding, picnics, overnight camping, and family packages. **Circle Bar B Stables and Guest Ranch**, 1800 Refugio Road, Goleta (20 miles north of Santa Barbara), 805/968-3901, also offers horseback riding, riding instruction, and rides at all times of day, including sunset and sunrise. They also have overnight accommodations and meal plans.

Boating and fishing enthusiasts will want to check out the following outfitters. **Captain Don's Charters and Cruises**, 805/969-5217, has 45-minute coastal cruises (with no reservations required), two-hour dinner cruises, and a two-hour sunset cruise. **Captain McCrea's Santa Barbara Sportfishing**, 805/687-FISH, offers sportfishing.

To see the region from above, call **Helicopter Excursions by Heli-Tours**, 805/964-0684, for scenic tours of the city and harbor, and picnic tours to Santa Cruz Island. Rates vary.

If you're keen on jet-boating while you're in Santa Barbara, **Santa Barbara Jet Boats**, 805/962-0887, offers rentals; rates vary. Be aware that a sizable security deposit is required.

SANTA BARBARA REGION

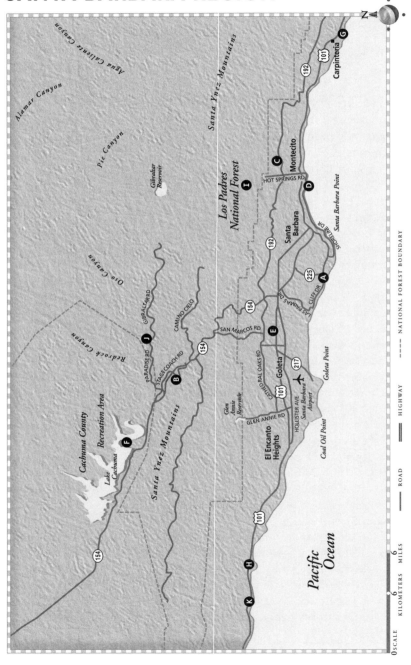

Looking for a weight room so you can pump some iron? **Gold's Sports and Fitness Center**, 805/965-0999, has workout rooms with equipment; daily rates available.

And if your idea of recreation is relaxation, try **The Hourglass** hot tubs, 805/963-1436, open from noon to midnight, with rates for two.

FOOD

Santa Barbara and the vicinity offer a wide assortment of restaurants catering to national and international tourists as well as the local University of California–Santa Barbara student population. These restaurants come in a wide range of prices and cuisines. Most eateries in Santa Barbara have views of the ocean, the mountains, or both.

Eliado's, One State Street, 805/963-4466, features a seafood and pasta menu, a large wine list, and a view of the beach and wharf. Dinner entrees start at $9.95.

Two restaurants on the wharf with views of the harbor and ocean are the **Harbor Restaurant**, 210 Stearns Wharf, 805/963-3311, which features oak-grilled fresh fish and seafood, prime rib, steak, chicken, and a Sunday Champagne Brunch, with dinner entrees starting at $12.95; and **Longboard's Grill** (same address and phone, directly above the Harbor Restaurant), offering casual dining: burgers, fish 'n' chips, soft tacos, and oyster bar. Longboard's sandwiches start at $4.95.

The Brown Pelican, 2981½ Cliff Dr., 805/687-4550, farther up the coast, features an ocean view and an excellent choice of seafood (seafood linguine, baked salmon fillet, roasted halibut, grilled ahi tuna) and land food (free-range chicken, filet mignon, grilled portobello) as well as a selection of local

---

FOOD
A The Brown Pelican
B Cold Spring Tavern
C Stonehouse Restaurant

LODGING
D Four Seasons Biltmore
E Ramada Limited
G San Ysidro Ranch

CAMPING
F Cachuma Lake Recreation Area
G Carpinteria State Beach
H El Capitan State Beach
I Los Padres National Forest
J Rancho Oso
K Refugio State Beach

Note: Items with the same letter are located in the same area.

---

wines. Their breakfasts and lunches range from around $5 to $9, dinner entrees range from $11 to $20.

For sushi and other Japanese dinners (and a great all-you-can-eat special), **Something's Fishy**, 502 State St., 805/966-6607, is the ticket. Lunch meals start at $5.95, dinner meals start at $10.45, and there's also Sushi a la Carte—but if you really like sushi, try the All You Can Eat Sushi for $16.95. Reservations are suggested.

Next to Something's Fishy is the **Natural Cafe**, 508 State St., 805/962-9494. This is the place to come if you're looking for smoothies, rice-and-bean dinners, and nachos grande with avocado dip and blue-corn chips. Meals start at $4.40.

Sojourner Cafe, 134 E. Canon Perdido, 805/965-7922, located right across the street from the Presidio, is a vegetarian restaurant serving fresh and wholesome natural foods (they don't even carry regular or diet colas): curried chicken and rice salad, Dijon chicken sandwich (very tasty!), sweet tomato linguine, Baked Potato Supreme (with broccoli, cauliflower, and assorted veggies packed into the baked potato), natural ginger ale, mulled cider, juices, smoothies and shakes, and rice dream ice cream. Meals with beverage average just under $10. Also serving very healthful multicourse meals is **Roy**, 7 W. Carrillo St., 805/966-5636. Meals average $12.50, and the menu also features beer, wine, and a gourmet coffee bar.

Nearby, serving local award–winning Mexican food (Best Dinner, Best Take-Out, Best Fish Taco, Best Restaurant For Eating Alone, per the *Santa Barbara Independent*), is **Julian's**, 421 N. Milpas St., 805/564-2322. The menu features burritos, tacos, soups, and salads for less than $6. They also serve breakfast.

Outside of Santa Barbara, high atop San Marcos Pass, is **Cold Spring Tavern**, 5995 Stage Coach Road, San Marcos, 805/967-0066. Specializing in game dishes, this tavern features the rustic decor of an old stagecoach line stop. It serves breakfast, lunch, and dinner on weekends; lunch and dinner on weekdays. Dinner entrees start at $6.75.

Atop San Ysidro Lane at the San Ysidro Ranch is the **Stonehouse Restaurant**, 900 San Ysidro Lane, 805/969-5046. This historic ranch/hotel is a getaway for the stars and other VIPs. (The Kennedys honeymooned here; Jack Benny, Groucho Marx, and Audrey Hepburn were all regulars at one time. Famous folk still come here, though usually under assumed names.) The impressive menu features everything from pan-roasted black sea bass to pepper-honey glazed lamb shank, bacon-wrapped venison chop, and grilled dry aged New York steak, as well as vegetarian dishes. Entrees are $27 and up. Reservations are suggested.

PAINTED CAVE ROAD

Painted Cave Road got its name because at some time someone found Chumash paintings in a cave. No one seems to know where they are, and there are no signs, but in looking for them I found a great view. Take Highway 154 through Los Padres National Forest toward San Marcos Pass. Before you get to the pass, keep your eyes open for a wooden "Painted Cave Road" street sign on your right and turn there. It's a steep, narrow, winding road, mostly well-paved. About 2.5 miles up this drive is a turnout with a terrific view of the valley, the city, the channel, the Channel Islands, and the ocean. And let me know if you find those paintings.

LODGING

Known for its B&Bs and resorts, Santa Barbara offers a wide variety of lodging, from the moderately priced to the incredibly pricey, some family-owned and some chains. Call Santa Barbara's free reservation service at 800/92-2222; for B&Bs, call 800/557-7898.

For moderately priced hotels, try one of the following. **Hotel State Street**, 121 State St., 805/966-6586, is a family-operated European-style hotel with complimentary continental breakfast; rates are $40 to $85. The **Santa Barbara City Center Travelodge**, 1616 State St., 805/569-2205 or 800/255-3050, is desirable because of its central locale on State Street and rates that range $65 to $95.

Among the B&Bs is the **Ivanhoe Inn**, 1406 Castillo St., 805/963-8832. This inviting spot, built in the 1880s, offers five rooms, including the Windsor Rose Room, the Isabella (sleeps three), and the Captain's Quarters (sleeps four); and a two-bedroom cottage. Complimentary bicycles are available. Sunday through Thursday rates start at $57 and weekend rates at $95. Weekly rates and discounts are also available for those not wishing to include breakfast.

Among those lodgings with ocean views are **Casa Del Mar**, 18 Bath St., 800/433-3097 or 805/963-4418, a Mediterranean-style inn, steps from the beach and near the harbor and wharf, offering a variety of room types with early summer rates from $84 to $209, late-summer rates $99 to $229, and winter rates $64 to $174. **The Radisson**, 1111 Cabrillo Blvd., 805/963-0744 or 800/643-1994, also featuring Mediterranean-style architecture, is directly across from East Beach, and most rooms have an ocean or mountain view.

CHANNEL ISLANDS

Five islands lie off the coast of Santa Barbara—Anacapa, Santa Rosa, Santa Barbara, Santa Cruz, and San Miguel—known collectively as the Channel Islands. Once connected to each other (many, many years ago), they were never connected to the mainland. Because of this, their geology and marine and animal life exhibit shades of differences from that of the mainland. Santa Rosa, for example, features the Santa Rosa blue jay, different from any other blue jay in the world and found only on Santa Rosa Island.

Each island offers its own excitement and its own hiking trails and kayak adventures:

Anacapa *is closest island to the mainland (1 1/2-hour boat ride) and consists of dramatic, steep cliffs, with hundreds of sea birds and marine mammals. There's a visitors center, lighthouse exhibits, primitive campground, and picnic area. Snorkeling, kayaking, and diving are all excellent in the rich kelp beds, and there are opportunities for bird-watching, fishing, and observing marine mammals.*

Santa Cruz *features over 650 species of plants and trees. Historic ranch houses and evidence of the Chumash people, along with rugged mountain ranges, deep canyons, and springs and streams, can be explored.*

Santa Rosa *is excellent for a multi-day visit. It offers hiking trails, a primitive campground, beach exploration, wildlife observation, ranger-led hikes, vehicle tours, and beach camping.*

San Miguel, *the farthest out from the mainland, is known for its seals and sea lions and hosts the most diverse pinniped rookery in the West. There are many undisturbed archaeological sites. The island is often fog-covered or very windy. San Miguel features a memorial to Juan Rodriguez Cabrillo, the explorer who discovered the islands.*

Santa Barbara, *the smallest of the islands, is also known for its sea lions and rookeries, and offers opportunities for hiking, bird-watching, scuba diving, snorkeling, fishing, and marine mammal observation. There's a visitors center, picnic area, and primitive campground.*

On each of your boat trips to, from, and among the islands, you may see dolphins, sharks, and whales. Keep in mind the islands have no stores, restaurants, or overnight accommodations; you must bring all your own food, water, and camping equipment.

The **Channel Islands Visitor Center**, on the mainland, provides interpretive programs, a movie about the park, tide-pool display, native plant garden, bookstore, and island exhibits. The facility is fully accessible and offers a picnic area overlooking the Ventura Harbor. The Channel Island Web site, with very useful links, is at www.nps.gov/chis/.

Several outfitters offer tours of the islands. **Truth Aquatics**, 301 W. Cabrillo Blvd., 805/962-1127, www.truthaquatics.com, is an authorized concessionaire to Channel Islands National Park offering single- and multi-day trips to the four islands from Santa Barbara and opportunities to hike, kayak, scuba dive, camp, or relax on the beaches. Schedules and prices vary with the season. They also offer "live aboard" trips from which you can go diving and explore the islands. (Diving equipment is not provided.) Because of the time involved in traveling from the mainland to the islands, a full day is recommended to visit the park.

Island Packers, 805/642-1393, is also an authorized concessionaire, leaving from Ventura. They offer half-day, full-day, and two-day excursions seven days a week. Their packages vary in duration and cost, and also change depending on the season. For example, Island Packers trips to West Anacapa Island tide pools (Frenchy's Cove) run only on specific dates November through April; trips depart at 9 or 10 a.m. and take seven to eight hours. The fare is $37 adults, $20 children 12 and under. Their Santa Cruz trip goes every day but Thursday, all year; leaves at 8 a.m.; lasts seven to eight hours; and is $42 adults and $25 children. The blue and humpback whale-watching tour runs only July through September, departs at 7 a.m., and lasts seven to eight hours; fare is $57 adults, $40 children 12 and under, and $52 seniors.

If you're interested in kayaking and/or scuba diving, be sure to mention this when you call Island Packers about their trips; some of these activities are run by other outfitters in cooperation with Island Packers. For kayaking, you'll need to call **OAARS**, 805/642-2912.

Be sure to ask about facilities on the island—in most cases you must bring your own food, drink, and film—and about the weather: It can get very chilly crossing the channel, and can be cold on the islands.

Summer rates are $169 to $259, winter rates $129 to $209. **Harbor View Inn**, 28 W. Cabrillo Blvd., 805/963-0780 or 800/755-0222, has a prime beach-and-harbor view and rates ranging $150 to $350. The **Four Seasons Biltmore**, 1260 Channel Dr., Montecito, 805/969-2261 or 800/332-3442, on 20 acres overlooking Butterfly Beach, features extensive health and recreational facilities, all with ocean views. Rates range from $245 to $550.

Farther from the ocean but still centrally located and near the airport is **Ramada Limited**, 4770 Calle Real, 805/964-3511 or 800/654-1965. Mountainside rooms start at $75, garden-side rooms at $85, and garden suites at $120. All rates include a buffet-style continental breakfast.

The historic **San Ysidro Ranch**, 900 San Ysidro Lane, 805/969-5046 or 800/368-6788, a dream resort with tennis courts and virtually everything else you could want, offers rooms and cottages from $350 to $3,000. Reservations are accepted up to a year in advance.

CAMPING

Among the numerous campgrounds around Santa Barbara are **Cachuma Lake Recreation Area**, Star Route, Highway 154, 805/686-5054; **Rancho Oso**, Star Route, Paradise Road, 805/683-5686; and **Santa Barbara Sunrise RV Park**, 516 S. Salinas St., 805/966-9954.

Carpinteria State Beach, 805/684-2811, a half-mile south of Santa Barbara on Highway 101, has 262 sites, many with hookups. Fishing and swimming are allowed. **El Capitan State Beach**, 805/968-3294, 20 miles northwest of Santa Barbara on Highway 101, has 140 sites and accommodates tent and RV campers. Fishing, hiking, and swimming facilities, nature trails, and food service and supplies are available. **Refugio State Beach**, 805/968-3294, 23 miles west of Santa Barbara on Highway 101, has 85 sites with swimming, fishing, hiking, and supplies and food service available.

Los Padres National Forest, 805/583-6711, includes sites at Juncal (21 miles northeast of Santa Barbara off Highway 154, six primitive tent sites), McGill (73 tent sites and 16 RV sites, with water and a $6 fee), Middle Santa Ynez (44 miles northeast of Santa Barbara off Highway 154, nine primitive tent sites), and Mono (48 miles northeast of Santa Barbara off Highway 154, seven primitive tent sites).

NIGHTLIFE

After your busy day of playing, sightseeing, and eating, there's plenty to do at night in Santa Barbara. You'll find live country-and-western music at **Cold**

Spring Tavern, 5995 Stage Coach Road, San Marcos, 805/967-0066; varied music every night with dancing on Friday and Saturday nights at the **Four Seasons Biltmore**, Channel Drive and Olive Mill Road, 805/969-2261; and folk-rock, folk, and jazz at **Soho**, 1221 State St., 805/962-7776. Admissions and show times vary.

For sports enthusiasts, there's **O'Malley's Sports Bar**, 523 State St., 805/564-8904. And there's always the beautiful outdoors under the night sky.

HELPFUL HINT

To assist in your sightseeing, the **Santa Barbara Trolley Company** offers an all-day fare of $5 ($3 for children 12 and under) to see the city. The trolley route includes Stearns Wharf, the mission, the courthouse, and numerous other tourist and cultural attractions as well as major hotels and shopping areas. Call 805/965-0353 for details and departure times.

Santa Barbara's Wine Country

Less than an hour from Santa Barbara, in the Santa Ynez Mountains, lies Santa Barbara's wine country. For a scenic drive, take Highway 101 north to Highway 154. Proceed up into Los Padres National Forest, through San Marcos Pass, past Lake Cachuma, and into Los Olivos. From there you can turn north on Foxen Canyon Road or continue west on 154.

If you drive through **Los Olivos**, a left turn on Alamo Pintado Road takes you to the Danish town of **Solvang**. From there you can take Highway 246 west to Highway 101, where you can head south to return to Santa Barbara. A left turn on 246 takes you through Santa Ynez and back to Highway 154, where you can turn right to go back through San Marcos Pass and back to Santa Barbara. Any variation of this trip takes less than half a day. As you drive up to San Marcos Pass, take in the ocean views.

If you want to add wine tasting to this drive, note that many vineyards don't open for tasting until 10 a.m. or later, and some wineries don't have tasting rooms. For further wine-country and wine-tasting information, contact the **Santa Barbara County Vintners' Association**, 800/218-0881, Monday–Friday 9 a.m. to 5 p.m.

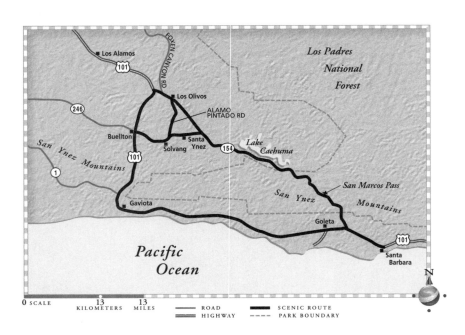

10
SAN LUIS OBISPO

Midway between Los Angeles and San Francisco is beautiful San Luis Obispo County. Within the county, surrounded by ancient volcanic peaks and rolling foothills, lies the village of San Luis Obispo, famous for its food and wine. Site of one of California's famous missions, San Luis Obispo is also known for what's nearby: San Simeon (Hearst Castle), Morro Rock, and the breathtaking Montana de Oro State Park.

A visit to San Luis Obispo is a visit to a mix of cultures and possibilities. San Simeon presents an opulent collection of art and antiques all wrapped up in a huge mansion. Morro Rock is home to the endangered peregrine falcon and sits amid an estuary of wildlife and civilization. Montana de Oro's eucalyptus trees were planted by an investor looking to make a fortune in wood products, but the eucalyptus proved unsuitable for that use and now they flourish, part of the beauty of this impressive park. The prevailing weather conditions nurture the growth of grapevines that support the local wine industry. Apples, other delicious fruits, herbs, and vegetables are also grown in the area. San Luis Obispo can be as wild and gaudy as the Madonna Inn, as quietly statuesque as downtown's Mission San Luis Obispo de Tolosa, as beautiful as the creek-side walkway that runs through downtown, and as friendly as the Market and Street Fair every Thursday night.

In San Luis Obispo the warmth prevails, the outdoors is beautiful to behold, and the town is an easy and interesting place to spend some time.

SAN LUIS OBISPO

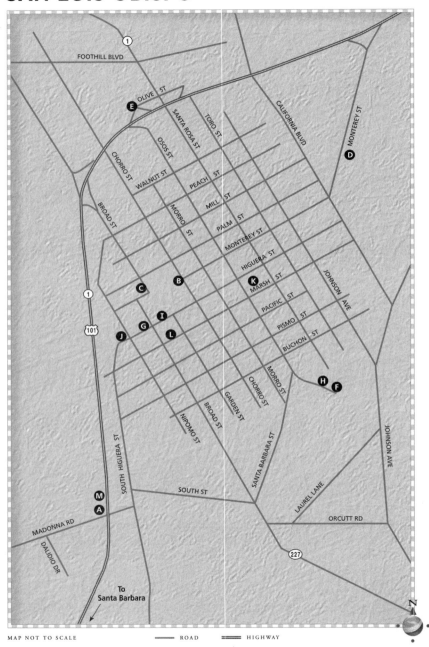

MAP NOT TO SCALE   ━━━ ROAD   ▨▨▨ HIGHWAY

A PERFECT DAY IN SAN LUIS OBISPO

If you've awakened at the Heritage Inn B&B, you're in for a great breakfast. After breakfast see the mission and the museum, then take a drive through wine country. Check out the wacky Madonna Inn for lunch. Next, drive over to Morro Bay and admire that rock. When you're ready for a real hike, drive over to Montana de Oro State Park and walk along the bluffs, watching the waves crash on the rocky coast below. For dinner, relax at the Rhythm Creekside Cafe; or if it's Thursday, attend the weekly Street Fair, have some barbecue, then settle into Linnaea's for some acoustic folk-rock before calling it a night.

SIGHTSEEING HIGHLIGHTS

★★★★ MISSION SAN LUIS OBISPO DE TOLOSA
941 Chorro St., 805/781-8220
This was the fifth in the chain of 21 California missions, built in 1772 from adobe bricks made by the local Chumash Indians. It was one of the few missions to be attacked by Indians, who shot fire-arrows into the thatched roof. The padres and Chumash began manufacturing red tiles for protection from flaming arrows, and it worked. As with the other missions in the chain, this one was secularized after Mexico won its independence from Spain and was returned to the Catholic Church under the U.S. government in the 1850s. The mission has an excellent museum featuring many artifacts and vivid displays of mission and Chumash history, evoking the spirit and the hardships of the times. There's also a gift shop.

SIGHTS
- **A** Madonna Inn
- **B** Mission San Luis Obispo de Tolosa
- **C** San Luis Obispo County Historical Museum

FOOD
- **D** The Apple Farm
- **E** Bon Temps Creole Cafe
- **F** Cafe Roma
- **G** F. McLintock's Saloon
- **A** Madonna Inn
- **H** Pete's Southside Cafe
- **I** Rhythm Creekside Cafe

FOOD (continued)
- **J** Tortilla Flats
- **K** Woodstock Pizza

LODGING
- **D** Apple Farm Inn
- **E** Embassy Suites
- **L** Garden Street Inn
- **E** Heritage Inn
- **A** Madonna Inn
- **M** Vagabond Inn

Note: Items with the same letter are located in the same area.

Details: Open daily 9–4 in winter, 9–5 in summer. Admission is $3. (1 hour)

★★★★ MONTANA DE ORO STATE PARK
Off Los Osos Valley Road, 805/528-0513
This beautiful and, in many places, breathtaking park has over seven miles of shoreline within its 8,000-plus-acre boundary. Located 25 miles west of San Luis Obispo, the park offers a variety of opportunities for outdoor activities, but even if time doesn't permit you to hike or camp here, it's definitely worth a drive-through. The lush eucalyptus forest (planted in the nineteenth century) and the views of the rocky shoreline are spectacular! The Ranger Station is located on the coast in the park and includes a small but worthy museum.

Details: Drive south on 101 past the Madonna Road exit to the Los Osos Valley Road exit. Take Los Osos Valley Road west for approx. 13 miles—it will lead right to the State Park. No admission fees, but fees for camping. (See Camping.) (2 hours)

★★★★ MORRO BAY
Morro Bay State Park Road, 805/772-2694
A few miles northwest of San Luis Obispo, Morro Bay features the stunning **Morro Rock**, also known as "the Gibraltar of the Pacific." Jutting out of the bay to an elevation of 576 feet, it was first spotted (presumably after the Chumash saw it) by Juan Cabrillo, and is now a home to the endangered peregrine falcon and other migratory birds. The **Morro Bay Estuary** is 2,300 acres of mud flats, eel-grass beds, tidal wetlands, and open water, and is home to the brown pelican, sea otter, steelhead trout, and over 70 migratory bird species. A self-guided tour of the estuary includes views of sand dunes, marsh, salt marsh, and mud flats. The estuary includes Tideland Park, an overlook at Black Hill, an observation point for Morro Bay heron and the cormorant rookery, and other observation points, including the Baywood pier and the Sweet Springs Nature Preserve. Don't miss the **Morro Bay State Park Museum of Natural History**, set on the coastline and featuring displays of peregrine falcons and migratory birds, land and sea mammals, the estuary, beaches, and the Chumash Indians. There are hands-on opportunities to meet sea otters and whales, and area artists' work is also exhibited. There's a museum store.

Details: Open daily 10–5 (except major holidays). Admission is $3 adults, $1 children 6–12, free for children under 6. (2 hours)

★★★★ SAN LUIS OBISPO COUNTY HISTORICAL MUSEUM
696 Monterey St., 805/543-0638
Although smaller than many other museums throughout the state, this museum is clearly the work of people who love history and love this county. The many exhibits and artifacts convey what life was like as the county developed through the mission and rancho days of the 1700s and 1800s up to the present time. On display are Chumash and Salinan tools, Spanish and Mexican relics, a fully furnished Victorian-era parlor, a postal-delivery wagon, and hundreds of historic photos. The museum is housed in the Carnegie Library Building, built in 1904.
> **Details:** *Open Wed–Sun 10–4; closed holidays. Free admission; donations are accepted. (1 hour)*

★★★ MADONNA INN
Madonna Road, 805/543-3000 or 800/543-9666
Not that Madonna. Or that Madonna . . . This inn is simply a motel and restaurant. So what makes it worth being designated a sightseeing highlight? Well, pardon what I hope is the only cliché in this book: it's got to be seen to be believed. The inn was created by architect Alex Madonna and his interior designer wife, Phyllis, in 1958. They built and designed 109 rooms, each with its own special theme and color scheme.

Many rooms feature hand-placed native rock; many have fireplaces; some are decorated Hawaiian-style; others have a Spanish, Old West, or European flavor. Some have waterfall-over-rocks showers. Some rooms are all rock and have a "caveman" atmosphere. Each is furnished according to the theme, with beds, tables, dressers, phones, light switches, doorknobs, and faucets all playing a part in the design symphony. It's ornate, it's opulent, it's camp, it's garish, it's baffling. And that's not all: the lobby, ladies' boutique, wine cellar, and gourmet gift shop are equally unique, and the balustrade on the way to the boutique is made of sculpted marble originally from San Simeon. The coffee shop and bakery have a copper theme, with virtually everything in the place designed or engraved exclusively for the inn. There are busy murals, Tiffany-style stained-glass lamps, and custom-made Axminster carpeting from England.

The pièce de résistance? The men's room downstairs has giant clamshell sinks and features a genuine waterfall urinal!
> **Details:** *Take the Madonna Road exit off Highway 101. (1 hour)*

★★ SYCAMORE FARMS

Route 1, Highway 46 West, Paso Robles, 805/238-5288

Located north of San Luis Obispo, this herb farm and vineyard has a nursery with 250-plus varieties of herbs. You can walk through the garden of culinary, medicinal, and other unique herbs. The bookstore and shop offer gardening accessories and, of course, herb soaps, herb vinegars, and other herb products.

Details: Open daily 10:30–5. (1 hour)

★★ WINE COUNTRY

San Luis Obispo is also wine country, with several vineyards surrounding the town. Most wineries are open for tastings. (Stopping and tasting will take longer than the two-hour suggested time for the scenic drive noted below. For tasting hours, contact the wineries.) The gently rolling hills dotted with vineyards, the sea air, and indigenous vegetation remind you that you are not in other agricultural parts of the country. If you hail from the big city, this is your ideal drive in the country—if you're from the country, this area, although it's flanked by mountains and ocean, may remind you of home.

For a self-guided tour, you can head either south or north. To the south, proceed down Highway 227. **Claiborne and Churchill Vintners**, 805/544-4066, are on Carpenter Canyon Road; and **Cottonwood Canyon Vineyard**, 805/549-WINE, is on Santa Fe Road off Tank Farm Road. Farther south, **Edna Valley Vineyard**, 805/544-9594, is on Biddle Ranch Road; and **Corbett Canyon Vineyards**, 805/544-5800, is on Corbett Canyon Road. Still further south, where Highway 227 hits Huasna Road and then joins Highway 101, are **The Wine Guy**, 805/546-8466 (a retail outlet for area wines), and **Laetitia Winery**, 805/481-1763.

North of San Luis Obispo are **Wildhorse Winery**, 805/434-2541, off Templeton Road between Eureka and Lupine Lanes; **Pesenti Winery**, 805/434-1030, and **Mastantuono Winery**, 805/238-0676, are both on Vineyard Drive in Templeton. In Paso Robles are **Sycamore Natural Herb Farm, Vineyards and Winery** (see Sycamore Farms, below); **Trianna Winery**, 805/238-6979, on Highway 46 West; **Martin Brothers**, 805/238-2520, on Buena Vista Drive off East Highway 46; **Meridian Vineyards**, 805/237-6000, on Highway 46 East; and **Twin Hills Ranch Winery**, 805/238-9148, on Lake Nacimiento Drive. (2 hours)

FITNESS AND RECREATION

Golfers will enjoy **Laguna Lake Golf Course**, 11175 Los Osos Valley Road, 805/781-7309, a nine-hole executive course that also has a driving range and barbecue facilities. (For a more complete list of golf courses in this coastal region, contact the Morro Bay Chamber of Commerce at 800/231-0592 and ask for the pamphlet called "Your Guide to Golf Courses on the Central Coast.")

Families will enjoy **Crux Climbing Gym**, 1150 Laurel Lane, 805/544-2789. It's a stand-alone climbing gym that's been designed to bring the mountain to you in a controlled environment. Call for hours.

San Luis Obispo city and county are a hiker's paradise. Within the city are the Laguna Lake, Poly Canyon, and El Chorro Trails. **Laguna Lake Trail** is a very easy hike in Laguna Lake Park on Dalidio Drive Southwest, off Madonna Road from Highway 101. It's less than two miles long and includes a lakeshore, a eucalyptus grove, and a rocky hill. **Poly Canyon Trail** is a moderately easy hike of just over five miles, originating in and passing through the California Polytechnic State University (Cal Poly) campus. The trailhead is at an elevation of 350 feet and about the halfway point you're at 1,000 feet. **El Chorro Trail** is a little less than three miles long, originating in El Chorro County Regional Park (seven miles north of San Luis Obispo on Highway 1, across from Cuesta College); it proceeds across hillsides, over creeks, and past old and military buildings and an abandoned dairy. *Note: Stay on the trail! This area holds unexploded ammunition from the old military base.*

At **Morro Bay State Park** are Black Hill Trail, Chorro Willows Trail, and Bautista Ranch Trail. And **Montana de Oro State Park** has numerous trails, including Morro Bay Sand Spit Trail, Valencia Peak Trail (a rugged 10-mile hike), Coon Creek Trail, and the absolutely beautiful **Montana de Oro Bluffs Trail**. If you have time for only one hike, the Bluffs Trail is the one, with spectacular views of the surf-carved coastal rocks and the possibilities of seeing cormorants, pelicans, albatrosses, and (in season) whales!

There are also several trails in the Northern Santa Lucia Mountains, the La Panza Range, and the Southern Santa Lucia Mountains. **Kvnia/Roffe Botanicals**, 805/543-4372, offers guided herb walks throughout the county.

For more fitness and recreation, **Horseback Adventures**, 805/238-5483, offers trail rides throughout the area; **Noland's Carriage**, 805/544-2042, provides romantic horse-drawn carriage rides in the Madonna Inn area, in the Apple Farm area, and in Cambria, just south of the Hearst Castle; and **Alamo Bicycle Touring Company**, 805/781-3830, and **SLO Coast Hostel and Adventure Tours**, 805/544-4678, rent bicycles. There's fishing at **Lopez Lake**, 805/489-1006, south of San Luis Obispo; **Nacimiento Lake**, 805/238-3256, north of San Luis Obispo; and **Santa Margarita Lake**,

SAN LUIS OBISPO REGION

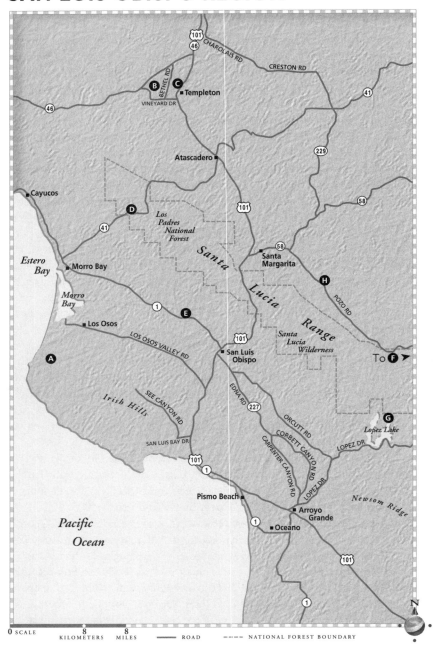

Pacific
Ocean

0 SCALE   8   8
         KILOMETERS   MILES ———— ROAD ----- NATIONAL FOREST BOUNDARY

N

805/438-5618 or 805/438-5485, northeast of San Luis Obispo. For hot-tub-bing, **Sycamore Mineral Spring Resort**, 1215 Avila Beach Dr., in nearby Avila Beach, 805/595-7302, features private hot tubs and massages.

Morro Bay provides opportunities for surfing, deep-sea fishing, sportfishing, sub-sea tours (in a semi-submersible vessel; call **Sub-Sea Tours** at 805/772-9463), kayaking, canoeing, and shopping.

FOOD

Rhythm Creekside Cafe, 1040 Broad St., 805/541-4048, a half-block from the mission, overlooking the creek, is a casual bistro offering California cuisine and featuring seafood, ribs, and lamb, with dinner entrees starting at $11.95. The breakfast buffet (Saturdays and Sundays until 1 p.m.) is less than $11. **Cafe Roma**, 1819 Osos St., 805/541-6800, serves award-winning Italian cuisine in an atmosphere the dressy side of casual. Entrees range from $8 to $19. Next door to Cafe Roma, **Pete's Southside Cafe**, 1815 Osos St., 805/549-8133, is a casual restaurant serving Mexican-style cuisine, with specialty dinners rang-ing from $8.50 to $11.95. Also serving Mexican-style cuisine is **Tortilla Flats**, 1051 Nipomo St. (in the Creamery), 805/544-7575. Meals generally run less than $10, and the Sunday champagne brunch is $8.95, the buffet is $9.95.

In the downtown area, **F. McLintock's Saloon**, 686 Higuera St., 805/541-0686, a family steak house (with some seafood, like calamari, on the menu), serves lunches and dinners. Entrees range between $4.25 and $16.50. The Kid's Corral menu features meals priced around $3.

Serving up American fare (and a few ethnic dishes) in a family-style setting, The **Apple Farm**, 2015 Monterey St., 805/544-6100, has meals that are generally less than $15. Reservations are recommended. Offering authentic Cajun Creole is **Bon Temps Creole Cafe**, 1000 Olive St., 805/544-2100

SIGHTS

Ⓐ Montana de Oro State Park
Ⓑ Sycamore Farms
Ⓒ Wine Country

CAMPING

Ⓓ Cerro Alto—Los Padres National Forest

CAMPING *(continued)*

Ⓔ El Chorro Regional Park
Ⓕ Hi Mountain—Los Padres National Forest
Ⓖ Lopez Lake Recreation Area
Ⓗ Santa Margarita Lake
Ⓐ Montana de Oro

Note: Items with the same letter are located in the same area.

MORRO BAY

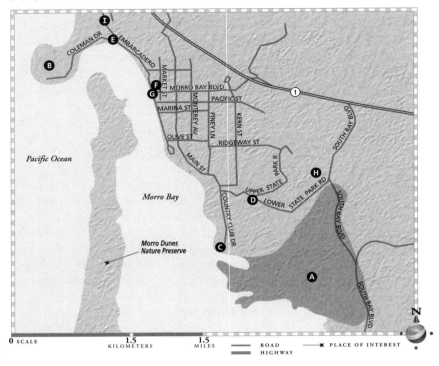

Pacific Ocean

Morro Bay

*Morro Dunes
Nature Preserve*

0 SCALE   1.5 KILOMETERS   1.5 MILES   ═══ ROAD   ──► PLACE OF INTEREST   ═══ HIGHWAY

SIGHTS
Ⓐ Morro Bay Estuary
Ⓑ Morro Rock
Ⓒ Morro Bay State Park
   Museum of Natural
   History

FOOD
Ⓓ Paradise

LODGING
Ⓔ Adventure Inn
   on the Sea
Ⓕ Blue Sail Inn

CAMPING
Ⓖ Bay View RV Park
Ⓗ Morro Bay State Park
Ⓘ Morro Dunes Travel
   Trailer Park
Ⓙ Morro Strand
   State Park

(right next to the Heritage Inn). Breakfasts (Cajun *pain perdu*, a Cajun French toast) are generally less than $7, lunches less than $10, and dinners less than $14. They're open every day for breakfast and lunch and Wednesday through Sunday for dinner. Although I haven't listed too many pizza places, this one deserves mention: **Woodstock Pizza**, 1000 Higuera St., 805/541-4420—and they deliver. Their large premier pizzas run around $17.

On the coast in Morro Bay and offering a beautiful view of the bay and especially the rock, **Paradise** (at the Inn at Morro Bay), 60 State Park Road, Morro Bay, 805/772-5651, specializes in seafood and pasta. Entrees range from $12.95 to $22. And again, in a world of its own, the **Madonna Inn**, Highway 101 and Madonna Road, 805/543-3000, is known mostly for its flamboyant decor (and "flamboyant" is almost too tame a word), but this original-style restaurant also serves desserts. (You really should take a look at this place, even if you don't eat here.) Coffee-shop meals range between $5.95 and $17.25; the Gold Rush Dining Room is pricier. There's dancing to live music Tuesday through Saturday evenings.

LODGING

The charm of San Luis Obispo is probably best experienced in a B&B, and at the top of the list is the very appealing **Heritage Inn**, 978 Olive St., 805/544-7440. This turn-of-the-century inn offers seven antique-filled guest rooms, a sitting parlor, a fireside breakfast room, and a view of the mountains, all a few blocks from downtown. Three rooms have private baths; the other four have a fireplace and sink in each room, with baths down the hall. Each morning proprietor Georgia serves a wonderful breakfast in the dining room, where you can enjoy an intimate meal with your traveling companions or join the rest of the guests in breakfast conversation. Wine and cheese are served in the evening in the parlor. Rates range from $85 to $120.

Other possibilities include the **Vagabond Inn**, 210 Madonna Road, 805/544-4710 or 800/522-1555, with rooms ranging from under $60 to $114; and the **Garden Street Inn** (B&B), 1212 Garden St., 805/545-9802, with nine guest rooms and four suites ranging from $90 to $160.

Offering a spa is the **Apple Farm Inn**, 2015 Monterey St., 805/544-2040, with rooms from $59 to $229; offering an indoor spa, a sundeck spa, Jacuzzis, and a health club is **Embassy Suites**, 333 Madonna Road, 805/549-0800, with rooms from $104 to $149. At the **Madonna Inn** (see Sightseeing Highlights), rooms run from $97 to well over $198 for single rooms. 805/772 - 7132

In Morro Bay, with ocean views, are **Blue Sail Inn**, 851 Market Ave., 805/772-2766, with rooms from $65 to $120; and **Adventure Inn on the Sea**, 1150 Embarcadero, 805/772-5607, with rooms from under $40 to $125.

CAMPING

While no camping is available in San Luis Obispo proper, there are many camping sites around the city. **Lopez Lake Recreation Area**, 805/489-8019,

SAN SIMEON (HEARST CASTLE)

San Simeon is a celebration of opulence, grandeur, excess, what was, what might still be, and what might always be. It's huge, and to many it's gorgeous. Built by the newspaper magnate and purveyor of "yellow journalism" William Randolph Hearst, the castle sits on 127 acres on a hilltop (La Cuesta Encantada, or "Enchanted Hill") in the Santa Lucia Mountains overlooking the Pacific Ocean. It took 28 years for craftsmen to build the 165-room estate, the terraces, the pools, and the walkways, all under the supervision of the remarkable architect Julia Morgan. Its rooms are furnished with Spanish and Italian antiques and art. Today it is owned and operated by the State of California (and apparently Patricia Hearst is persona non grata there since the publication of her novel in which a murder occurs in the castle). If you have to make a choice between here or Montana de Oro and Morro Rock, I'd urge the latter two natural sites; but all three are pretty spectacular.

Details: 750 Hearst Castle Road, San Simeon (about 30 miles north of San Luis Obispo), 800/444-4445. There are a variety of tours and prices. All tours include a half-mile walk and 150 to 400 stairs; some last two hours, some take all day.

---

south of San Luis Obispo off Highway 101, has 355 tent/RV spaces and water, flush toilets, showers, and other amenities; nightly fees are $13 to $21. **Santa Margarita Lake**, 805/438-5485, north of San Luis Obispo off Highway 58, offers 46 campsites; no hookups, but they have water, flush toilets, showers, and other amenities; nightly fees are $13. At **El Chorro Regional Park**, 805/781-5219, four miles northwest of San Luis Obispo on Highway 1, are 44 tent/RV spaces and water, flush toilets, showers, and other amenities; nightly fees range from $18 to $20.

In Los Padres National Forest, 805/683-6711, **Hi Mountain** has 11 tent/RV spaces, limited amenities, and no fees. **Cerro Alto**, northeast of Morro Bay off Highway 41, with 24 tent/RV spaces and water; no fees.

Morro Bay State Park, 805/772-7434, off Highway 1, has 115 tent/RV spaces and flush toilets, showers, and other amenities; nightly fees start at $14. Water is available. And at **Morro Strand State Beach**, 805/772-2560, north of Morro Bay, are 104 tent/RV spaces and water, flush toilets, and some amenities; nightly fees are from $14.

For RV travelers in Morro Bay, **Bay View RV Park**, 714 Embarcadero, 805/772-3300, offers electric, water, and cable TV and sewer hookups but no restrooms or showers, and daily rates starting at $23 (weekly and monthly rates are also available). **Morro Dunes Travel Trailer Park and Resort Campground**, 1700 Embarcadero, 805/772-2722, has full hookups, restrooms, laundry, a clubhouse and more; nightly rates start at $23.

Montana de Oro, 805/528-0513, west of San Luis Obispo off Los Osos, has 50 primitive campsites with RV hookups; nightly fees are from $7.

NIGHTLIFE

Every Thursday night (unless it rains) San Luis Obispo presents the **Thursday Night Outdoor Market and Street Fair**. Four blocks of downtown are closed to traffic and transformed into an outdoor market where local farmers sell fresh fruits and vegetables, and everyone enjoys live music, entertainment, and street-side eats, especially barbecued chicken and ribs. This is fun for the whole family and, really, every town ought to do this. The fair starts at 6:30 p.m., ends at 9 p.m., and parking is available in the municipal garages at Palm and Morro Streets or Marsh and Chorro Streets.

San Luis Obispo has a number of clubs featuring dancing and live music. **Mother's Tavern**, 725 Higuera, 805/541-8733, features blues, rock, swing, and jazz and on Sundays the Royal Garden Swing Orchestra, a big-band extravaganza. **SLO Brewing Co.**, 1119 Garden St., 805/543-1843, features world beat and reggae music Thursdays through Saturdays; cover varies. **Linnaea's Cafe**, 1110 Garden St., 805/541-5888, offers acoustic, folk-rock, blues, and jazz almost every night of the week.

For a more complete guide, pick up a copy of San Luis Obispo's *New Times*.

This six-hour, twisty, exciting scenic route takes you out of San Luis Obispo, over the **La Panza Range** of the Sierra Madres, through a valley that features the **San Andreas Fault**, over the **Temblor Range**, across the California Aqueduct, across the Kern River, through Bakersfield, into the **El Tejon Mountains**, through Tehachapi, up through the **El Paso Mountains**, past **Red Rock Canyon**, over the **Panamint Mountains**, and into **Death Valley**. (If you like, you can break it up with lunch in Bakersfield, or spend the night there and take in **Buck Owens' Crystal Palace** restaurant, museum, and nightclub, on Pierce Road off Highway 99, Bakersfield, 805/328-7560; this stop is a must for country-and-western fans!)

Fill up with gas before you start, take the 101 north out of San Luis Obispo to Highway 58, and head east on 58. You'll ascend the La Panza Range in the beautiful Los Padres National Forest, on a winding road with many views. As you descend you'll see **Black Mountain**, elevation 3,625 feet, on your right. Then you're in the Carrizo Plain, with almost nothing but flat expanse and the Temblor Range in the distance. You'll pass a few buildings and a school (people do live around here), cross the San Andreas Fault, and then ascend the Temblors, elevation roughly 3,000 feet. You'll descend into **Willow Springs Valley**, ascend again, cross the rest of the range, and

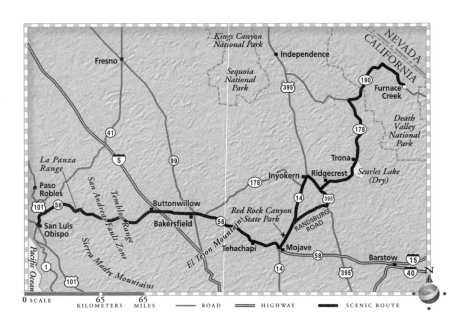

drop into the huge **San Joaquin Valley**. When you cross the California Aqueduct and Buena Vista Slough, you'll begin to see signs of civilization.

Stop for gas in **Bakersfield**, then continue through on Highway 58 (you're about halfway to Death Valley). Leaving the San Joaquin Valley, you'll enter the Sequoia National Forest and El Tejon Mountains. At Bealville you can see Bear Mountain on your right, elevation 6,919 feet. Continue through the mountains, through Tehachapi, and follow signs for Highway 14 North or Randsburg Cutoff. Take the cutoff, then take Highway 14 north. On your right is Fremont Valley and the Mojave Desert; on your left are the Sierra Nevadas and Sequoia National Forest.

Continuing on Highway 14 you'll pass through **Red Rock Canyon State Park** (unless you want to stop; it's a beautiful place, and if you're planning to spend the night in Ridgecrest before going into Death Valley, you have time). Continue north and follow signs for Highway 178 and Ridgecrest. You'll turn east on Highway 178, pass through the town of Inyokern and into Ridgecrest. From Ridgecrest you continue on 178 to 190 and into Death Valley (see next chapter).

An alternate, desolate route (if you're in the mood for solitude) that will skip Red Rock but take you through a very old mining town is to take Randsburg Road (about 13 miles north of where you joined Highway 14; it's about two miles south of Red Rock State Park) east to Randsburg, then take Highway 395 north to Ridgecrest. If you do this, make sure you have at least 40 miles worth of gas because there's no gas in Randsburg (or in nearby Johannesburg).

11
DEATH VALLEY

Death Valley is the middle of nowhere, and to drive to the middle of nowhere you must drive through the edge of nowhere. But when you get there you realize it's not nowhere, it's just like no place you've been before. OK, perhaps that's too philosophical.

Maybe it's the name of the place that generates such thoughts. Death Valley is huge; it's rocky; it's bordered by very high mountains; it contains the lowest spot in North America (282 feet below sea level) and only has around 400 human residents; it has marvelous alluvial fans, volcanic craters, salt flats, sand dunes, and petroglyphs; it's the place borax comes from (Ronald Reagan hosted *Death Valley Days*, brought to you by 20-Mule Team Borax); and in summer it's "hot as Hell." The highest temperature recorded here was 134°F, in 1913.

During your visit, you'll see several kinds of cactus (beavertail, strawtop cholla, grizzly bear, calico, mound, cottontop barrel); spring wildflowers, if you visit between February and April (desert star, blazing star, desert gold, poppies, evening primrose, and more); common desert plants (creosote bush, desert holly, desert trumpet, sprucebush, honey mesquite, arrowweed, pickerelweed); and perhaps local wildlife (roadrunner, black-tailed jackrabbit, zebra-tailed lizard, and coyote). And you can see the date palms planted by the Pacific Borax Company in 1920 and buy some very tasty dates. The stunning geography, the views, the wildlife—all found in the solitude of Death Valley—will be among your most memorable Southern California experiences.

DEATH VALLEY

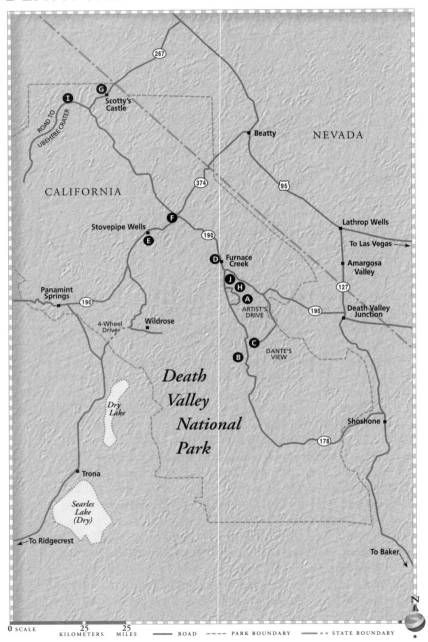

267

G Scotty's Castle

I

ROAD TO UBEHEBE CRATER

Beatty

NEVADA

374

95

CALIFORNIA

Stovepipe Wells

F

Lathrop Wells

E

190

To Las Vegas

D Furnace Creek

Amargosa Valley

Panamint Springs

J

H

127

190

A

ARTIST'S DRIVE

190

Death Valley Junction

4-Wheel Drive

Wildrose

C

DANTE'S VIEW

B

Death Valley National Park

Dry Lake

Shoshone

178

Trona

Searles Lake (Dry)

To Ridgecrest

To Baker

N

0 SCALE   25   25
KILOMETERS   MILES   ——— ROAD   ---- PARK BOUNDARY   ——-·— STATE BOUNDARY

A PERFECT DAY IN DEATH VALLEY

Arise early. If it's the right time of year, it's daylight but the moon is still in the sky, and as you look around at the landscape, with the mountains in the distance and both the sun and the moon above, you might just think you're on another planet. If you spent the night at Stovepipe Wells, check out Mosaic Canyon and the Sand Dunes. You'll also want to visit Scotty's Castle and Ubehebe Crater. See the visitors center and the museum and learn a little more about this fascinating place. Have lunch at Furnace Creek, then spend your afternoon seeing more sights: Artists Palette, Dante's View, Twenty Mule Team Canyon, and Zabriskie Point. If you're done hiking and driving, take a horseback ride out of Furnace Creek Ranch. As the sun sets, pick a spot and watch as it sets behind the Panamint Mountains: maybe Dante's View or Zabriskie Point. Then it's time for dinner and perhaps a swim in the heated pool under the stars; or a moonlight horseback ride, if the moon cooperates; or a quiet walk in this beautiful middle of nowhere.

GETTING TO DEATH VALLEY

Because it's a huge place, there's a lot to see; and because each person's trip is individual, what follows is meant to be a suggestion, one version of what you can see and do on your visit.

If you're reading this as you plan your Southern California trip, I strongly urge you to see this place. Death Valley is not just a desert, nor is it merely barren land. Admittedly, when I moved to California years ago and was asked if I'd been to Death Valley, I pictured a flat expanse of nothing and wondered why anyone would go there. Now I'm amazed at anyone who doesn't go take a look, and I can't wait to return.

SIGHTS

- **Ⓐ** Artists Palette
- **Ⓑ** Badwater
- **Ⓒ** Dante's View
- **Ⓓ** Death Valley Museum and Furnace Creek Visitor Center
- **Ⓔ** Mosaic Canyon
- **Ⓕ** Sand Dunes
- **Ⓖ** Scotty's Castle
- **Ⓗ** Twenty Mule Team Canyon
- **Ⓘ** Ubehebe Crater
- **Ⓙ** Zabriskie Point

If you're following the general route of this book (San Diego up the coast to San Luis Obispo) and you're coming from San Luis Obispo, you can continue east on Highway 58 through Bakersfield to Highway 14, then go north to Highway 178 to Ridgecrest. If you're coming from Los Angeles you can take I-5 to Bakersfield, then turn east on Highway 58. On your way to Ridgecrest you'll pass Red Rock Canyon and on your way out of Ridgecrest you'll pass Trona. Bakersfield to Red Rock Canyon is very scenic; east of Ridgecrest gets a little desolate until you approach the Panamint Mountains. Make sure you gas up in Ridgecrest!

From Ridgecrest, take Highway 178 to Highway 190 (otherwise designated SR 190), turn east, and begin your ascent of the Panamint Range. You'll go through Towne Pass (4,956 feet) and down into Death Valley. On the floor of the valley, SR 190 will take you to Stovepipe Wells Village, Furnace Creek, and Scotty's Castle (follow the signs). If you have a four-wheel-drive vehicle and the Wildrose Road is open, you can take Highway 178 into the park, over the mountains, and through Emigrant Pass (elevation 5,318 feet), and intersect SR 190 southwest of Stovepipe Wells.

If you want to enter from the south, from Los Angeles, take I-10 east and turn north on I-15; stay on I-15 to Baker, then turn north on Highway 127. At Shoshone, go west on Highway 178. This takes you into the national monument and intersects with SR 190 at Furnace Creek. You can also continue on Highway 127 to Death Valley Junction, intersect with SR 190 there, and enter the monument.

SIGHTSEEING HIGHLIGHTS

★★★★ ARTISTS PALETTE
Off SR 178
Painted by nature (oxidation), the red, orange, yellow, green, brown, and black colors on these rocks are gorgeous. This is another site best seen right at sunset. The one-way route off the highway allows you to gaze at the colors; you can park and walk around, too.

Details: *About 30 miles south of the Furnace Creek Visitor Center (see below). (1 hour)*

★★★★ DANTE'S VIEW
Off SR 190
This is one of the best panoramic views of the valley. From here, at 5,475 feet elevation, you can see Badwater and the multitude of

geologic configurations in the valley floor, Starvation Canyon and other canyons in the Panamint Range foothills, Telescope Peak (21 miles away), Aguereberry Point (farther to the north in the Panamints), Furnace Creek, and the Grapevine Mountains, which form the valley's northeastern ridge. To the northwest, the Sierra Nevadas are sometimes visible.

Details: *Almost 27 miles south of Furnace Creek Visitor Center (see below). (30 minutes)*

★★★★ DEATH VALLEY MUSEUM AND FURNACE CREEK VISITOR CENTER
Furnace Creek, 760/786-2331

This is the logical place to start your adventure. The Furnace Creek Visitor Center offers up-to-the-minute information on weather and all kinds of excellent maps, many of which feature distances and time estimates for getting to and from various sites; information on hiking trails, flora, and fauna (so you can identify what you're seeing); an orientation film shown periodically throughout the day; a bookstore with numerous books about Death Valley history, geology, flora, fauna, and sites, many featuring glorious photos; a gift shop; and a

ARTISTS PALETTE

Chuck Kurtz

museum. The museum displays photos and artifacts of the valley's history, starting with its geological beginnings, moving on to the activities of early Native American settlers, and then to the prospectors, settlers, and miners who followed them. The first known Anglos reached Death Valley by accident, taking a wrong-turn shortcut on their way to the mother-lode goldfields. As one of the leaders of the first errant wagon train noted upon seeing Death Valley, "Pretty near all creation was in sight." (Note: Many distances from and directions to different sites use the visitors center as a starting point, as in, "The Devil's Golf Course is 13 miles from Furnace Creek Visitor Center.")

Details: Open daily 8–4. (1 hour)

★★★★ UBEHEBE CRATER
Off SR 190
One of many awe-inspiring sites, Ubehebe Crater was created a few thousand years ago when a huge volcanic eruption blasted out this 600-foot-deep hole. A half-mile wide, the crater reflects various layers and colors of rock. Dark gray soil from the cinders surrounds the crater.

Details: About 65 miles north of Furnace Creek Visitor Center. (30 minutes)

★★★ BADWATER
On SR 178
This is close to the lowest spot in North America. Park and look out over the salt flat, then turn around, look up, and note the mark on the mountain wall behind you, which indicates sea level. If you're here at sundown, watch the sun set behind Telescope Peak (11,049 feet) in the Panamint Range. You can walk out on the flats, too.

Details: About 20 miles south of Furnace Creek Visitor Center. (30 minutes)

★★★ MOSAIC CANYON
Off SR 190
This canyon, near Stovepipe Wells, offers a unique, panoramic view of the northern valley. The multicolored walls look as if they've been polished. This site, unlike many others, is best seen around noon; that's when the sun really brings out the colors.

Details: About 32 miles from Furnace Creek Visitor Center. (1 hour)

★★★ SAND DUNES
Off SR 190

Located northeast of Stovepipe Wells, these dunes are visible from both SR 190 and Grapevine Road. This 14-square-mile area looks like it's right out of *Lawrence of Arabia*, and it is perhaps what most people think of when they think of a desert. Because of the valley's wind patterns, these dunes shift but don't migrate. In the morning you can often find footprints left by nocturnal animals.

Details: *About 30 miles north of Furnace Creek Visitor Center. (30 minutes)*

★★★ SCOTTY'S CASTLE
On SR 267, off SR 190, 760/786-2392

This huge Spanish-Moorish-style house was built by so-called prospector Walter Scott and millionaire Albert Johnson in the late 1920s (until the Depression stopped both the flow of money and the construction). What is a huge estate doing in the middle of nowhere? Who knows for sure? There are many stories about Scotty, his exploits, and his partnership with Johnson, but this huge, $2.5 million estate with lavishly decorated rooms, an impressive kitchen, a huge pipe organ, and other unseemly (for a desert) features is more impressive than any stories.

Details: *About 55 miles north of Furnace Creek. Open daily 9–5. Guided tours (only) inside the house are $8 adults, $4 children 6–11; free for children 5 and under. (1 hour)*

★★★ TWENTY MULE TEAM CANYON
On SR 190

This lonely, three-mile, dirt-road loop takes you through some of the badlands where prospectors mined for ore: borax, not gold. There are some close-up views of colorful rock in the remnants of this ancient lakebed. Ironically, no 20-mule team ever worked out of this canyon. But one of the first buildings in Death Valley was originally constructed and used here. It's now at the Borax Museum at Furnace Creek.

Details: *About six miles south of Furnace Creek Visitor Center. (20 minutes)*

★★★ ZABRISKIE POINT
On SR 190

Another beautiful view, this point was named after Christian

DEATH VALLEY

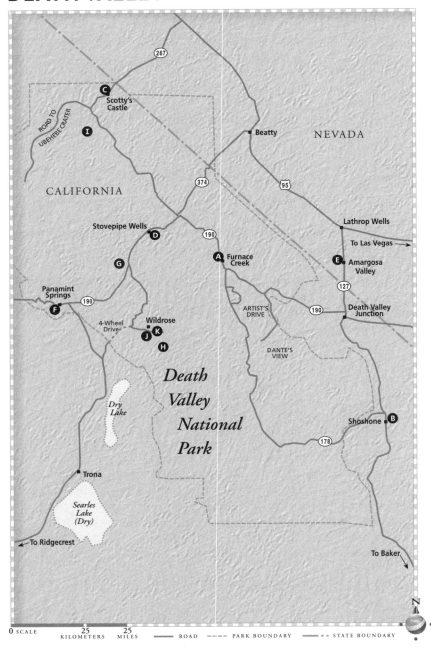

267

C Scotty's
Castle

ROAD TO UBEHEBE CRATER

I

Beatty

NEVADA

CALIFORNIA

374

95

Stovepipe Wells

D

190

Lathrop Wells

To Las Vegas →

A Furnace
Creek

E Amargosa
Valley

G

Panamint
Springs

190

F

127

4-Wheel
Drive

Wildrose

J K

H

ARTIST'S
DRIVE

190

Death Valley
Junction

DANTE'S
VIEW

Death
Valley
National
Park

Dry
Lake

Shoshone B

178

Trona

Searles
Lake
(Dry)

← To Ridgecrest

To Baker

N

0 SCALE   25   25
        KILOMETERS   MILES   ▬▬▬ ROAD   ▬ ▬ ▬ PARK BOUNDARY   ▬ ▪ ▬ STATE BOUNDARY

Zabriskie, one of the borax-mine superintendents. Geologically, the view is of an ancient lakebed, but to the layperson it's a gorgeous panorama of rippling, colorful rock. It's one of several places to be at sunrise or sunset.

Details: *Almost five miles south of Furnace Creek Visitor Center. (30 minutes)*

★★ OTHER SIGHTS

If time permits, there is much more to see, such as Golden Canyon and the trail from there to Zabriskie Point, the Devil's Golf Course, Harmony Borax Works, Keane Wonder Mine, Salt Creek Nature Trail, the Devil's Cornfield, Titus Canyon, and Charcoal Kilns.

FITNESS AND RECREATION

Death Valley offers opportunities for hiking, biking, horseback riding, and even golf (at the 18-hole **Furnace Creek Inn** course).

There are hundreds of hiking trails throughout the valley. Day hiking possibilities include **Bridge Canyon, Desolation Canyon, Golden Canyon, Gower Gulch Loop, Salt Creek, Keane Wonder Mine Trail, Sand Dunes, Mosaic Canyon, Titus Canyon Narrows, Little Hebe Crater Trail,** and **Ubehebe Peak Trail.** For adventurous backcountry hikes, look for **Coffin Peak, Death Valley Buttes, Corkscrew Peak, Fall Canyon, Red**

FOOD

A Furnace Creek Inn Dining Room
A Furnace Creek Ranch restaurants
B Red Buggy Cafe and Crowbar Lounge
C Scotty's Castle snack bar
D Stovepipe Wells Inn Restaurant

LODGING

E Amargosa Hotel and Opera House
A Furnace Creek Inn
A Furnace Creek Ranch
F Panamint Springs Resort
B Shoshone Inn
D Stovepipe Wells Inn

CAMPING

G Emigrant
A Furnace Creek Campground
H Mahogany Flat
I Mesquite Springs Campground
F Panamint Springs Resort Campground
B Shoshone Trailer Park
D Stovepipe Wells
A Sunset
A Texas Spring
J Thorndike
K Wildrose

Note: Items with the same letter are located in the same area.

Wall Canyon, Little Bridge Canyon, and the Panamint Range hike to Wildrose Peak (this trail ascends 2,000 feet in four miles, taking you through pines and offering a spectacular view from the 9,000-foot-elevation summit). Also accessible by hiking (from Mahogany Flat) is Telescope Peak.

When hiking, always drink at least a gallon of water per day—more is better—and drink every hour even if you're not thirsty. As for biking, bikes are allowed only where cars are allowed: no cross-country biking is permitted.

Furnace Creek Stables offers horseback riding (if you enjoy horseback riding, it's fun to do in Death Valley; with your imagination on the run, you can feel what the pioneers and settlers must have felt as they trekked across the valley floor). Packages include a two-hour daytime ride, a moonlight ride (during the full moon), a champagne carriage ride, and hay-wagon rides for groups of 10 or more. The stables are located on Furnace Creek Ranch, 760/786-2345, ext. 230 or 222.

Death Valley Tours, 760/786-2345, ext. 222, offers a variety of tours in vans and motor coaches from Furnace Creek Ranch to Scotty's Castle, Titus Canyon, the Lower Valley, Darwin Falls/Charcoal Kilns, Dante's View, and more. Some tours include hikes, some require a minimum number of passengers, and tour rates and lengths vary.

FOOD

Outside the park, **Red Buggy Cafe and Crowbar Lounge** (across from the Shoshone Inn), Shoshone, 760/852-9908, serves home-cooked meals for breakfast, lunch, and dinner in a cozy mom-and-pop diner atmosphere. Breakfasts generally run less than $6, dinners generally less than $12. The adjacent bar has a pool table and sometimes live entertainment.

Food within the park is the same story as gas and lodging: there are only three major providers. **Furnace Creek Inn Dining Room** is the antithesis of its outside surroundings. It's a formal, elegant place requiring semiformal attire; dinners average $35. The **Furnace Creek Ranch** restaurants are more casual, with prices running a little higher than you might expect. The menus feature American and Southwestern cuisines. **Stovepipe Wells Inn Restaurant** offers casual dining and American fare with most meals less than $20. There's a snack bar at **Scotty's Castle**.

LODGING

There are only three places to stay in Death Valley if you're not camping. **Furnace Creek Inn**, SR 190, just south of the visitors center, 760/786-2361 or 800/236-7916, is a historic resort hotel in a scenic location overlooking the valley. There are saunas, an exercise room, a heated pool, four lighted tennis courts, and a restaurant (see Food, above). Rates range from $215 to $325 October to May, and $135 to $225 May to October. **Furnace Creek Ranch**, SR 190, also just south of the visitors center, 760/786-2345 or 800/236-7916, is a resort complex with 224 rooms, 27 cabins, lighted tennis courts, playground, gas station (very important to keep track of these!), restaurant, cafeteria and coffee shop, Borax Museum, grocery, and a shipping outlet for dates grown in the valley. Rates range from $90 to $130. **Stovepipe Wells Inn**, SR 190, about 25 miles northwest of the visitors center (you'll encounter this first if you enter from Ridgecrest), 760/786-2387, is a functional 83-room motel with a heated pool (this is a nice feature: on a cool desert night—jump into the pool and float, your eyes on the stars above). There's also a restaurant and, across the street, a gas station and grocery. Compared to the "civilization" at Furnace Creek, this place is relatively isolated. Rates range from $58 to $80.

Near the southeast entrance of the park is **Shoshone Inn**, Shoshone, 760/852-4335. It's a small, very comfortable motel with 16 rooms, HBO, a nearby natural spring pool with temperatures ranging from 85 to 90 degrees year round (it's *very* relaxing!), and a restaurant and saloon across the street. Next door is a gas station. Room rates range from $46 to $70.

East of the park is the **Amargosa Hotel and Opera House**, 760/852-4441, at Death Valley Junction on SR 127, about 30 miles from Furnace Creek, offering 12 rooms with rates ranging from $45 to $60. This has been an on-again, off-again operation . . . good luck. It's fun when it's open, and it is right now . . .)

West of Death Valley but still in the park is **Panamint Springs Resort**, 702/482-7680 or 760/482-7680 direct, panamint@ix.netcom.com. An hour from Furnace Creek. it features 15 rooms, a restaurant, and a gas station; rates range from $56.50 to $89.50; $129 for the new two-bedroom cabin suite (the only room that includes satellite TV—but do you really want to watch TV when there's Death Valley to see?). They also have RV sites and camping spots under tamarisk trees.

Ridgecrest, two hours west, has many chain motels (including Econo Lodge, Heritage Inn, and Motel 6).

CAMPING

Death Valley has several campgrounds for tent and RV campers. Some are open seasonally, most have maximum-stay restrictions, and national park rules apply.

ROY ROGERS AND DALE EVANS MUSEUM, VICTORVILLE

If you ever wore a Roy Rogers or Dale Evans cowboy hat when you were a kid, or were ever a fan of TV and movie cowboys, or loved the way TV and movies portrayed the Wild West, this museum is for you.

The exterior is designed to look like a frontier fortress from the 1850s, and the new courtyard also presents the setting of the interior area of a fort.

Inside, the museum features the radio, television, and motion-picture careers of Roy Rogers and Dale Evans through photos, costumes, and artifacts. The theater shows short films about Roy and Dale's life, their sidekicks, and other movie and television memories. Roy's world-famous horse, Trigger; along with Pat Brady's Jeep, Nellybelle; pictures of Gabby Hayes and the Sons of the Pioneers, and Roy and Dale's Remington collection are included in the exhibits.

Details: 15650 Seneca Road, Victorville (take the Roy Rogers Drive exit off I-15, about 40 miles south of Barstow), 760/243-4548 (760/243-4547 gives you a recorded message), www.royrogers.com. Open daily 9–5; closed Thanksgiving and Christmas. Admission is $7 adults, $6 seniors and ages 13–16, $5 ages 6–12, free for children under 6.

Stovepipe Wells, SR 190, at the north end of Stovepipe Wells Village, has 200 tent/RV spaces, a disposal station, flush toilets, no showers, and a $6-per-night fee, and it's closed May through September. **Emigrant**, off SR 190 about nine miles southwest of Stovepipe Wells Village, has 10 spaces, piped water, flush toilets, and no fee, and it's closed November through April.

Near Furnace Creek, **Furnace Creek Campground**, off SR 190 about a mile north of Furnace Creek Ranch, has 33 tent sites and 103 tent/RV spaces on 30 acres, a disposal station, flush toilets, and a $10 fee. **Sunset**, on SR 190 across the street from Furnace Creek Ranch, has 1,000 tent/RV spaces, a disposal station, flush toilets, no showers, and a $6 fee, and is closed May through September. **Texas Spring**, behind Sunset Campground just east of Furnace Creek Ranch, off SR 190, has 36 tent spaces and 60 tent/RV spaces, a disposal station, flush toilets, no showers, and a $6 fee, and is also closed May through

September. The National Park Reservation System takes reservations for Furnace Creek and the Texas Springs campground group sites: 800/365-2267.

Off the Trona-Wildrose Road are **Mahogany Flat**, about 40 miles south of Stovepipe Wells Village, with 10 tent/RV spaces, no showers or drinking water, pit toilets, and no fee, closed December through March; **Thorndike**, with eight tent/RV spaces, no water, pit toilets, and no fee, closed November through March; and **Wildrose**, about 30 miles southeast of Stovepipe Wells, with 30 tent/RV spaces, no drinking water, no showers, pit toilets, and no fee. The roads to these sites are open seasonally, weather permitting, and despite the RV spaces, the road to Thorndike and Mahogany Flat is not passable for trailers, campers, or motor homes. Four-wheel-drive vehicles may be necessary.

Mesquite Springs Campground, on Grapevine Road, is about five miles south of Scotty's Castle, with 30 RV spaces on two acres, a disposal station, flush toilets, no showers, and a $6 fee.

Outside the valley, **Panamint Springs Resort Campground**, SR 190, 702/482-7680, about 30 miles west of Stovepipe Wells (not in Death Valley), has 12 RV spaces, 40 tent/RV spaces, several hookups, flush toilets, groceries and supplies, varying rates, and a motel and restaurant nearby. **Shoshone Trailer Park**, in Shoshone, 760/852-4569, has full hookups, showers, laundry, a warm-springs pool, and tent camping available; rates range $10 to $15 daily and monthly rates are also available.

NIGHTLIFE

If you're a nocturnal desert animal, I suspect the nightlife is very active. For humans, however, night is when things quiet down. The lounge next to the restaurant at Stovepipe Wells features live music on some nights, and the heated pool at the Stovepipe Wells Inn feels great. Sitting and looking at the night sky may be the right thing to do, or maybe a moonlight horseback ride.

If it's between October and May and you're up for an hour's drive, head for Marta Becket's **Amargosa Hotel and Opera House**, on SR 127 at Death Valley Junction, 760/852-4441. Ms. Becket is an artist, ballet dancer, and desert lover who presents unique performances, starting at 8:15 p.m., seasonally, on various nights. Admission is $10 adults, $5 children 12 and under. Call for program schedule. Ballet in the desert is too good to miss.

HELPFUL HINTS

Water. Gas. Death Valley is hot; summer temperatures can exceed 120°F, so water is a must. Always travel with plenty—at least one gallon per person per day. Bring suitable clothing (including something warm—winter nights can get cold), a hat, and sunscreen. The valley is also huge, so always make sure you've got enough gas to do the traveling you want to do. Turn off your vehicle's air-conditioning on uphill grades. There's radiator water (not suitable for drinking) available along the main roads. *Most important:* If trouble develops, *stay with your vehicle*; rescuers can spot it more easily than they can a person wandering around.

There are three service stations in Death Valley: Furnace Creek Chevron, open 7 a.m. to 7 p.m.; Stovepipe Wells, open 7 a.m. to 8 p.m.; and Scotty's Castle, open 9 a.m. to 5:30 p.m.

For further information, the official National Park Service Web site and this unofficial Web site are helpful and current: www.nps.gov./deva, and www1.ridgecrest.ca.us/~matmus/DeathV.html.

12
JOSHUA TREE

Joshua Tree is a small town along the Twentynine Palms Highway, but the key attraction, here long before the town, is the desert area that in 1994 became Joshua Tree National Park. The desert is full of fascinating plant life and huge rock configurations that look like they've been placed by giants. (Actually, what you see are the tips of rock formations mostly buried underground.) One of Southern California's most stunning sights is also here: Keys' View.

Joshua Tree National Park actually contains two deserts: the northern region, at a higher elevation, is part of the Mojave; the lower, southern region is part of the Colorado. The park is inhabited by a variety of wildlife, including coyote, kangaroo rat, bobcat, tarantula, sidewinder, and roadrunner. Flora include the Joshua tree, along with teddybear cactus, ocotillo, California juniper, and California fan palm. Despite the desert's harsh climate, there have been and are oases, so there have been (and are) human inhabitants. Remains of Pinto Basin culture from 5,000 to 7,000 years ago have been found, and petroglyphs are scattered throughout the park (their locations mostly unadvertised, to prevent their thoughtless destruction). Chemehuevi, Cahuilla, and Serrano people lived here until the early 1900s. In the late 1800s prospectors and miners explored the area, and with them came the legends: Did the Lost Horse, Eldorado, and Desert Queen mines yield $40,000 or was it $40 million? Rediscover the past as you explore present-day Joshua Tree.

A PERFECT DAY IN JOSHUA TREE

Enjoy breakfast at the friendly Country Kitchen. Then choose your scenic drives and hikes and get to it. Start with Keys' View to see what it looks like in the morning. After that, since you're near the Lost Horse Mine, pull into the parking area and hike to the ruins. Check out the Cap Rock Nature Trail, Skull Rock, and the Jumbo Rocks. Ask at the Visitor Center about a tour of the Desert Queen Ranch. After lunch, explore Indian Cove or drive down to the Cottonwood Visitor Center and do the Mastodon Peak and Lost Palms Oasis hikes; or just sightsee, driving around the park to view the Cholla Cactus Garden or Black Rock Canyon. As sunset approaches, return to Keys' View and watch the sun set behind the mountains. At night, enjoy a home-cooked dinner at Kim's Coffee Shop and, if you're camping, relax under the stars.

GETTING TO JOSHUA TREE

If you're coming from Death Valley, don't think that this place is the same as the last. It's not. Take the scenic drive from Highway 127 south to I-15, head west to Highway 247 in Barstow, take that southeast to Highway 62, and you're a few miles west of Joshua Tree. If you're coming from Los Angeles, take I-10 to Highway 62 and turn north; coming from the Palm Springs area, take 62 north. You're about two hours away from L.A. and less than an hour from Palm Springs.

Joshua Tree's average high springtime temperature is 82°F, in summer it's 103°F, fall reaches 83°F, and winter's average low is 35°F. If you want to experience quiet, beauty, and a different kind of desert, Joshua Tree is for you.

JOSHUA TREE NATIONAL PARK SIGHTSEEING HIGHLIGHTS

As in Death Valley, your experience here can be magical if you like unusual rocks, rock formations, and plants, and the tactile and spiritual character of the high desert. You may want to see most of its many sights by car, or you may decide to hike or bike. There are three entrances: in Joshua Tree at Twentynine Palms Highway and Park Boulevard, in Twentynine Palms at Twentynine Palms Highway and Utah Trail/National Park Drive, and on the south side on Highway 195 off I-10.

The following park sites are clearly marked on the map provided when you pay your entrance fee. The times listed are guidelines if you just want to see the site. Stopping to "smell the flowers" may take longer.

JOSHUA TREE

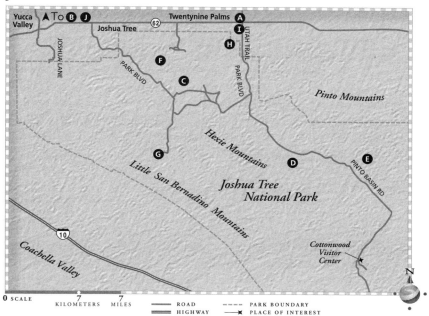

SIGHTS

Ⓐ Hi-Desert Nature Museum
Ⓑ Pioneertown

JOSHUA TREE NATIONAL PARK

Ⓒ Barker Dam
Ⓓ Cholla Cactus Garden

JOSHUA TREE NATIONAL PARK (continued)

Ⓔ Cottonwood Spring
Ⓕ Desert Queen Ranch
Ⓖ Keys' View
Ⓗ Oasis of Mara
Ⓘ Visitor Center and Museum

FOOD

Ⓙ Country Kitchen
Ⓙ Kim's Coffee Shop
Ⓙ Jeremy's Cyber Cafe & Beer Haus
Ⓙ 29 Palms Inn Restaurant

Note: Items with the same letter are located in the same area.

★★★★ BARKER DAM

This dam was built by C.O. Barker in the early 1900s (after previous ranchers had identified the area and done some preliminary work). Bill Keys (of Keys' View) did more work on it in the 1950s. The dam was part of the cattle and mining industry and today works as a reservoir. The trail also offers views of the Wonderland of Rocks.

Details: *Accessed by Barker Dam trail (a one-mile loop). (1 hour)*

★★★★ COTTONWOOD SPRING

This is a peaceful oasis at the park's southern end, with palms, cotton-woods, and a little water seeping from the rocks. One hundred years ago, over 3,000 gallons of water a day moved through the rocks. The change is attributed to shifting land and earthquakes. According to one park ranger, the water has increased since the 1994 Northridge quake.

Details: *Easily accessed by car. (30 minutes)*

★★★★ DESERT QUEEN RANCH

Accessed by dirt road out of the Hidden Valley campground, this ranch was last worked by Bill Keys until he died in 1969 and looks as it did then. The McHaneys built the barn in 1893 and Keys came along in 1917. The ranch features exhibits of days past, when a few pioneers, ranchers, and miners tried to make the land work: an old tractor, homemade rakes, canning jars, and other old tools and wares. Mostly, the ranch is a study of the nature of man in the nature of the desert.

Details: *760/367-1488. Viewable only through guided tours coordinated from the Visitor Center. (1 hour)*

★★★★ KEYS' VIEW

More than just a spectacular vista, this view, named after one of the area's pioneers, puts Southern California in perspective. From this 5,185-foot elevation, you can see San Gorgonio Mountain, the highest point in Southern California (11,500 feet); San Gorgonio Pass, gateway for bad air from Los Angeles; San Jacinto Peak (10,800 feet), which you might have visited or plan to visit as part of your Palm Springs stop; and, at the base of San Jacinto Mountain, Palm Springs. This point also shows you the San Andreas Fault; Indio and the Coachella Valley (where dates and other fruit are grown); and the Salton Sea (230 feet below sea level), which was dry when the Spanish were here but became a lake when the Colorado overran its banks. On a clear day, you can even see Signal Mountain in Mexico.

Details: *With extra time and energy, climb to the peak for an even better view. (At least 30 minutes)*

★★★★ VISITOR CENTER AND MUSEUM
74485 National Park Dr., Twentynine Palms, 760/367-1488
Stopping here is the best way to orient yourself in Joshua Tree. The museum features exhibits and information on the park's natural and human history, and the center provides up-to-the-minute climatic information.
Details: *Open daily 8–6. (1 hour)*

★★★ CHOLLA CACTUS GARDEN
This "garden" is a natural rather than a tended garden, made up primarily of Bigelow cactus (also known as teddybear cholla or jumping cholla), along with calico cactus and desert senna.
Details: *Take a self-guided tour here; the trail is marked. (20 minutes)*

★★★ OASIS OF MARA
This is a desert, so oases are rare. California fan palms and the water served as much of the basis of civilization for the Serrano and Chemehuevi Indians, who lived here before Anglos arrived. Then came the Spanish, the Mexicans, and the Americans. The spring water stopped flowing in 1942; piped-in water now keeps the area alive.
Details: *Accessed by a half-mile-long trail from the Visitor Center. (20 minutes)*

OTHER JOSHUA TREE SIGHTSEEING HIGHLIGHTS

Like Death Valley, this area features many other sites and sights, some popular enough to have accepted names (such as Jumbo Rocks, Cap Rock, and Skull Rock); some just interesting or fascinating to see. If you have one day, you can drive through and hike a little; with more time, you can do more hiking.

★★ HI-DESERT NATURE MUSEUM
57117 Twentynine Palms Highway, Yucca Valley; 760/228-5452
This museum features a natural-history diorama with animals from the desert and other California regions, a kids' corner for activities related to the exhibits, a mini-zoo with small desert animals, a rock and mineral collection, including fossils from the Paleozoic era, and "Artist of the Month" exhibits of outstanding contemporary Morongo Basin art.
Details: *Open Wed–Sun 1–5. Free. (1 hour)*

★★ PIONEERTOWN

Built by Gene Autry and Roy Rogers, this was the site of many movie gunfights and includes a version of the famous OK Corral. Although it's now a community of private residences, the Old West flavor remains. Running Deer petting zoo is for the kids. The main attraction is **Pioneertown Palace** (760/365-5956). With homemade country-style cooking, this palace has dancing to live country music on weekends and country-music jam sessions on Wednesday nights.

Details: *On Pioneertown Road, off Twentynine Palms Highway. (1 hour)*

FITNESS AND RECREATION

The main thing to do in the Joshua Tree area is hike and rock-climb in **Joshua Tree National Park**. Among the hiking trails are **Barker Dam Trail** (see Barker Dam, under Sightseeing Highlights), and the following:

Lost Horse Mine Trail is off Keys' View Road south of the Cap Rock junction. It's a two-mile hike from the small parking area to the Lost Horse Mine ruins. Although shafts have been sealed off, be careful. **Ryan Mountain Trail** begins at the Ryan Mountain parking area between Sheep Pass and Cap Rock and is a strenuous 1.5-mile hike up the mountain. You'll have wonderful views of San Gorgonio Mountain and San Jacinto Peak. **Lost Palms Oasis Trail** from Cottonwood Spring is an almost-four-mile hike across the lower reaches of this desert area, with an exciting overlook into a palm tree–filled canyon. You can hike into the canyon—but remember: what climbs down must climb up. **Mastodon Peak Trail** also starts at Cottonwood Springs and leads to a point just below the summit, then past mine ruins (be very alert for open mine shafts) and to the ruins of a small town called Winona (it had a gold mill in the 1920s), then back to Cottonwood Springs. It's a three-mile hike. The nature trails—**Cap Rock**, **Hidden Valley**, **Indian Cove**, and **Arch Rock**—are all loop-walks of less than a mile, each offering its own unique mix of geology, plant life, and views.

For mountain biking or four-wheel-drive recreation, there are several roads, including 20-mile Pinkham Canyon Road (beginning at Cottonwood Visitor Center), 6.5-mile Black Eagle Mine Road, north of Cottonwood Visitor Center; 23-mile Old Dale Road (which starts at the same place as Black Eagle Mine Road); Queen Valley Roads, a network of roads beginning at Hidden Valley campground (with several bike racks in the area, bikers can lock up and go hiking); **Geology Tour Road**, an 11.5-mile stretch from west of Jumbo Rocks campground to Pleasant Valley; and several dirt roads in

JOSHUA TREE

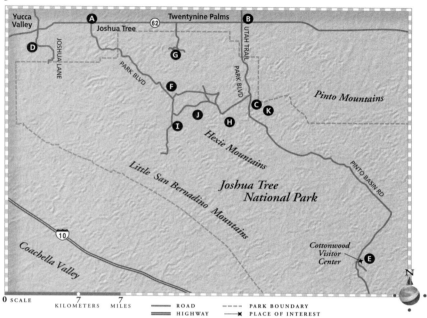

LODGING

- **A** High Desert Motel
- **A** Joshua Tree Inn B&B
- **B** 29 Palms Inn

CAMPING

- **B** 29 Palms RV Resort
- **C** Belle
- **D** Black Rock

CAMPING (continued)

- **E** Cottonwood
- **F** Hidden Valley
- **G** Indian Cove
- **H** Jumbo Rocks
- **I** Ryan
- **J** Sheep Pass
- **K** White Tank

Note: Items with the same letter are located in the same place.

Covington Flats, which holds some large Joshua trees.

For hiking, climbing, biking, and camping supplies, water, firewood, guide-books, shoe rental, shoe repair, and tent rental, stop at **Coyote Corner**, 6535 Park Blvd., Joshua Tree, 760/366-9683. Chris and Ethan are very helpful.

To see the area from atop a horse, contact **Yucca Trails**, 760/365-2818, or **Full Moon Adventures**, 760/366-3507.

FOOD

Joshua Tree has only a few restaurants. **Country Kitchen**, 61768 Twentynine Palms Highway, Joshua Tree, 760/366-8988, is my favorite. This is a friendly, down-home place with a small-town atmosphere. They serve breakfast all day and lunch at lunch time. Most meals are less than $6, it's good, and the portions are what you need with a day of rock-climbing ahead of you. **Kim's Coffee Shop**, 61761 Twentynine Palms Highway, 760/366-3650, also unpretentious and casual, serves home-cooked, filling dinners for less than $12.

Jeremy's Cyber Cafe & Beer Haus, 61597 Twentynine Palms Highway, 760/366-9799, is not so much a restaurant as an activity center with food. They have sandwiches, juices, fresh baked goods, Haagen Das ice cream, hummus, and pitas, all moderately priced with sandwiches at less than $6. They have a killer homemade chocolate cheesecake (you should only eat this if you did some hiking today) made with Jeremy's mom's secret recipe. And they feature a large selection of off-the-beaten-path microbrewed and exotic beers—not to mention Guiness on tap. They sell premium cigars, and they have four computers (three Macs and one PC), which many travelers use these to check e-mail.

Over in Twentynine Palms is the **29 Palms Inn Restaurant**, 73950 Inn Avenue, Twentynine Palms, 760/367-3505, serving lunch from Monday through Saturday 11 a.m.–2 p.m., brunch on Sundays 9 a.m.–2 p.m. and dinner every night from 5–9 (9:30 on Fridays and Saturdays). Lunches include tasty sandwiches like a turkey salad pita, a grilled breast of chicken and veggie pita, a Santa Fe grilled chicken sandwich, and the "Grunt Burger." They also have salads and soups. Most lunches are $5 or less. Dinners include steaks, seafood (including fresh fish and broiled Australian Lobster Tail, as well as chicken, pastas, and salads. Dinners with beverage and dessert average $20; more with an appetizer.

LODGING

There are really only two places to stay in Joshua Tree; both are comfortable and cater to different tastes and budgets. The **Joshua Tree Inn B&B**, 61259 Twentynine Palms Highway, Joshua Tree, 760/366-1188 or 800/366-1444, is a lovely, hacienda-style B&B less than a mile from one of the park's entrances. This inn has the historical distinction of being the place where songwriter/musician Gram Parsons died and has become something of a mecca for his fans. The Gram Parsons room features posters from the 1960s Fillmore West era, and once a year there's a memorial gathering attended by many well-known musicians. Full breakfasts feature gourmet cooking, and box lunches and candlelight dinners can be arranged. Rates range from $85 to $220.

GENERAL GEORGE S. PATTON MEMORIAL MUSEUM

Just off I-10 at the Chiriaco exit is a vivid and unusual sight: WWII tanks—at least 10 of them. They're part of this memorial museum. What are they, and this museum, doing here? It seems that this vast area of desert, stretching into Arizona, was a training ground for U.S. Army troops preparing to fight during WWII, and Gen. George S. Patton was the first commanding officer here. He trained troops in this desert, then led them into battle in the North African desert; over 1 million soldiers trained here. In April 1944, the camp was closed.

The museum is not the official Patton museum (that's at Fort Knox), so these exhibits contain almost none of Patton's personal memorabilia. But they do have many WWII artifacts, and displays from other wars and other aspects of war (like the home front); many pieces are from soldiers who served with Patton. There's also a video on Patton, and, having nothing to do with Patton, a fascinating relief map of the Southern California water system. This map, coupled with Keys' View, your memories of Cabrillo Point (if you went), and your drive up the coast, should bring into focus all the natural aspects of Southern California. Open daily 9:30–4:30. Museum admission is $4 adults, $3.50 seniors, children under 12 are free with an adult. Call 760/227-3483 for details.

For a comfortable motel experience, **High Desert Motel**, 61310 Twenty-nine Palms Highway, Joshua Tree, 760/366-1978, also at the park's entrance, has spacious rooms and reasonable rates, less than $60.

Further east, Twentynine Palms offers several chain motels and the **29 Palms Inn**, 73950 Inn Avenue, Twentynine Palms, 760/367-3505, www.29palmsinn.com, just off the main highway, which features several unique cottages and cabins tucked between trees. The inn's Adobe Bungalows have fireplaces and sun patios; Irene's Historic Adobe is a one-bedroom unit with a bunk room, living room, fireplace, kitchen, and enclosed garden patio. There are also cabins with decks and cabins with wood stoves. All the rooms have evaporative coolers and heaters, and firewood for the rooms with fireplaces. Rates range from $65 to $260.

CAMPING

Joshua Tree National Park is a camper's heaven. The sites are limited to six people and two cars each; campground capacities range from 10 to 70 people. Sites at Black Rock and Indian Cove, and all group sites, require reservations: 800/365-2267; other are first-come, first served. Water is available at Oasis of Mara, Indian Cove Ranger Station, and the Black Rock and Cottonwood campgrounds. Bring your own firewood; all park vegetation is protected. There are no showers and no RV hookups. All campsites have fire grates and tables.

Campgrounds include **Belle** (17 sites, chemical toilet), **Black Rock** (100 sites, $10 fee, water, flush toilets, dump station), **Cottonwood** (62 sites, $8 fee, water, flush toilets, dump station), **Hidden Valley** (39 sites, chemical toilets), **Indian Cove** (101 sites, $10 fee, chemical toilets), **Jumbo Rocks** (125 sites, chemical toilets), **Ryan** (29 sites, chemical toilets), **Sheep Pass** (six group sites, $10 group fee, chemical toilets), and **White Tank** (15 sites, chemical toilets). All campsites are at 3,000 feet elevation or higher.

For RV travelers, **29 Palms RV Resort**, 4949 Desert Knoll Ave., Twentynine Palms, 760/367-3320, has 196 RV spaces with water, flush toilets, showers, some other amenities, and nightly rates of $19.

NIGHTLIFE

There isn't much in the way of nightlife if you define it as live music, dancing, bars, concert halls, and theaters. **Jeremy's** features live music every weekend; it varies in styles from folk to light rock to spiritual and features singer-songwriters and bands. And you may very well find some fine conversation. The **Pioneer Palace** (see Pioneertown under Sightseeing Highlights) has live country-western music Friday, Saturday, and Sunday evenings. There also are a few bars on the main highway just down the road in Twentynine Palms . . . but you might want to ask yourself: did you come to Joshua Tree to experience this beautiful desert, only to spend your night at a bar?

13
PALM SPRINGS AND COACHELLA VALLEY

In Palm Springs and the Coachella Valley, different worlds—geographically, culturally, and economically—have bumped up against each other over the years,
making the area an interesting and exciting place. The desert abuts the mountains here, and the lifestyles of Native Americans, farmers, and laborers collide
with the ones celebrated by Robin Leach. The result is an area diverse in
lifestyles, natural features, and opportunities for visitors.

Long before the Spanish entered the territory, Yuman Indians inhabited
the area around Lake Cahuilla. For the past 500 years, Agua Caliente Indians
have lived here. In 1884 Judge John McCallum moved to Palm Springs and
began planting fruit trees. In 1886 Dr. Welwood Murray built a hotel and san-
itarium for patients seeking the restorative effects of dry desert air. In the
1930s actors Ralph Bellamy and Charles Farrell bought a few hundred acres
and built tennis courts. The courts, which became the Palm Springs Racquet
Club, put the area on the map: Indio became known as a place to grow fruit,
and Palm Springs was celebrated for its curative air, mineral waters, and hot
springs.

Plenty of wide open space remains; the air is still dry; the springs are still
good for you. The temperatures can heat up between June and September, with
average highs above 100°F. The average high the rest of the year is 80°F. In addition to tennis, visitors enjoy top-notch golf courses, desert hiking and camping,
museums, and fine restaurants.

PALM SPRINGS REGION

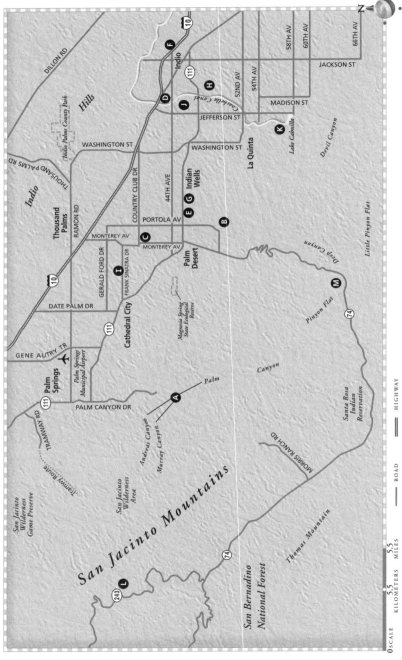

A PERFECT DAY IN PALM SPRINGS AND COACHELLA VALLEY

Start with breakfast at Bit of Country, then ride the tram up to San Jacinto Peak. Return to the valley and visit such museums as Agua Caliente Cultural Museum Center, Palm Springs Desert Museum, Moorten Botanical Garden, Ruddy's General Store Museum, and the Living Desert. Have lunch at Papa Dan's or Sherman's Deli and Bakery, then head to Indian Canyons for a horseback ride. If shopping or golf is your thing, you may want to skip the museums and canyons to do that. For dinner, enjoy a touch of the exotic at St. James. After dinner, sample some blues at the Blue Guitar, some jazz at Billy Reed's, some piano music at the piano bar at The Nest, or some acoustic music at the Ice House.

SIGHTSEEING HIGHLIGHTS

★★★★ AGUA CALIENTE CULTURAL MUSEUM CENTER
219 S. Palm Canyon Dr., Palm Springs, 760/323-0151, www.prinet.com/accmuseum
This Cahuilla Indian museum traces the history of the Agua Caliente Indians from early prehistoric times to the present, through artifacts left by their ancient ancestors and the stories and photographs left by more recent ancestors. A desert landscape diorama and patio exhibit demonstrate vividly how the early Cahuilla people used the resources of their natural environment.
    Details: Open Wed–Sat 10–4, Sun noon–4. Admission is free. (1 hour)

SIGHTS
Ⓐ Indian Canyons
Ⓑ The Living Desert

FOOD
Ⓒ Papa Dan's

LODGING
Ⓓ Best Western Date Tree Hotel
Ⓔ Embassy Suites

LODGING (continued)
Ⓕ Holiday Inn Express–Indio
Ⓔ Holiday Inn Express–Palm Desert
Ⓖ Miramonte Resort
Ⓓ Motel 6–Indio
Ⓔ Palm Desert Lodge
Ⓖ Sands Hotel of Indian Wells
Ⓔ Vacation Inn

CAMPING
Ⓓ Arabian Gardens Mobile Estates
Ⓗ Desert Aire RV Resort
Ⓘ Emerald Desert RV Resort
Ⓙ Fiesta RV Park
Ⓚ Lake Cahuilla
Ⓛ Mount San Jacinto Wilderness State Park
Ⓜ Pinyon Flats

Note: Items with the same letter are located in the same area.

★★★★ INDIAN CANYONS
Off South Palm Canyon Drive, 760/325-3400

The Agua Caliente Band of the Cahuilla Indians trace their presence on these lands back many centuries, and through some combination of good luck and the spirit willing, they still own this land and have chosen to preserve its natural beauty.

The canyons, (Palm, Andreas, and Murray), offer a beautiful array of scenic vistas, towering cliffs, and natural beauty along with picnicking, hiking, and horseback riding opportunities (riders, call **Smoke Tree Stables** at 760/327-1372).

Palm Canyon is 15 miles long and has 14 hiking trails varying in length and difficulty: as short as one-half mile and an elevation gain of only 30 feet, and as long as 15 miles and elevations gains of over 3,200 feet. It has the largest palm-stand oasis in Northern America, with more than 3,000 palms. Among the trails in Palm Canyon is the West Fork Falls Trail, a short, very easy hike with little elevation gain and a beautiful view of the waterfalls. There's also the West Fork Trail-South, a fairly strenuous hike of 2.5 miles with an elevation gain of 1,500 feet. This trail offers the opportunity to climb. (Maps of these trails are posted throughout the canyons and can be purchased at the Trading Post.)

Andreas Canyon features two trails. One is about a mile, takes about 45 minutes (the Andreas Canyon Trail), and parallels a creek; the other (The Maynard Mine Trail) is about four miles and leads to an old mine.

Near Andreas is **Murray Canyon**, the most secluded of the canyons. Named for Dr. Wellwood Murray, the second Anglo citizen of Palm Springs, who built the first hotel in the area, the canyon offers the Murray Canyon Trail, a two-mile trail (four miles round trip) that's fairly easy to hike (there are stream crossings), has an elevation gain of 500 feet, and leads to a group of waterfalls known as the Seven Sisters.

If you have all day, check out trails in all three canyons; if you're short on time, take the Andreas Canyon Trail hike, then drive to the Trading Post in Palm Canyon and take a couple of the shorter trails (there's one called the Fern Canyon Trail, just past the restrooms, that leads to a creek and a cave and takes less than 30 minutes).

Details: Five miles from the center of Palm Springs, off South Palm Canyon Drive, Palm Springs. Open year-round, 8–5 in winter and fall, 8–6 in summer. Admission is $6 adults, $3.50 students and military with ID and seniors, $1 children 6–12, free for children under 5. (2 hours)

★★★★ THE LIVING DESERT
47-900 Portola Ave., Palm Desert, 760/346-5694
This fascinating 1,200-acre wildlife and botanical park combines the elements of a zoo, a botanical garden, and a scenic wilderness, and features rare desert animals and some African wildlife. Along with bighorn sheep, mountain lions, Mexican wolves, cheetahs, and zebras are exhibits of Indian culture and geology, a picnic area, hiking trails, a café, and a gift shop. Guided tram and walking tours available.

Details: Open daily 9–5 (closed in August and on Christmas). Admission is $7.50 adults, $6.50 seniors, $3.50 ages 3–12, free for children 2 and under. Tour and rate schedules vary. (2 hours)

★★★★ MOORTEN BOTANICAL GARDEN
1701 S. Palm Canyon Dr., Palm Springs, 760/327-6555
A garden in the desert? Three thousand varieties of cactus? Yes! And the San Jacinto Mountain Range as a backdrop. If you think of the saguaro when you think of cactus, come here and rearrange your thinking. Set along a winding path, the cacti are displayed according to the area of their origin: the Sonoran Desert region, the Mojave Desert region, the Arizona Desert region, the Colorado Desert region, the Yuman Desert region, and so on. In addition to petrified ironwood, beautiful agaves, mesquite and Joshua trees, ocotillo, and creosote bushes, you'll see Turk's cap cactus, organ ape cactus, beavertail cactus, barrel cactus, mink cactus, grizzly bear cactus—many of the names aptly describe the appearance. There's also a "Cactarium," a Quonset hut filled with numerous varieties of rare cacti—it's a fascinating yet slightly spooky place: About halfway down the aisle you might start remembering all those movies where strange plants surround people and devour them. At the end of the path are some historical artifacts (the first plow in Palm Springs) and a nursery where you can purchase plants.

Details: Open Mon–Sat, 9–4:30, Sun 10–4. Admission is $2 adults, 75 cents children. (1 hour)

★★★★ PALM SPRINGS AERIAL TRAMWAY
Tramway Drive, Chino Canyon off Highway 11 North, Palm Springs, 760/325-1391
Here's a thrilling ride up to 8,516 feet! You gain approximately 6,000 feet in about 14 minutes. At the top you'll find both civilization and wilderness: a restaurant, cocktail lounge, gift shop, picnic area, movie

theater, and Mount San Jacinto Wilderness State Park, with 54 miles of hiking trails, a wilderness trail ride, and camping (with permit). Bring a jacket; temperatures atop Mount San Jac can be 30 to 40 degrees cooler than in Palm Springs.

Details: *Open at 10 a.m. weekdays and 8 a.m. weekends; the last car up leaves at 8 p.m., the last car down returns at 9:45 p.m.; later during Daylight Savings Time. Closed for two weeks in August. Ticket prices and packages vary, including a Ride 'N' Dine package for $20.95. Call for details. (2 hours)*

★★★ PALM SPRINGS AIR MUSEUM
745 N. Gene Autry Trail, Palm Springs, 760/778-6262

Opened in November 1996, this museum features one of the largest collections of World War II aircraft, including the B-17, B-25, P-38, Spitfire, Grumman Wildcat, Grumman Hellcat, Bell King Cobra, Vought Corsair, North American Mustang, Douglas Invader, and more. On average, there are at least four temporary exhibitions running simultaneously, plus movies, videos, numerous vehicles, artifacts, memorabilia, photographs and original murals and art. There is a "History and Heritage Program" scheduled most Saturdays at 1 p.m. year-round.

Details: *Open daily 10–5. Admission is $7.50 adults, $6 seniors, $3.50 children 6–12, free for children under 6. (1 hour)*

★★★ PALM SPRINGS DESERT MUSEUM
101 Museum Dr., Palm Springs, 760/325-7186

This magnificent art and natural-science museum encompasses several galleries and a sculpture garden, with permanent collections and changing exhibitions of Western (civilization) art, American Indian artifacts and artworks, and displays on the performing arts. Permanent collections include nineteenth-century landscapes and classic Western American art.

Details: *Open Tue–Sat 10–5, Sun noon–5; closed Mon. Admission is $7.50 adults, $6.50 seniors, $3.50 ages 6–17, students, and military with ID; free for children under 6. (2 hours)*

★★★ RUDDY'S GENERAL STORE MUSEUM
221 S. Palm Canyon Dr., Palm Springs, 760/327-2156

This is a re-creation of a general store of the 1930s and early '40s, with authentic showcases and over 6,000 unused products. Without spoiling the surprise, the products are amazing! We've come a long way, but which way?

Details: *Open Oct–June Thu–Sun 10–4; July–Sep Sat and Sun, 10–4. Admission is 50 cents. (1 hour)*

FITNESS AND RECREATION

Palm Springs and Coachella Valley are perfect for outdoor fun: Biking, hiking, horseback riding, ballooning, golfing, and myriad other activities are all available.

Biking trails are marked in Palm Springs; ask for a guide from one of the outfitters listed here. Bike rental outfits include **Mac's Desert Cyclery**, Rancho Mirage, 760/321-9444; **Bighorn Bicycle Tour and Rental Co.**, Palm Springs, 760/325-3367; and **Tri-A-Bike**, Palm Desert, 760/340-2840.

There's plenty of territory for hiking, including the **Mount San Jacinto Wilderness** via the tram. **Big Morongo Canyon Preserve**, I-10 to Highway 62 to East Drive in Morongo Valley, 760/363-7190, features picnic areas and hiking trails; open Wednesday through Sunday, 7:30 a.m. to sunset. **Coachella Valley Preserve**, 10 miles east of Palm Springs near Thousand Palms (Ramon Road to Thousand Palms Canyon Road), 760/343-1234, has 13,000 acres of mesas, bluffs, dunes, and clear springs. Two outfits lead hikes: **Palms to Pines Hikes**, 760/251-1717, and **Trail Discovery Hiking Guide Service**, 760/325-HIKE.

Lake Cahuilla, about six miles outside of Indio, 760/564-4712, is a county park with fishing, boating, pool swimming, picnicking, hiking, and camping; open Sunday through Thursday, 6 a.m. to 7 p.m.; Friday and Saturday, 6 a.m. to 10 p.m. Admission is $2 ages 13 and up, $1 children 12 and under.

For horseback riding, horses are available in Palm Springs at **Smoke Tree Stables**, 760/327-1372, and **Los Compadres Stable**, 760/327-5411. **Ivey Ranch Equestrian Center** offers trail and overnight rides in Thousand Palms, 760/343-4251. **Rancho of the 7th Range**, La Quinta, 760/777-7777, offers rides and evenings in the desert with meals and special entertainment (gunfight shows, Indian dancers, Western dancing). **Willowbrook Riding** in nearby Desert Hot Springs has a cross-country course as well as guided trail rides, 760/329-7676.

Camelot Park Family Entertainment Center, 67-700 E. Palm Canyon Dr., Cathedral City, 760/321-9893, features a batting cage, go-karts, bumper boats, a games pavilion, and three 18-hole miniature-golf courses. Open Sunday through Thursday, 10 a.m. to 11 p.m.; Friday and Saturday, 10 a.m. to midnight. Admission is free; each activity has a ticket price, generally running less than $5. Package tickets are available.

PALM SPRINGS

Thousand Palms · Palm Desert · Rancho Mirage · Cathedral City · Palm Springs

To Los Angeles

VARNER RD · RAMON RD · COUNTRY CLUB DR · FRED WARING · PORTOLA AVE · MONTEREY AVE · BOB HOPE DR · DATE PALM DR · EL CIELO RD · E PALM CANYON DR · INDIAN TRAIL · GENE AUTRY TRAIL · PALM DR · INDIAN AVE · TRAMWAY RD · PALM CANYON DR · INDIAN CANYON · BELARDO · VISTA CHINO · ALEJO · TAHQUITZ CANYON · MESQUITE AVE · S. PALM CANYON DR

N

MAP NOT TO SCALE — ROAD === HIGHWAY

The **Children's Discovery Museum of the Desert**, 71-701 Gerald Ford Dr., Rancho Mirage, 760/321-0602, offers kids several interactive and hands-on activities with art, rock-climbing, and more. There's an archaeological dig where children dig up pottery, a science lab, a workshop area for playing at fixing radios and TVs, and a pretend grocery store and pizza restaurant where children can play at being shoppers and pizza cooks.

Jeep tours of the area during the season, and summer sunrise and sunset tours, are offered by **Desert Adventures**, Cathedral City, 760/324-JEEP. **Adventure Bike Tours**, Palm Desert, 760/341-221, offers bike and rollerblade tours of The Living Desert, Indian Canyons, and more. Packages and prices vary. **Desert Safari**, Palm Springs, 760/776-6087, offers guided tours of Indian Canyons. Call for tour times and prices.

You can also jump out of airplanes (**Parachutes Over Palm Springs**, 760/345-8321) or dogfight in WWI planes (**Classic Dogfights**, 760/322-7703; package includes flying in biplanes decorated as WWI fighters, smoke, machine guns with noise, and dogfight-tactics instruction).

How about sailplaning with **Sailplane Rides**, 800/586-7627; hot-air ballooning with **American Balloon Charters**, 760/327-8544, **The Balloon Ranch**, 760/398-0682, **Desert Balloon Charters**, 760/398-8575, **Dream Flight**, 760/321-5154, or **Fantasy Balloon Flights**, 760/398-6322; touring

SIGHTS
- Ⓐ Agua Caliente Cultural Museum Center
- Ⓑ Moorten Botanical Garden
- Ⓒ Palm Springs Aerial Tramway
- Ⓓ Palm Springs Air Museum
- Ⓔ Palm Springs Desert Museum
- Ⓐ Ruddy's General Store Museum

FOOD
- Ⓕ Bangkok Five
- Ⓖ Bit of Country
- Ⓗ Captain Cook's Sea Grill
- Ⓘ The Europa Restaurant
- Ⓖ Flower Drum
- Ⓗ French Club 74
- Ⓙ Jeremiah's Steak House
- Ⓚ Kokopelli Caffe
- Ⓗ Midori Restaurant
- Ⓛ Sherman's Deli and Bakery
- Ⓐ St. James at the Vineyard
- Ⓜ Trilussa
- Ⓐ Village Pub
- Ⓕ Zorba's Greek Restaurant

LODGING
- Ⓑ Budget Host Inn
- Ⓝ Cactus Flower Hotel
- Ⓞ Desert Hills
- Ⓞ Korakia
- Ⓙ L'Horizon
- Ⓟ Motel 6
- Ⓠ Orchid Tree Inn
- Ⓡ Shilo Inn
- Ⓢ Spa Hotel and Casino
- Ⓣ Villa Royale
- Ⓣ The Willows

CAMPING
- Ⓤ Happy Traveler RV Park

Note: Items with the same letter are located in the same area.

(the outsides of) movie stars' homes with **Celebrity Tours**, 760/770-2700; or enjoying a Western covered-wagon cookout with **Covered Wagon Tours**, 760/347-2161? And let's not forget golf: 20-plus golf courses in the area are open to the public (this non-golfer won't presume to tell you where to start!). For further information, contact the **Palm Springs Visitor Information Center** at 800/347-7746.

The Palm Springs area and neighboring Desert Hot Springs are a hotbed of spas; most that are part of hotels are open to the non-guest public. Palm Springs spas include **Givenchy Hotel and Spa**, 760/324-6104; **Spa Hotel and Casino** (see Lodging, below); and **Spa du Jour**, 760/864-4150. In Desert Hot Springs, look for **Desert Hot Springs Spa Hotel**, 760/329-6000, and the **Moors Motel and Spa**, 760/329-7121. Prices vary and discounts are usually given to guests.

For those who define "recreation" as "shopping," there are numerous stores and shopping areas throughout the valley. **Downtown Palm Springs'** row of boutiques features designer sportswear and European fashions. **Desert Fashion Plaza**, Palm Springs, features Saks Fifth Avenue and 45 other stores, as well as a Walk of Stars (including Frank Sinatra, Bob Hope, and Ginger Rogers). **El Paseo** boasts over 150 shops and restaurants, and **Palm Desert Town Center** has more than 100 stores. Both are in Palm Desert.

FOOD

Palm Springs and the Coachella Valley offer a full range of dining possibilities, including continental, American, Chinese, Californian, Mediterranean, Mexican, French, Italian, kosher, international, Cajun, Japanese, and Greek cuisine.

Bit of Country, 418 S. Indian Canyon, Palm Springs, 760/325-5154, is the choice for a home-style breakfast. Open from 6 a.m. to 2 p.m., its meals are less than $5.

For superb Continental cuisine in an intimate setting, the **Europa Restaurant**, 1620 Indian Trail, Palm Springs, 760/327-2314 or 800/245-2314, www.villaroyale.com, offers the best. Whether it's steak Europa, roast rack of lamb, roasted duck, free-range chicken, or salmon in parchment, these folks know how to prepare and present fine food. Appetizers include buffalo mozzarella and beefsteak tomato on a pool of fresh basil vinaigrette; smoked salmon with garlic toast points, Bermuda onion, capers, and herb vinaigrette; and deviled crab fritters on a bed of mango and papaya chutney. The Villa Royale salad and the classic Caesar are both excellent. Entrees start at $17; the veal and lamb are $28. Appetizers average $9, salads $5. Dinner is served Tuesday through Sunday 5:30 'til 10 p.m.

For outstanding international cuisine in an exotic setting, **St. James at the Vineyard**, 265 S. Palm Canyon Dr., Palm Springs, 760/320-8041, offers a wonderful menu with pepper-seared venison loin, shrimp Bangkok, and other delicious appetizers, and entrees that include grilled lamb rack Mediterranean, sea bass roasted in olive oil, lobster medallions, baked veal chop, and more. The wine cellar has over 200 selections from around the world, and the relaxed ambiance features a collection of masks, golden Buddhas, and other artifacts. Entrees average $28.

For outstanding Italian cuisine, **Papa Dan's**, 73-131 Country Club Dr., Palm Desert, 760/568-3267, is a casual mom-and-pop, family-style restaurant that's so tasty and popular they have to keep expanding; they've done so while retaining the cozy atmosphere. All the regular Italian cuisine favorites are served—lasagna, tortellini, manicotti, cannelloni—and the recipes are excellent! The antipasto salad is delicious and light, and they have a full bar. Open for lunch and dinner; most meals are less than $10; pizzas run to $17.

Also serving excellent Italian cuisine in a spacious dining room on Palm Springs' main street is **Trilussa**, 123 N. Palm Canyon Dr., Palm Springs, 760/323-4255. Their menu includes salads, appetizers such as *insalata flamminga* (radicchio, Belgian endive, Gorgonzola cheese, and walnuts), roasted Tuscan bread, pizza, wonderful pasta dishes featuring homemade pasta, and entrees like *petto di pollo al funghi* (chicken breast with mushrooms), *scaloppine di vitello piccata* (veal scaloppine in a lemon-caper sauce) and *gamberoni al limone* (jumbo shrimp in a lemon-garlic sauce). The gnocchi *di patate al pomodoro* is excellent, the service is fine, they have a variety of fine wines, and they serve complimentary Amaretto with your order of an after-dinner coffee. The outdoor patio is heated in winter. Dinners range between $8.50 and $22.

For kosher deli, one of the best in all Southern California is **Sherman's Deli and Bakery**, 401 Tahquitz Canyon Way, Palm Springs, 760/325-1199. It's a family-style restaurant with meals from $3.25 to $10.25; the choices are fresh and made from scratch. And I must recommend one of their chef specialties, the Beef 'n' Latkas sandwich, invented by the owner's father. This sandwich should be enshrined as one of the all-time great deli sandwiches: lean corned beef served sandwich style between two potato latkas, served with applesauce and sour cream. And the chocolate eclairs are excellent, too. Eat here, then walk it off in the Indian Canyons.

For Chinese food, **Flower Drum**, 424 S. Indian Canyon Dr., Palm Springs, 760/323-3020, offers dinners from $6.95 to $28. For American steak and seafood, **Jeremiah's Steak House**, 1201 E. Palm Canyon Dr., Palm Springs, 760/327-1469, has meals from $7.95 to $19.95 and a sports bar.

For Cajun and seafood, try **Captain Cook's Sea Grill**, 72-191 Highway

111, Palm Desert, 760/341-8333, with meals from $12.50 to $22. **Kokopelli Caffe**, 44-150 Town Center Way, Palm Desert, 760/776-1500, serves Southwestern breakfast and lunch with meals ranging from $2.50 to $8. Japanese cuisine and a sushi bar can be found at **Midori Restaurant**, 73-759 Highway 111, Palm Desert, 760/340-1466, with meals from $8.50 to $18. For Thai food, **Bangkok Five**, 69-930 Highway 111, Rancho Mirage, 760/770-9508, has meals from $11.95 to $22.95. At **French Club 74**, 73-061 El Paseo, Palm Desert, 760/568-2782, meals range from $16 to $28. **Zorba's Greek Restaurant**, 42-434 Bob Hope Dr., Rancho Mirage, 760/340-3066, serves meals priced from $10.95 to $19.95.

For modestly priced meals in a very casual atmosphere, **Village Pub**, 266 S. Palm Canyon, Palm Springs, 760/323-3265, serves burgers, sandwiches, chicken, seafood, food from all over the globe, and homemade desserts, with most items less than $10.

LODGING

You don't have to be rich to stay in Palm Springs, despite its reputation. The variety of motels and hotels in Palm Springs and throughout the Coachella Valley includes many chain and budget places. On the other hand, if you have some disposable income (to dispose of), you can spend it and live very comfortably while passing through.

At the top of the list is the beautiful and wonderfully comfortable **Orchid Tree Inn**, 261 S. Belardo Road, Palm Springs, 760/325-2791 or 800/733-3435, styled as a 1930s desert-garden retreat, nestled between the San Jacinto Mountains and the South Palm Canyon Drive hub of shopping and dining activity. This inn, featuring Spanish bungalows (built in 1934), motel-style rooms, and suites, all carefully and painstakingly restored in the style of the Palm Springs of the 1930s, has been a decades-long labor of love for proprietor Bob Weithorn, and the heart-and-soul effort shows. The Orchid Tree has been family-owned and -operated since 1952. The 40 rooms offer the modern amenities of TVs, VCRs, and stereo systems, combined with period and sometimes antique (or specially commissioned) furniture featuring ranch oak, Spanish colonial, Queen Anne, lodgepole pine, Old West–style leather and saddle blankets, and California wicker; and most of the rooms have kitchens with 1940s-era gas stoves—all clean and in excellent working order—with dishware from the period. Several rooms offer microwaves, electric citrus juicers, coffee-bean grinders, and blenders. Each room is one-of-a-kind, with themes woven between the paintings, tile, and bedspreads. Many of the rooms have private patios, gardens, or balconies. The beautifully landscaped grounds also house a lodge with a guest library, board games, a video theater, a fireplace, and a breakfast dining area for the complimentary continental breakfast served November through May (and it's more than just a sweet roll and coffee: Breakfast includes choices of hot and cold cereals, fresh cut-up fruit, bagels and cream cheese, fresh juice, and a choice of coffees!). And there are two pools and a spa area. Although there is no restaurant, more than 80 restaurants are within close walking distance (including St. James, the Village Pub, Sherman's Deli, and Trilussa; see Food, above). Rates range from $65 to $295, depending on the room and the season—there are discounts for stays of one week or longer.

The **Villa Royale,** 1620 Indian Trail, Palm Springs, 760/327-2314 or 800/245-2314, is a European style bed-and-breakfast offering spacious and unique rooms off interior courtyards framed with statuesque pillars, cascading bougainvillea, and hovering shade trees. The wandering brick paths and bubbling fountains add to the intimate atmosphere, and there are two pools on the lush 3.5 acres. Gourmet meals are prepared at the renowned Europa restaurant (see Food, above). Lunch or dinner may be served outdoors, in the beautiful poolside courtyard, with shady desert palms; you'll dine while gazing at the majestic San Jacinto Mountains. The room decor offers a variety of styles—Dutch, Spanish, German, Italian, Swiss, Moorish, English, Irish, or Greek—and many rooms have their own romantic wood-burning fireplaces and private spas. Rates range from $95 to $295, depending on the size of the room and the season. A complimentary breakfast is served.

The Willows, 412 W. Tahquitz Canyon Way, Palm Springs, 760/320-0771, is an eight-room Mediterranean-style villa built in 1927, each room lavishly designed and appointed, with rates from $250 to $500. **L'Horizon**, 1050 E. Palm Canyon Dr., Palm Springs, 760/323-1858, a 22-room hotel in Palm Springs' residential area, offers privacy, his-and-hers bicycles, and a Jacuzzi, with rates ranging from $95 to $250. **Shilo Inn,** 1875 N. Palm Canyon, Palm Springs, 760/320-7676, has a spa, sauna, and gazebo; all rooms have gardens and refrigerators, and rates range from $95 to $129. **Spa Hotel and Casino**, 100 N. Indian Canyon Dr., Palm Springs, 760/325-1461, provides 230 luxury rooms and suites, a spa and casino, and rates starting at $119 (they offer many specials and packages; for special rate promotions call 800/854-1279).

Other Palm Springs lodgings include **Korakia,** 257 S. Patencio Road, 760/864-6411, a historic 12-room Mediterranean-style villa with rates from $109 to $365; **Desert Hills**, 601 W. Arenas Road, 760/325-2777, offering bicycles, Jacuzzi hot pools, and outdoor barbecues, with rooms ranging from $70 to $160; **Cactus Flower Hotel**, 220 Avenida Palmera, 760/325-6046, an eight-room lodge with kitchen facilities, laundry, barbecue grills, and rates from $49 to $69; the **Budget Host Inn**, 1277 S. Palm Canyon Dr., 760/325-5574,

IDYLLWILD

For an escape to what feels like an alpine village, far from the urbanity of L.A. or the busy resort feel of Palm Springs, **Idyllwild**, nestled within the Santa Rosa Mountains and the San Bernardino National Forest, surrounded by state and national parks, bordering the Mount San Jacinto Wilderness Area, is ideal. Approachable from I-10 to the north on a stunning, scenic drive on State Road 243; or from Highway 74 out of Palm Springs/Palm Desert to the east; or the 74 via 79 from Temecula to the southwest, Idyllwild offers comfortable lodgings, restaurants, shops, hiking, fishing, camping, and mostly the serenity of a small, beautiful, remote mountain village. And it's only about two hours from Venice, an hour from Temecula, and 45 minutes from Palm Desert.

The **Mount San Jacinto Wilderness** and **Santa Rosa Mountains** offer hiking and backpacking, nature trails, and mountain-biking and horseback-riding trails, and have several locations for picnicking and fishing. And many of the views are absolutely spectacular. For information about trails, camping, and permits, contact the San Jacinto Ranger District, San Bernardino National Forest, 54270 Pinecrest Ave., Idyllwild, 909/659-2117.

Thousand Trails, 24400 Canyon Trail, 909/659-2526, also offers camping and hiking opportunities; their facilities include a swimming pool and volleyball.

Among the restaurants in the village, **Arriba**, 25980 Highway 243, 909/659-4960, features tasty Mexican food and offers an outdoor patio with a view. Breakfasts and lunches generally run less than $5; dinners are less than $10. **Jan's Kettle**, 54220 N. Circle Dr.,

with a giant therapy pool, in-room refrigerators available, and rates starting at $39; and several chains, many with relatively low rates, such as **Motel 6** at 595 E. Palm Canyon Dr. 760/325-6129 and 660 S. Palm Canyon Dr., 760/327-4200, where rooms start at $36.

Indio has several chain motels, including **Best Western Date Tree Hotel**, 81-909 Indio Blvd., 760/347-3421, with whirlpool and kitchen suites available; summer rates start at $45 and winter rates at $59. Other Indio lodgings include **Motel 6–Indio**, 82-195 Indio Blvd., 760/342-6311, where year-round rates start at $26; and the **Holiday Inn Express–Indio**, 84-096 Indian

909/659-4063, serves breakfasts and lunches in a casual dining room for less than $8. **Chelsea's**, *54200 N. Circle Dr., 909/659-4540, offers 12 blends of gourmet coffee with 25 flavored coffees to choose from, and homemade chili and ice cream, along with breakfasts and lunches that generally run less than $7.*

In keeping with the idyllic setting, there's the **Idyllwild Inn**, *54300 Village Center Road, 909/659-2552 or 888/659-2552. It's convenient, a close walk from "downtown," but offers a feeling of seclusion. The cozy cabins and theme rooms (Indian, French, Old West) all have fireplaces, with weeknight rates as low as $47 for the theme rooms and as low as $53 for a cabin; weekend rates run as high as $129 for a three-bedroom cabin and $65 for a theme room. Weekly rates range from $411 to $693 for cabins; $5 extra for extra persons. The grounds include a playground for the kids.*

Strawberry Creek Inn, *26370 Highway 243, 909/659-3202 or 800/262-8969, also walking distance from the village circle (although a slightly longer walk), is a B&B with nine rooms and a separate cottage, serving gourmet country breakfasts. Most rooms have fireplaces; each room has a private bath and a queen bed. Rates range from $70 to $105. And there are many other inns throughout the village and the mountainside.*

For further information about Idyllwild, call their Visitor Information Center at the Chamber of Commerce, 909/659-3259, Web site www.idyl.com.

Springs Dr., 760/342-6344, with a whirlpool, summer rates starting at $49, and winter rates starting at $69.

In Palm Desert, **Palm Desert Lodge**, 74-527 Highway 111, 760/346-3875, has kitchens, saunas, and rates starting at $40 to $60, depending on the season (higher during special events like the Bob Hope Classic). **Vacation Inn**, 74-715 Highway 111, 760/340-4441, has kitchens, a putting green, therapy pools, and rates starting at $98 in winter, $70 in summer. **Embassy Suites**, 74-700 Highway 111, 760/340-6600, features a whirlpool and tennis courts, where summer rates start at $69 and winter rates at $119. **Holiday**

Inn Express–Palm Desert, 74-675 Highway 111, 760/340-4303, has a whirlpool, summer rates starting at $39, and winter rates at $79.

In Indian Wells, **Sands Hotel of Indian Wells**, 75-188 Highway 111, 760/346-8113, has a whirlpool, golf course, and kitchenettes, with summer rates starting at $55 and winter rates at $99. **Miramonte Resort**, 76-477 Highway 111, 760/341-2200, also has a whirlpool and golf course, with summer rates starting at $89 and winter rates at $169.

CAMPING

Camping is available around but not in the Palm Springs cities area. **Lake Cahuilla** (see Fitness and Recreation, above) has campsites and partial hookups for RVs; for camping reservations, call 800/234-PARK. **Mount San Jacinto Wilderness State Park**, 760/323-3107 or 909/659-2607, has primitive campsites. **Pinyon Flats**, 14 miles southwest of Palm Desert on Highway 74 in the San Bernardino National Forest, 909/383-5588, has 18 tent and RV spaces, is open October through May, has water and toilets, and is within five miles of fishing opportunities and a grocery.

For RV travelers, **Emerald Desert RV Resort**, 76000 Frank Sinatra Dr., Palm Desert, 800/426-4678, offers a clubhouse, billiard room, executive golf course, putting green, pro shop, grocery, barbecues, tennis courts, fitness center, indoor and outdoor spas, laundry facilities, security gates, and more. Rates vary seasonally.

In Palm Springs, the **Happy Traveler Recreational Vehicle Park**, 211 W. Mesquite Ave., 760/325-8518, has water, toilets, and showers, and is near other facilities and services.

Indio has several RV parks, including **Arabian Gardens Mobile Estates**, 81-600 Fred Waring Dr., 760/347-0872; **Desert Aire RV Resort**, 81-620 Ave. 49, 760/347-9181; and **Fiesta RV Park**, 46-421 Madison St., 760/342-2345. All have full hookups, laundries, and swimming pools.

NIGHTLIFE

The best live music entertainment in Palm Springs, especially if you like the blues, can be found at the recently opened **Blue Guitar**, 120 S. Palm Canyon Dr. (in the heart of downtown Palm Springs above the Plaza Theater), 760/327-1549. This intimate club, a labor of love created by bandleader and blues guitarist extraordinaire Kal David, features comfortable seating with no one sitting more than 20 feet from the stage, great lighting, great sound, a great band (Kal David and the Real Deal, featuring vocalist Lauri Bono—no relation) and, very often, blues greats from all over the country. David, who toured with Muddy Waters, B.B. King, and John Mayall, among others, has done what every musician dreams of and what every audience needs: He's put together a club with music, performance, and the audience in mind. And for those into vintage guitars, David's collection is on display. There are usually two shows a night. Show times and cover vary; reservations are suggested.

Unique to this destination is the **Fabulous Palm Springs Follies**, a cabaret of performers over age 50, all professional dancers (Donald O'Connor headlined the 1998–99 season). The season runs from November to May (call for precise dates and prices) at the historic Plaza Theater, 100 Jack Benny Plaza, Palm Springs, 760/327-0225. Also at the Plaza are the Hollywood Museum, a photo gallery, and a Walk of Fame.

Palm Desert is home to the **McCallum Theater for the Performing Arts**, featuring shows from around the world at the Bob Hope Cultural Center, 73-000 Fred Waring Dr., 760/346-6505. The **Rock Garden Cafe**, 777 S. Palm Canyon Dr., Palm Springs, 760/327-8840, presents dinner theater; dinner and show costs around $29.95; show alone is around $15.95.

The Nest, 75-188 Highway 111, Indian Wells, 760/346-2314, is a casual piano bar. For blues and R&B lovers, **Gumbo Joe's** (at Captain Cook's—see Food, above), 72-191 Highway 111, Palm Desert, 760/341-8333, has live music on weekends. Acoustic music lovers, try the **Ice House**, 67-501 E. Palm Canyon Dr., Cathedral City, 760/321-8558, featuring live music Thursday through Saturday. For jazz lovers, **Billy Reed's**, 1800 N. Palm Canyon Dr., Palm Springs, 760/325-1946, is the place for live music on weekends; **Club 340**, 340 N. Palm Canyon Dr., Palm Springs 760/320-1758, has live music (jazz, honky-tonk, and more) every night; and **Cunard's Sandbar**, 78-120 Calle Tampico, La Quinta, 760/564-3660, has a piano bar Tuesday through Sunday. For dancing, billiards, and comedy on Sundays, head for **Zeldaz**, 169 N. Indian Canyon Dr., Palm Springs, 760/325-2375. **Village Pub** (see Food, above) has acoustic folk, rock, and blues.

Palm Desert to Temecula

There are several ways to get to **Temecula** from the desert. One of the easiest from Palm Springs is to take I-10 west to Highway 215 south, but a very scenic route is to take Highway 74 from Palm Desert, follow it through the San Bernardino National Forest to **Idyllwild**, and down to the citrus-growing town of Hemet, then to Highway 215 south.

For a scenic route that takes a little over an hour and offers twisting roads, mountain vistas, and rural agriculture views, take Highway 74 out of Palm Desert (elevation 243 feet) up into the Santa Rosa Mountains. On your left is Sheep Mountain (5,100 feet). Continue up past Alpine Village, where the summit peaks at around 8,000 feet, then begin to descend. At around 4,900 feet you'll take Highway 371 through the Cahuilla Indian Reservation, with Cahuilla Mountain (5,640 feet) off to your right. Pass through the small outpost of **Aguanga** and turn north on Highway 79, skirt the Agua Tibia Wilderness Area to the south, and drive through beautiful Temecula Valley and into Temecula.

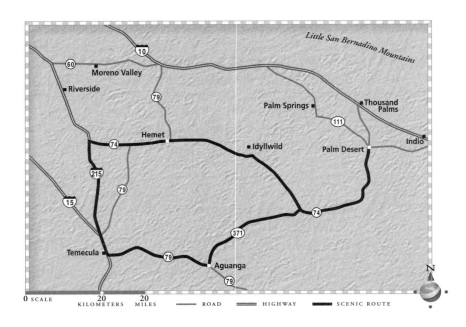

14
TEMECULA

If Southern California has a living reminder of the Wild West, then Temecula is it. Now a wine-country center, Temecula Valley was home to the Pechanga Indians. Father Juan Norberto de Santiago, a Franciscan padre, is the first known European to enter the valley; he came in 1797, searching for a mission site. American trappers arrived in 1831; Jedediah Smith and Kit Carson reportedly traveled through the area. In 1847 a bloody battle was fought as part of the Mexican-American War when Temeculan Indians captured and killed 11 Mexican soldiers. Other Mexican soldiers gave chase and, with the help of the Cahuilla Indians, slaughtered the Temeculans.

After that war the territory became part of the United States, and in 1858 the first of the Butterfield Overland Stages en route from St. Louis to San Francisco stopped in Temecula. With the stage run came bandits and stage holdups. In 1875 the local Indians were evicted from their lands; the Pechanga Indian Reservation was created nearby in 1885. In 1882 a rail line from National City to Temecula was completed, sparking a business boom. The city of Temecula, however, was not incorporated until 1989.

Today, Temecula offers many tourist activities, from balloon rides, to sightseeing and shopping in historic Old Town, to wine tasting. It offers a tantalizing climate as well—warm summers and moderate winters with prevailing ocean breezes. July temperatures can approach 99°F, but the average yearly temperature is 80°F; the coolest days average 65°F, sinking to 36°F at night.

TEMECULA

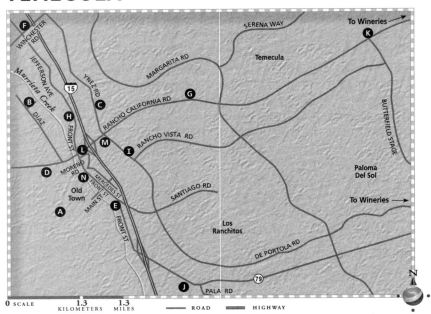

SIGHTS

A Old Town
B Temecula Valley Beer & Ale Works

FOOD

C Baily Wine Country Café
D Captain's Cabin
E Cosantino's Silver Spoon
F Mexicana
E Penfold's Cafe and Bakery
G Prestos
H Rocky Cola Cafe
E Rosa's Cantina Restaurant
I Scarcella's

J Temet Grill
E Texas Lil's Mesquite Grille
H Tony's Spunky Steer
K Vineyard Terrace

LODGING

H Best Western Country Inn
L Best Western Guest
H Comfort Inn
M Embassy Suites
L Motel 6
N Ramada Inn
J Temecula Creek Inn

Note: Items with the same letter are located in the same area.

A PERFECT DAY IN TEMECULA

Wake up early, real early, and take a thrilling hot-air balloon ride over the beautiful valley. Enjoy breakfast at Penfold's, then check out the historic buildings and shopping in Old Town, visit the vineyards and breweries, and lunch at Rosa's Cantina Restaurant or any of the other restaurants in the Old Town area. Hikers can head to the Santa Rosa Plateau Ecological Preserve; or if you're in the mood to be pampered, spend the afternoon at Glen Ivy Day Spa, just up the road. For dinner, you can't beat the Temet Grill for fine dining or Prestos for family dining.

SIGHTSEEING HIGHLIGHTS

★★★★ VINEYARDS AND WINERIES

Temecula's unique microclimate, created by the breezes from the Pacific Ocean only 21 miles away, provides a growing environment comparable to the coastal wine-producing regions of central and northern California. The beautiful Temecula Valley is home to 14 wineries. Originally considered primarily a white wine–producing area, with excellent chardonnay, sauvignon blanc, and Riesling, the Temecula Valley is now known for its outstanding red wines as well: cabernet sauvignon, merlot, and petite sirah.

All wineries are open to the public and offer tastings; several give tours as well. Many offer picnic areas where visitors can have lunch and enjoy a bottle right there. Most of the wineries charge a tasting fee. One outfit, **Temecula Shuttle**, 909/695-9999, offers several types of tours through the wine country; some include a light lunch and tasting. Rates vary.

To see the wine country, head east on Rancho California Road. You'll come across **Callaway Vineyard and Winery**, 32720 Rancho California Road, 909/676-4001, open daily 10:30 to 5; **Thornton Winery**, 32575 Rancho California Road, 909/699-0099, open daily 11 to 5 (they serve lunch and dinner); **Baily Winery**, 33833 Rancho California Road, 909/695-1895, open daily 10 to 5; **Mount Palomar Winery**, 33820 Rancho California Road, 909/676-5047, open daily 10 to 5; **Maurice Carrie Winery**, 34225 Rancho California Road, 909/676-1711, open daily 10 to 5; and **Van Roekel Vineyards and Winery** (Temecula's newest), 34567 Rancho California Road, 909/699-6961, open daily 10 to 5.

Taking Glenoaks Road to De Portola Road, you'll come upon **Filsinger**, 39050 De Portola Road, 909/626-4594, open weekends

Dean Alden Ekdahl

10:30 to 5; and **Keyways**, 37338 De Portola Road, 909/676-1451, open daily 10 to 5. Backtracking to Calle Contento, you'll find **Temecula Crest Winery**, 40620 Calle Contento, 909/676-8231, to the north of Rancho California Road, open daily 10 to 5; and **Cilurzo Vineyard and Winery**, 41220 Calle Contento, 909/676-5250, open daily 10 to 5, to the south.

Held approximately the last weekend of April, the **Temecula Valley Balloon and Wine Festival**, 909/676-6713, features over 50 colorful hot-air balloons, wine tasting, gourmet food demonstrations, live entertainment, an arts and crafts fair, and more. (All day)

★★★ OLD TOWN
Front Street

Old Town is a six-block-long stretch of historic buildings and replicas of late-nineteenth-century structures. Mostly a commercial shopping and tourist area, Old Town's most notable buildings include the **Welty Building**, built as a store and saloon in 1902, today an antiques store and deli; the **Wine Cellar/Temecula Jail**; the **Welty Hotel/Temecula Hotel**, originally built in 1882, burned down and rebuilt in 1891, now a private residence; **Temecula Mercantile**, built in 1891, now an antiques mall; **First National**

Bank of Temecula, built in 1914 and robbed once in 1930, now a Mexican restaurant; **St. Catherine's Catholic Church**, built in the early 1920s, now to be the new museum; and **Machado's Store**, built in 1892, originally a store and now an antiques mall.

Details: *Located on Front Street, between I-15 and Murrieta Creek. (2 hours)*

★★ BREWERIES

Not only is Temecula a wine center, it's got brews, too! Check out **Temecula Valley Beer & Ale Works**, 43122 Via Dos Picos, 909/693-0222, which features a tasting bar and gift shop, and offers bottling and packaging tours on weekends; and **Murrieta Home Brew**, 39872 Los Alamos Road, Murrieta, 909/587-0021, a beer, wine, and soda producer offering tours Wednesday through Sunday.

Details: *Call for tasting and tours info. ($^1/2$–1 hour)*

FITNESS AND RECREATION

Temecula's outdoor activities include golfing, biking, hiking, and lots of ballooning. Among the outfits offering balloon rides are **A Grape Escape Balloon Adventure**, 909/698-9772, featuring sunrise flights from the wineries; **Above All Balloon Charters**, 800/942-RIDE or 909/694-6287, offering sunrise flights over Temecula Wine Country; and **California Dreamin'**, 800/373-3359, for "balloon adventures."

For volleyball, basketball, picnicking, and the like, the **Rancho California Sports Park/Temecula Community Recreation Center**, 30875 Rancho Vista Road, has a children's play area, a community building, barbecue pits, a gym, picnic tables, swimming, volleyball, and restrooms. **Pala Community Park**, 44900 Temecula Lane, features a children's play area, barbecue, picnic tables, outdoor basketball, volleyball and tennis facilities, and restrooms.

Golfers will enjoy **Redhawk Golf Club**, 45100 Redhawk Pkwy., 800/451-HAWK, a public course with 18 holes; **Temecula Creek Inn Golf Resort**, 44501 Rainbow Canyon Road, 800/96-CREEK, a 27-hole public course; and **Temeku Golf Course**, 41687 Temeku Drive, 800/839-9949, a public championship course with 18 holes. There are also golf courses in nearby Murrieta, Sun City, and Fallbrook.

Gravity Activated Sports, 800/985-4GAS, offers bike tours, complete with equipment. Parks and lakes around Temecula that provide fishing, swimming, boating, and picnicking include **Lake Elsinore** (about 16 miles away, I-15

TEMECULA REGION

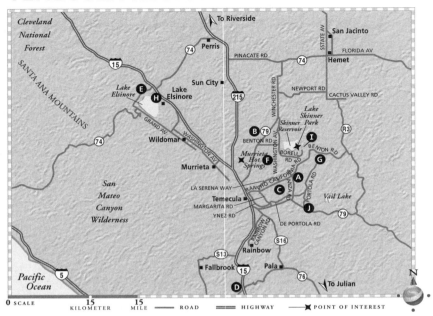

SIGHTS

A Vineyards and Wineries
B Murrieta Home Brew

LODGING

C Loma Vista Bed and Breakfast
D Pala Mesa Resort

CAMPING

E Cleveland National Forest
F Domenigoni Valley Reservoir
G Indian Oaks Trailer Ranch
H Lake Elsinore
I Lake Skinner
J Woodchuck

to Highway 74); **Vail Lake** (about 12 miles away on Highway 79); and **Lake Skinner** (about 10 miles northeast of Temecula on Rancho California Road).

Nearby hot springs include **Glen Ivy Hot Springs**, 25000 Glen Ivy Road, 909/277-3529 (about 25 miles away off I-15, see sidebar, p. 214); and **Murrieta Hot Springs Resort**, 39405 Murrieta Hot Springs Road, 909/677-7451 (about five miles north off I-15).

For hikers, the **Santa Rosa Plateau Ecological Preserve**, 909/699-

1856, a 7,300-acre wildlife preserve, is open sunrise to sunset. (To reach the reserve at the Sycamore Trails entrance and trailheads, take I-15 north to the Clinton Keith Road exit and go west to Santa Rosa Preserve, Sycamore Trails entrance.) Hikers, sailors, or fisherfolk will like the **Domenigoni Valley Reservoir**, 800/273-3430, east on Highway 79 between Temecula and Hemet.

FOOD

Temecula's locally owned and chain restaurants serve a variety of food. Among the best is the **Temet Grill**, 44501 Rainbow Canyon Road, Temecula, 909/694-1000, www.jcresorts.com, located at the Temecula Creek Inn, which sits perched on a hillside with a panoramic view of the Inn's golf course and the San Jacinto Mountains in the distance. Serving breakfast, lunch, and dinner, it's a relaxing, friendly place to eat. Breakfasts include Eggs Benedict and omelettes, and there's a breakfast croissant with scrambled eggs, Gruuyere cheese and Canadian bacon, all generally less than $10. Lunches include grilled salmon and grilled chicken breast, but it's the tasty sauces in addition to the fine food that really make the meal. Lunches run less than $12. Dinners include mouthwatering roast salmon with thyme crust, red wine sauce and Yukon potatoes (I recommend this) and roasted rack of lamb. Entrees average $20. The restaurant has an extensive wine list, featuring many local wines. And of course there's an overwhelming selection of delicious desserts.

Prestos, 30590 Rancho California Rd., C3, Temecula, 909/699-0019, offers comfortable family dining for lunch and dinner with a variety of Italian-influenced cuisine including chicken piccata, eggplant parmesan, garlic chicken linguine salad and, from the Texan part of Italy, Texas pork chops. Entrees are generally less than $11, salads less than $8. They deliver.

The Captain's Cabin, 28551 Rancho California Road, Temecula, 909/6769334, with two very comfortable dining rooms and the Wine Cellar bar, serves fresh seafood, prime rib, and steaks. Entrees start at $13.95. They're open Wednesday–Sunday.

For Italian food in a home-style setting, try **Scarcella's**, 27525 Ynez Road, Temecula, 909/676-5450, with most entrees under $10 and pizzas up to $30. For Mexican food, it's **Mexicana**, 41125 Winchester Road, Temecula, 909/676-8226, with meals less than $10. **Rocky Cola Cafe**, 27405 Jefferson Avenue, Temecula, 909/699-9667, serves breakfasts and lunches for less than $5. **Penfold's Cafe and Bakery**, 28250 Front Street, Temecula, 909/676-6411, is a popular and tasty breakfast place that also serves lunch and dinner; most meals are under $12.

Old Town has **Texas Lil's Mesquite Grille**, 28495 Front Street,

Mission Inn, Riverside

Riverside's **Mission Inn**, 3649 Mission Inn Ave., 909/784-0300, is one of California's most dramatic, historic buildings and is worth seeing. The inn opened in 1902; it was designed in the architectural style of the California missions and took more than 30 years to complete. Its architectural features include flying buttresses, domes, a bell tower, clock towers, interior courtyards, fountains, and a five-story open-air rotunda with a circular wrought-iron staircase.

The inn is situated on an entire city block, encompassing 320,000 square feet, and offers over 235 rooms, many of which have domed ceilings, wrought-iron balconies, leaded- and stained-glass windows, and carved pillars. The Presidential Lounge was originally built as a suite for President Theodore Roosevelt when he dedicated the inn in 1902, and was the site of Richard and Pat Nixon's wedding in 1940. Many famous politicians, actors, and celebrities have stayed here, including Presidents Taft, Harding, Hoover, and Reagan (he and Nancy honeymooned here); Jack Benny, Charles Boyer, Jacques Cousteau, Albert Einstein, Cary Grant, Bob Hope, Robert Redford, Oliver Stone, Will Rogers, Dr. Jonas Salk, Elizabeth Taylor—it's a huge list. Several movies were filmed at the inn, including *Sword and the Sorcerer*, *The First Legion*, and *Man in the Iron Mask*.

Walk in and take a look around. If you're interested in eating, there are dining facilities: the **Spanish Patio** serves fine breakfast and **Duane's Prime Steaks and Seafood** serves the best steak I've enjoyed outside of Chicago. If you're interested in staying, rates range from $115 to $600.

As a destination, **Riverside**, the birthplace of California's citrus industry, also offers several museums, restaurants, shops, and lodgings. The **Municipal Museum**, **Art Museum**, and **Museum of Photography** are all within walking distance of the Mission Inn, and the shop-lined **Pedestrian Walkway** in downtown Riverside is only a block from the inn. Every Wednesday night, April through October, it's **Riverside Wednesday Night on Main Street** at the Pedestrian Walkway, featuring a farmer's market, arts and crafts, food, and activities for the kids (pony and other rides, petting zoo). **Citrus Heritage Park** and the **UC-Riverside Botanical Gardens** are beautiful, and **Mt. Rubidoux** is excellent for hiking. For further information, contact Riverside Visitor & Convention Bureau, 909/787-7950.

Temecula, 909/699-5457, with meals under $10; **Rosa's Cantina Restaurant**, 28636 Front Street, Temecula, 909/695-2428, features tacos, burritos, and Rosa's specialties, with meals under $6; and **Constantino's Silver Spoon**, 28690 Front Street, Temecula, 909/6991015, with burgers, hot sandwiches, Italian and steak and lamb dinners, and several selections from "The Greek Connection": gyro plate, chicken souvlaki sandwich, and the "Ultimate Souvlaki" plate; lunches are generally less than $10, dinners less than $16.

For fried chicken, steaks, pork chops, and fish, you can't beat **Tony's Spunky Steer**, 27645 Jefferson Avenue, Temecula, 909/676-1963, with meals under $12.

And there are restaurants at some of the wineries: the **Baily Wine Country Cafe**, 27644 Ynez Road, Temecula, 909/676-9567, offers fine dining, featuring over 50 selections of wine and 25 selections of beer. They serve fresh fish daily, Salmon Wellington, steaks, and pork tenderloin. Dessert specialties include crème brûlée and Bailey's white chocolate cheesecake. Lunches run $6.95–$10.95 and dinner entrees $14.95–$20.95. And the **Vineyard Terrace**, Callaway Vineyard, 32720 Rancho California Road, 909/308-6661, offers fine dining and an extraordinary view of the valley with the hills and mountains in the background. (If you dine early, it's an excellent place to watch the sunset!) They serve lunches Thursday–Sunday, dinners only on Friday and Saturday nights, and reservations are suggested. Lunches feature Tuscan-style pizzetta bruschetta, a roasted-peppers-and-sausage sandwich, pasta Il Forno and Pinot Gris oven roasted salmon ,and are generally priced less than $8. Dinners include the same kind of unique, imaginative approach; entrees generally start around $18. And, of course, there's a fine selection of wine.

LODGING

The lone B&B in Temecula, **Loma Vista Bed and Breakfast**, 33350 La Serena Way, 909/676-7047, offers six rooms, with rates starting at $100 that include evening wine and cheese and a full champagne breakfast. Each room (they're named after wines) has a private bath.

Among the chain motels are **Best Western Country Inn**, 27706 Jefferson Road, 909/676-7378, with a spa/hot tub, a health club/sauna, and rooms starting at $47 (rooms with whirlpools start at $95). **Best Western Guest**, 41873 Moreno Road, 909/676-5700, offers views, a spa/hot tub, and rooms starting at $46. **Comfort Inn**, 27338 Jefferson Road, 909/699-5888, has a spa/hot tub and a health club/sauna, and rooms start at $46. **Ramada Inn**, 28980 Front St., 909/676-8770, has a spa/hot tub and rates starting at $49. **Embassy**

JULIAN

Julian is a historic gold-mining town where the clock seems to have stopped about a century ago. With the exception of modern telephones, ATMs, prices, and those newfangled horseless carriages that run on gasoline, almost everything else seems to be right out of the late 1800s. If your goal is to get away, this small, comfortable town, set against the lush mountains and adjacent to the beauty of the Anza-Borrego Desert, is the perfect place.

Roughly 1 1/2 hours from Temecula (on Highway 79 south), about the same distance from San Diego (I-8 west to Highway 79 north or I-15 north to Highway 78 to 79 south), and 2 1/2 hours from Palm Desert (Highway 74 to 371 to 79 south), Julian was founded in 1869 by ex–Confederate soldiers and ex-slaves. Thomas Coleman, a former slave, found gold in what was later called Coleman's Creek, and a gold rush was on. Julian became a center for hard-rock mining, with active gold mines from 1869 until World War I and again between World Wars I and II, after which the mines were shut down.

Now Julian is a quiet, peaceful B&B-type community, where the celebration centers not on gold but on apples and bakeries. There is a plethora of apple-pie venues. (Well, there really is no such thing as too much apple pie.)

If a pleasant drive with some shopping and dining is your goal, Julian and the surrounding area offer several scenic possibilities, several antique shops, and several restaurants.

If staying overnight interests you, you won't do better than the **Julian Hotel B&B**, 2032 Main St. (virtually in the center of town), 760/765-0201 or 800/734-5854, www.julianhotel.com. Known as The Queen of the Back Country, this hotel was established in 1897 by Albert Robinson, a former slave from Georgia. Each of the comfortable, quiet rooms is furnished with authentic American antiques (many original to the hotel) and includes a private bath. The roomy parlor has chairs for relaxed reading and tables for games, puzzles, or writing; and the spacious dining area offers that roll-out-of-bed-and-eat-a-big-lazy-breakfast feeling. The typical breakfast menu features eggs Florentine, toasted Dudley's date nut raisin bread (from Dudley's Bakery nearby, it's delicious!), fresh fruit, queen oats (oatmeal), chilled *orange juice, and coffee or tea. The hotel also offers a special tea time every afternoon. Weeknight rates range from $72 to $92; weekend rates from $90 to $125. The patio cottage rates are $110 to $145 and the beautiful, cozy but spacious Honeymoon House (with fireplace) is $125 to $175.*

There are many other B&Bs and lodgings in town and in the area. For more information, contact the Julian Bed and Breakfast Guild, 760/765-1555 or www.julianbnbguild.com.

*Besides shopping in Julian, you can visit nearby orchards and fruit stands, including a pick-your-own orchard at **Calico Ranch** on Highway 78 in Wynola, 619/586-0392. **Dudley's Bakery** (source of that terrific date nut raisin bread) is located at 30218 Highway 78, Santa Ysabel, 760/765-0488, about 30 minutes from Julian.*

*There are many hiking trails at **Cuyamaca Rancho State Park**, 760/765-0515, south of Julian on Highway 79. Camping is available there and at **William Heise County Park**, 619/694-3049, east of Julian; at **Lake Henshaw**, 760/782-3501, north of Julian; and at **Palomar Mountain State Park**, 760/742-3462, northwest of Julian. Heise Park, Lake Henshaw, and Palomar all also have RV sites.*

*To discover a dusty taste of Julian's history, don't miss the **Eagle & High Peak Mines**, at the end of C Street, 760/765-0036. These were real gold mines. Tour guides will lead you into crosscut tunnels on a winding path; they do an excellent job of teaching you about gold mining and processing, and share some tales about the glory (and not so glory-filled) days of Julian's gold-mining past.*

*As for scenic drives, Steve at the Julian Hotel has prepared several suggestions, including the **Anza-Borrego Desert Drive** (this takes just over two hours, depending on whether or not you stop for lunch in Borrego Springs). Take Highway 78 east to State Road 3 north to State Road 22 west to Highway 79 south, and back to Julian. This loop travels through a beautiful section of the Anza-Borrego Desert State Park, as does Steve's **Desert Journey Drive** (Highway 78 east to State Road 2 south to I-8 west to Highway 79 north, and back to Julian). Ask Steve about other scenic drives, including tours to Mt. Palomar and through Cuyamaca Rancho State Park.*

GLEN IVY HOT SPRINGS DAY SPA

For an absolutely relaxing day, take the brief trip to **Glen Ivy Hot Springs Day Spa** (south of Corona on I-15) and relax and enjoy and relax and enjoy and . . . relax and enjoy.

Nestled among rolling hills, this spa, dubbed "Club Mud," offers natural mineral-water baths, seven pools, including a covered hot pool and a lounge pool, beautiful and comfortable areas to lounge, and mud. The California red clay is reputed to have a purifying effect on the skin, drawing from the pores, absorbing impurities, and helping release wastes from the skin. (And it feels good.)

A daily admission covers all of these activities; for additional rates you can add a wide range of massage, aromatherapy, and other skin therapies and treatments. To indulge in any of these pleasures, be sure to make arrangements when you arrive.

If you've never been to a spa before, this is a great introduction— but you may be spoiled, because they're not all this good. (This is not a strip-mall spa.) Bring everything you would take to the beach (sunglasses, sunblock, sandals, hat or visor, book, Walkman, bathing suit— and maybe a second suit for the mud; and, if you prefer, a robe). Plan to spend at least four hours. There is a restaurant and snack bar (most sandwiches and salads are $6.95) and you should plan to suffer memory loss as you do nothing but relax.

Many nearby motels and hotels offer spa packages (**Embassy Suites** in Temecula, **Country Side Inn** and **Best Western Kings Inn** in Corona), and there are restaurants nearby if you want to dine after leaving the spa.

Details: 25000 Glen Ivy Road (off the Temescal Canyon exit off the 15), Corona, 909/277-3529. Open daily except Friday 10–5. Admission Mon–Thu $19.50, Sat and Sun $25. (4 hours)

Suites, 29345 Rancho California Road, 909/676-5656, offers many amenities (including a complimentary full breakfast) and rooms starting at $109. Rates at **Motel 6**, 41900 Moreno Road, 909/676-7199, start at $34.

The two resorts are **Pala Mesa Resort**, 2001 Old Highway 395, Fallbrook, 760/728-5881, with four lighted tennis courts, a lounge with live entertainment, an 18-hole golf course, and rooms with a view of the fairway that start at $110 (mountain-view rooms start at $135); and **Temecula Creek Inn**, 44501 Rainbow Road, Temecula, 909/694-1000, which features a 27-hole golf course, two tennis courts, and rates starting at $125.

CAMPING

Camping is available all around Temecula: at **Lake Skinner** and **Domenigoni Valley Reservoir** (see Fitness and Recreation, above), in the Trabuco district of the **Cleveland National Forest**, on Highway 74 between San Juan Capistrano and Lake Elsinore, 909/736-1811; and at **Lake Elsinore**, 909/674-3171.

In Temecula, **Woodchuck**, 37885 Highway 79 South, 909/676-4701, has RV and tent camping with 140 hookups, hiking trails, fishing ponds, swimming pool and spa, a Western town and saloon, and a playground. **Indian Oaks Trailer Ranch**, 38120 Benton Road, 909/676-5301, is a rural RV park with full hookups.

NIGHTLIFE

Most of Temecula's nightlife takes place in Old Town, on Front Street. The **Temecula Stampede**, 28721 Front St., 909/695-1760, is a country-western nightclub with a 4,000-square-foot dance floor and mechanical bull. Nearby **High Society Billiard Club**, 27309 Jefferson Ave., 909/699-3478, has a family atmosphere and offers a huge selection of beers in addition to the tables.

APPENDIX

Consider this appendix your travel tool box. Use it along with the material in the Planning Your Trip chapter to craft the trip you want. Here are the tools you'll find inside:

1. **Planning Map.** Make copies of this map and plot out various trip possibilities. Once you've decided on your route, you can write it on the original map and refer to it as you're traveling.

2. **Mileage Chart.** This chart shows the driving distances (in miles) between various destinations throughout the state/region. Use it in conjunction with the Planning Map.

3. **Special Interest Tours.** If you'd like to plan a trip around a certain theme—such as nature, sports, or art—one of these tours may work for you.

4. **Resources.** This guide lists various regional chambers of commerce and visitors bureaus, state offices, bed-and-breakfast registries, and other useful sources of information.

PLANNING MAP: Southern California

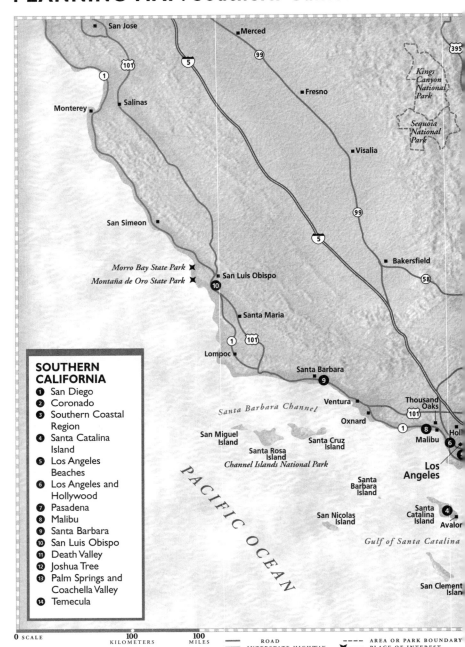

San Jose

Merced

99

395

101

5

Kings Canyon National Park

■ Fresno

Monterey ■   ■ Salinas

1

Sequoia National Park

■ Visalia

99

San Simeon ■

5

■ Bakersfield

Morro Bay State Park ✕
Montaña de Oro State Park ✕   ■ San Luis Obispo

58

10

■ Santa Maria

1   101

Lompoc ■

SOUTHERN CALIFORNIA

- ❶ San Diego
- ❷ Coronado
- ❸ Southern Coastal Region
- ❹ Santa Catalina Island
- ❺ Los Angeles Beaches
- ❻ Los Angeles and Hollywood
- ❼ Pasadena
- ❽ Malibu
- ❾ Santa Barbara
- ❿ San Luis Obispo
- ⓫ Death Valley
- ⓬ Joshua Tree
- ⓭ Palm Springs and Coachella Valley
- ⓮ Temecula

Santa Barbara
9

Santa Barbara Channel   Ventura ■   Thousand Oaks

101

Oxnard ■

1   ❽   Hol

San Miguel Island   Santa Cruz Island   Malibu   6

Santa Rosa Island
Channel Islands National Park   Santa Barbara Island   Los Angeles

PACIFIC OCEAN

Santa Catalina Island   ❹

San Nicolas Island   Avalor

Gulf of Santa Catalina

San Clement Islan

0 SCALE   100 KILOMETERS   100 MILES   ═══ ROAD   ----- AREA OR PARK BOUNDARY
═══ INTERSTATE HIGHWAY   ✕─── PLACE OF INTEREST

You have permission to photocopy this map.

NEVADA

95

93

15

374

190

95

Death Valley
National Park

190

11

Las
Vegas

Lake Mead National
Recreation Area

395

ARIZONA

178

93

14

15

95

CALIFORNIA

Kingman

58 Barstow

40

Needles

395 15

14

Lake
Havasu
City

San Bernardino

Twentynine
Palms

62

95

62

7
Pasadena

wood

10

Joshua Tree
National Park

13

12

177

95

Anaheim

Riverside

215

Palm
Springs

Blythe

10

Long
Beach 5

Newport Beach
Laguna Beach
San Juan
Capistrano San
Clemente 3

Temecula

14

15

Escondido

Anza-Borrego
Desert
State Park

95

Oceanside

5

San Diego

1

Coronado 2

8

El Centro

Yuma 8

Mexicali

Tijuana MEXICO

N

	Bakersfield	Burbank	Coronado	Death Valley	Joshua Tree	Long Beach	Los Angeles	Malibu	Oceanside	Ontario	Palm Springs	Pasadena	Ridgecrest	San Diego	San Luis Obispo	Santa Barbara	Santa Catalina	Santa Monica	Temecula
Burbank	95																		
Coronado	242	145																	
Death Valley	215	319	379																
Joshua Tree	212	161	186	270															
Long Beach	141	40	11	319	172														
Los Angeles	112	15	130	305	147	25													
Malibu	126	38	154	335	187	192	30												
Oceanside	196	108	52	344	154	68	93	111											
Ontario	152	57	117	262	104	57	43	73	82										
Palm Springs	225	114	136	315	45	127	114	142	109	69									
Pasadena	107	12	149	297	159	35	10	40	103	35	114								
Ridgecrest	92	139	244	123	160	179	154	177	209	127	182	145							
San Diego	236	139	6	373	180	108	124	148	40	111	130	143	238						
San Luis Obispo	125	193	325	356	342	212	195	172	280	229	309	205	229	319					
Sanata Barbara	148	99	222	397	239	118	92	78	186	135	206	111	120	216	103				
Santa Catalina	169	77	129	356	209	37	62	77	83	94	164	72	216	123	249	155			
Santa Monica	112	25	142	323	165	28	18	12	96	61	130	28	189	136	184	90	65		
Temecula	201	112	67	312	119	88	97	135	32	50	74	107	177	61	175	181	101	58	
Ventura	115	67	201	334	218	86	71	46	154	114	187	73	193	194	126	32	123	91	149

SPECIAL INTEREST TOURS

With *Southern California Travel•Smart* you can plan a trip of any length—a one-day excursion, a getaway weekend, or a three-week vacation—around any special interest. To get you started, the following pages contain five special interest itineraries geared toward a variety of interests. For more information, refer to the chapters listed—chapter names are in boldface, and chapter numbers appear inside black bullets. You can follow a suggested itinerary in its entirety, or shorten, lengthen, or combine parts of each, depending on your starting and ending points.

Discuss alternative routes and schedules with your travel companions—it's a great way to have fun even before you leave home. And remember: Don't hesitate to change your itinerary once you're on the road. Careful study and planning ahead will help you make informed decisions as you go, but spontaneity is the extra ingredient that will make your trip memorable.

NATURE LOVERS' TOUR

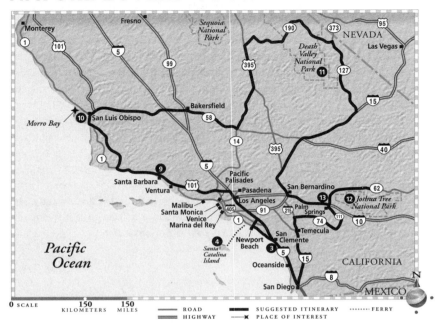

Southern California offers beautiful coastline, islands with unique species, lush coastal mountains, wine countries, high deserts, and high-desert mountains. In many cases you can go from one extreme environment to another within a day. Note that completing this itinerary in 10 days to 2 weeks means only driving through some of these places, not spending real time.

❽ Southern Coastal Region (Pacific Coast Highway drive; Laguna Beach beaches, coves, and views)
❹ Santa Catalina Island
❾ Santa Barbara (Channel Islands, wine country drive)
❿ San Luis Obispo (Montana de Oro Park, Morro Rock)
⓫ Death Valley (Ubehebe Crater, Sand Dunes, Artists Palette)
⓬ Joshua Tree (Keys' View, Joshua Tree National Park)
⓭ Palm Springs and Coachella Valley (Living Desert, Palm Springs Desert Museum, Moorten's Botannical Garden, Anza-Borrego Desert, drive to San Diego)

Time needed: 10 days to 2 weeks

FAMILY FUN TOUR

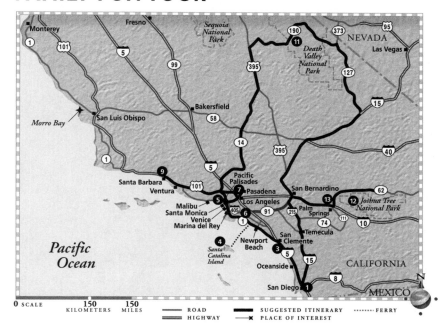

Southern California abounds with theme parks, real and make-believe. Consider checking out the natural theme parks: Santa Catalina Island, Death Valley, and Joshua Tree.

❶ San Diego (Wild Animal Park, Sea World, San Diego Zoo, Balboa Park)
❸ Southern Coastal Region (Balboa Fun Zone, Newport Beach)
❹ Santa Catalina Island (beach, glass-bottom boat, submerged boat)
❺ Los Angeles Beaches (Santa Monica Pier)
❻ Los Angeles and Hollywood (Disneyland, Knott's Berry Farm, Universal Studios, museums, Griffith Park and Observatory)
❼ Pasadena (Kidspace museum)
❾ Santa Barbara (Sea Center, natural history museum, zoo)
⓫ Death Valley
⓬ Joshua Tree (rock climbing)
⓭ Palm Springs and Coachella Valley (Palm Springs Aerial Tramway, Children's Discovery Museum)

Time needed: 2 to 3 weeks

ARTS AND CULTURE TOUR

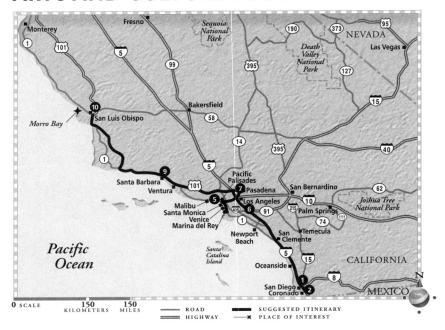

Art and culture are in the eyes of the beholder, and there are many beholders in Southern California, where self-expression seems endless.

❶ San Diego (Balboa Park museums, Old Town, Gaslamp Quarter)

❷ Coronado (Hotel del Coronado)

❺ Los Angeles Beaches (Venice Boardwalk, coffeehouses, Main Street and Abbot Kinney art galleries, Edgemar, Third Street Promenade, Montana Avenue)

❻ Los Angeles and Hollywood (art museums, Hollywood Entertainment Museum, Autry Western Heritage Museum, Mann's Chinese Theatre, Walk of Fame, Museum of Television and Radio, celebrity homes, Sunset Boulevard)

❼ Pasadena (Pacific Asia, Huntington, Southwest, and Norton Simon Museums, historic houses)

❾ Santa Barbara (San Ysidro Ranch)

❿ San Luis Obispo (Madonna Inn, Hearst Castle)

Time needed: 10 days to 2 weeks

HISTORY TOUR

The points below offer a taste of this area's rich history and culture.

❶ **San Diego** (Cabrillo Point, Maritime Museum, Mission San Diego de Alcala)

❷ **Coronado** (Hotel del Coronado)

❸ **Southern Coastal Region** (missions)

❻ **Los Angeles and Hollywood** (museums, La Brea Tar Pits)

❼ **Pasadena** (museums, San Gabriel Arcángel Mission)

❾ **Santa Barbara** (museum, Mission Santa Barbara)

❿ **San Luis Obispo** (Mission San Luis Obispo de Tolosa, San Luis Obispo County Historical Museum, Hearst Castle)

⓫ **Death Valley** (Scotty's Castle, Borax mine)

⓬ **Joshua Tree** (Desert Queen Ranch)

⓭ **Palm Springs and Coachella Valley** (Palm Springs Desert Museum)

⓮ **Temecula** (Old Town, Julian, Mission Inn)

Time needed: 3 weeks

OUTDOOR RECREATION TOUR

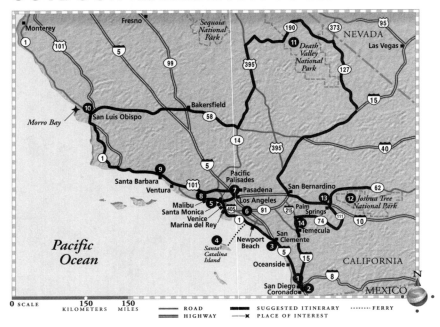

Southern California is an outdoor person's paradise. Hike, bike, balloon, rollerblade, fish, play tennis, or invent your own sport—just about anything goes.

❶ **San Diego** (boating, ballooning, horseback riding, hiking, golf)
❷ **Coronado** (boating, fishing, golf, tennis, biking, water sports)
❸ **Southern Coastal Region** (boating, golf, water sports, biking)
❹ **Santa Catalina Island** (hiking, biking, golf, water sports)
❺ **Los Angeles Beaches** (biking, rollerblading, water sports)
❼ **Pasadena** (golf, hiking)
❽ **Malibu** (water sports, hiking)
❾ **Santa Barbara** (hiking, biking, horseback riding, water sports)
❿ **San Luis Obispo** (hiking, golf, water sports in Morro Bay)
⓫ **Death Valley** (hiking, horseback riding)
⓬ **Joshua Tree** (hiking, rock climbing)
⓭ **Palm Springs and Coachella Valley** (golf, horseback riding, hiking)
⓮ **Temecula** (ballooning, hiking)

Time needed: 3 weeks

RESOURCES

General
Amtrak: 800/USA-RAIL
California Association of B&B Innkeepers: 408/464-8159
California Department of Fish & Game: 916/653-7664
California Department of Parks & Recreation: 916/653-6995
or 800/444-7275
California Division of Tourism: 800/GO-CALIF
California Hotel & Motel Association: 916/444-5780
California State Beach Parks Reservations: 800/444-7275
Caltrans 24-hour Highway Information Service: 213/628-7623
Coast Express Rail: 800/262-7837
Los Angeles Current Weather: 213/554-1212
National Parks & Forests: 414/556-0560
National Parks & Forests, California Info: 415/556-0560 or
916/644-6048
San Diego Current Weather: 619/289-1212

Lodging Chain Reservation Numbers
Best Western: 800/922-2336
Comfort Inn: 800/228-5150
Days Inn: 800/DAYS-INN
DoubleTree Inn: 800/222-TREE
Econo Lodge: 800/446-6900
Embassy Suites: 800/EMBASSY
Hilton: 800/HILTONS
Holiday Inn Express: 800/HOLIDAY
Hyatt Regency: 800/233-1234
Motel 6: 800/466-8356
Quality Inn: 800/228-5151
Radisson: 800/333-3333
Ramada Inn: 800/272-6232
Super 8: 800/800-8000
Travelodge: 800/255-3050
Vagabond Inn: 800/522-1555

Rental Cars
Alamo: 800/327-9633
Avis: 800/331-1212
Budget: 800/527-0700
Dollar: 800/800-4000
Hertz: 800/654-3131
National: 800/227-7368

Visitor Information
Anaheim Visitor Center: 714/999-8999
Catalina Visitor Center: 310/510-1520
Coronado Visitor Center: 800/622-8300
Death Valley National Park: 760/786-2331
Hollywood Visitor Center: 213/461-4213
Joshua Tree Chamber of Commerce: 760/366-3723
Joshua Tree National Park: 760/367-7511
Laguna Beach Visitor Center: 800/877-1115
Long Beach Visitor Center: 800/452-7829
Los Angeles Downtown Visitor Center: 213/689-8822
Los Angeles Visitor and Convention Bureau: 213/624-7300
Malibu Chamber of Commerce: 310/456-9025
Manhattan Beach Chamber of Commerce: 310/545-5313
Marina del Rey Visitor Center: 800/919-0555
Newport Beach Visitor Center: 800/94-COAST
Oceanside Visitor Center: 800/350-7873
Palm Desert Chamber of Commerce: 760/346-6111
Palm Springs Visitor Center: 800/347-7746
Pasadena Visitor Center: 818/795-9311
Redondo Beach Visitor Center: 800/553-3439
San Diego Visitor Center: 619/236-1212
San Luis Obispo Visitor Center: 805/781-2777
Santa Barbara Visitor Center: 805/966-9222
Santa Monica Visitor Center: 310/393-7593
Temecula Valley Chamber of Commerce: 909/676-5090
Twentynine Palms Chamber of Commerce: 760/367-3445
West Hollywood Chamber of Commerce: 310/858-8000

Web Sites

Coastal Parks: http://ca.living.net/trav/parks/reg5map.htm

Death Valley Unofficial Site: www1.ridgecrest.ca.us/~matmus /DeathV.html

Gateway to Various City Web Sites:www.city.net

Joshua Tree National Park: www.llbean.com/parksearch/parks /5277GD3772GD.html

National Parks: www.nps.gov./index_txt.htm

Santa Barbara Wineries: www.santabarbaraca.com/wine2.html

Santa Cruz - Board Walk

Carmel (Hog's Breath Inn - Clint Eastwood's B+B)
    Cypress Inn (Bug+ Erie)

Big Sur

INDEX

MAP INDEX

You'll Feel like a Local When You Travel with Guides from John Muir Publications

CiTY-SMaRT™ GUIDEBOOKS

Pick one for your favorite city: *Albuquerque, Anchorage, Austin, Calgary, Charlotte, Chicago, Cincinnati, Cleveland, Denver, Indianapolis, Kansas City, Memphis, Milwaukee, Minneapolis/St. Paul, Nashville, Pittsburgh, Portland, Richmond, Salt Lake City, San Antonio, St. Louis, Tampa/St. Petersburg, Tucson*

Guides for kids 6 to 10 years old about what to do, where to go, and how to have fun in: *Atlanta, Austin, Boston, Chicago, Cleveland, Denver, Indianapolis, Kansas City, Miami, Milwaukee, Minneapolis/St. Paul, Nashville, Portland, San Francisco, Seattle, Washington D.C.*

TRAVEL✦SMART®

Trip planners with select recommendations to: *Alaska, American Southwest, Carolinas, Colorado, Deep South, Eastern Canada, Florida Gulf Coast, Hawaii, Illinois/Indiana, Kentucky/Tennessee, Maryland/Delaware, Michigan, Minnesota/Wisconsin, Montana/Wyoming/Idaho, New England, New Mexico, New York State, Northern California, Ohio, Pacific Northwest, Pennsylvania/New Jersey, South Florida and the Keys, Southern California, Texas, Utah, Virginias, Western Canada*

Rick Steves' GUIDES

See *Europe Through the Back Door* and take along guides to: *France, Belgium & the Netherlands; Germany, Austria & Switzerland; Great Britain & Ireland; Italy; Russia & the Baltics; Scandinavia; Spain & Portugal; London; Paris; or the Best of Europe*

ADVENTURES IN NATURE

Plan your next adventure in: *Alaska, Belize, Caribbean, Costa Rica, Guatemala, Honduras, Mexico*

JMP travel guides are available at your favorite bookstores. For a FREE catalog or to place a mail order, call: 800-888-7504.

John Muir Publications ◆ P.O. Box 613 ◆ Santa Fe, NM 87504

GARY GORDON

Nick Bischoff

Gary Gordon lives in Venice, California, where he is a novelist, songwriter, playwright, screenwriter, producer, director, musician, and the film critic for the *L.A. Free Press*. Gordon grew up in Gainesville, Florida, and holds a Bachelor's of Science degree in journalism from Northwestern University.

He was director, co-producer, and co-writer (with Ron Birnbach) of the internationally recognized and critically acclaimed satire *O.J. Law*, which celebrated a six-month run at the Complex Theatre in Los Angeles during the trial. Gordon's most recent production, the satirical radio play *Elvis & Lady MacBeth at the Heartbreak Hotel* (about the Clinton-Starr scandal), can be heard on Broadcast.Com. (at www.broadcast.com).

Gordon is currently working on *Dragonfly Jones*, a screenplay, with actor-comic Tommy Davidson, and draws on his political activism and city hall background in Gainesville, working for the Santa Monica Main Street Merchants Association on parking, zoning, and related issues.

Gordon's album of original songs, *Warning Signs*, was recorded and released in 1986, and he is working on another CD of original songs, to be released in the fall of 1999.

Gordon performs his original songs periodically at the Unurban Cafe in Santa Monica and performs in comedy shows in West L.A.